ON OBEDIENCE

ON OBEDIENCE

CONTRASTING PHILOSOPHIES
FOR THE MILITARY,
CITIZENRY, AND COMMUNITY

PAULINE SHANKS KAURIN

NAVAL INSTITUTE PRESS
ANNAPOLIS, MARYLAND

Naval Institute Press
291 Wood Road
Annapolis, MD 21402

First Naval Institute Paperback edition published in 2025.
ISBN: 9798892410397 (paperback)

The Library of Congress has cataloged the hardcover edition as follows:
Names: Shanks Kaurin, Pauline, author.
Title: On obedience : contrasting philosophies for the military, citizenry, and community / Pauline Shanks Kaurin.
Identifiers: LCCN 2019040971 (print) | LCCN 2019040972 (ebook) | ISBN 9781682474914 (hardcover) | ISBN 9781682474921 (epub) | ISBN 9781682474921 (pdf)
Subjects: LCSH: Obedience.
Classification: LCC BJ1459 .S53 2020 (print) | LCC BJ1459 (ebook) | DDC 174/.9355—dc23
LC record available at https://lccn.loc.gov/2019040971
LC ebook record available at https://lccn.loc.gov/2019040972

♾ Print editions meet the requirements of ANSI/NISO z39.48–1992 (Permanence of Paper).
Printed in the United States of America.

9 8 7 6 5 4 3 2 1

Contents

ACKNOWLEDGMENTS

THIS BOOK BEGAN AS A SERIES of questions and intellectual explorations in my blog linked on Twitter, but in the immediate aftermath of the 2016 election, I had numerous colleagues and acquaintances (especially in the military community) who expressed concern about whether they could or should render obedience to the new administration. In response to these questions, I wrote a specific blog post on the unique context that many were facing after the election. I tried to frame the issue, to raise questions and issues for people to consider, and to discuss the issue in terms of the profession of arms and the community of practice of the U.S. military and political context. This event and the responses to the blog convinced me that the posts that I had been working on needed to be a much deeper and more philosophically nuanced project and that it was needed sooner rather than later. While these issues of obedience are as old as *Antigone* and the *Iliad*, they have taken on an increased urgency in the past few years. It also became clear that we needed a conversation about not just the military and obedience, but also how obedience should be viewed in the political context. This book is the result of a desire to open and deepen that conversation.

I would like to first thank my followers on various social media platforms for their engagement and comments that sharpened the ideas. Some of the ideas in chapters 4 and 8 were presented in an earlier form at the International Society of Military Ethics in 2017, and I thank those who attended that session and gave feedback.

Some of the material on disobedience and professional judgment and discretion was initially worked out in several articles published in *The Strategy Bridge* in 2017–18, and I thank the team there for their support, especially Nathan Finney, Ty Mayfield, and Eric Murphy.

Second, many of the ideas about professionalism and professional judgment and discretion were worked out in a project that ultimately became a volume on the nature of and challenges to the military profession, *Redefining the Modern Military*, published in 2018 by the Naval Institute Press. In particular, contributor Mike Denny, whose ideas about professionals being able to know when to break the rules, shares some of the points that I am making here, and thinking through his work on this was helpful in clarifying how my ideas are similar to and also depart from his. My ideas of military professionalism were also shaped by my contribution to that book and the process that led to it. Thank you to Nate Finney and Ty Mayfield for shepherding that project and supporting the conversation about professionalism, a discussion to which I hope this book will contribute.

Third, chapter 4 benefited from feedback from Dr. Samuel T. Shanks. Dr. Nikki Coleman was also kind enough to let me see a copy of her unpublished dissertation on obedience (soon to be published as a book by Routledge), and I benefited from conversations with her on the topic. When her work is published, it will fill in the legal aspects of this topic, which I intentionally did not address in this book as her work does a stellar job at that piece of the discussion.

In addition, I received support from Pacific Lutheran University, including sabbatical leave during 2018–19, for the completion of this manuscript. My colleagues in the Department of Philosophy were especially supportive of this project, and I thank them. The final work on this book was done at the start of my tenure at the U.S. Naval War College, and my colleagues there were very supportive. I also thank the editors, reviewers, and staff at Naval Institute Press for their hard work and willingness to support this project. I especially thank Dr. Benjamin Armstrong of the U.S. Naval Academy for his encouragement and for providing helpful connections to bring this project to publication.

Finally, my children McClellan and Trevan were an inspiration for the topic of obedience and even argued with me on several of the points in the book; without their love and patience, this book would not have been possible.

ON OBEDIENCE

CHAPTER 1

INTRODUCTION

If his cause be wrong, our obedience to the King wipes the crime of it out of us.
　　　　—William Shakespeare, *Henry V* [1]

Remember we are women . . . / I'm forced, I have no choice— I must obey.
　　　　—Sophocles, *Antigone* [2]

Good, well-behaved children are obedient. We take our dogs to training so they can learn to be obedient. We assume that our cats will *not* be obedient—or at least not on command or consistently. Members of the military are expected to give obedience to their superiors and obey all lawful orders, and they in fact take oaths to that effect when they join the military. Citizens are obligated to be obedient to political authority, with rare and carefully delineated exceptions that are subject to legal discretion and rulings. In Sophocles' play, Antigone might be viewed as prideful and arrogant for disobeying the orders of Creon not to bury her rebellious brother, and she was sentenced to death for the offense.

3

When the police officer pulls me over for speeding, it is expected that I will obey and subject myself to the authority of the state, within reasonable and prescribed limits.

Civil disobedience is generally acknowledged to be disruptive and a threat to the established order, even if there are cases (such as antiwar protests or the U.S. civil rights movement in the 1950s and 1960s) where it is eventually deemed appropriate and necessary. However, at the time of these actions and movements, figures such as Martin Luther King Jr. were viewed as a threat to law and order and were accordingly targeted and arrested. Disobedience in legal and political contexts is generally discussed in pejorative terms and must be well justified to avoid or mitigate punishment. The character of Kurtz in Joseph Conrad's *Heart of Darkness* illustrates the kind of perceived danger of disobedience for the breakdown of order and social control. We see this perception at work in the Black Lives Matter and other protests in Ferguson, Missouri, in 2015, as the media coverage focused on threats of violence, looting, and property damage potentially spinning out of control, thus justifying a quasi-military police response.

In the military, disobedience is seen as undermining good order and discipline, unit cohesion, and ultimately combat effectiveness, as it produces chaos and unpredictable behavior in stressful situations such as combat. Numerous mutinies in military history seem to bear out this idea, but lack of obedience and the resulting deficit in good order also create additional chaos in war. The Kwantung army was notorious for the lack of good order (and creation of chaos) in Japan in the early twentieth century.[3] More recently, the example of U.S. Army sergeant Bowe Bergdahl walking away from his post in Afghanistan in 2009 and the resulting impact and consequences seem to bear this out as well.

This is, I would hazard, conventional wisdom that many agree with. What is much less clear is exactly what counts as obedience and disobedience and why one ought or ought not to be obedient. The task of this book is to take up a philosophical exploration of the idea of obedience in both military and political communities of practice and examine how we think about what obedience is and what grounds its moral necessity.[4] In this introductory chapter, I highlight issues and themes that I will pursue in more depth later in order to set up the major questions and lines of debate and to clarify the nature of this project and how it fits into a larger landscape of discussions about obedience. I also highlight key terms and different categories of arguments I will use, as well as lay out the book's structure and major topics and my hope for how readers will use this material to engage the topic.

EXAMPLES FOR CONSIDERATION

To open discussion, we consider some classic examples of obedience and disobedience that serve as cases that will run throughout the book and what they might tell us about the topic from the standpoint of our initial intuitions and assumptions. Hachikō the dog waited for his owner at a Japanese train station every day for nine years even after his owner's death. While this behavior is often taken as a sign of loyalty, we can also see it as obedience, since presumably the dog had acquired this habit while his owner was alive. In a similar vein are stories and legends of soldiers fighting on in a jungle or other remote location long after a war is over, in obedience to orders not to surrender.

The film *A Few Good Men* takes up the question of obedience in relation to implicit and explicit orders and when that might be problematic. Marines are ordered to carry out a Code Red (a type of disciplinary action) against a Marine who is falling behind, and he ends up dying as a result. Jack Nicholson's character, Colonel Jessup, points out that Marines follow orders or people get killed in combat, but the plot of the film revolves around the question of what orders were given, whether they were implicit or explicit, and whether the Marines who followed them were correct in doing so. Here the Marines are put on trial for following these orders, which seems counterintuitive given the general presumption of obedience in the military.[5]

In the cases of war crimes, unquestioning obedience also seems more problematic and much less laudatory. In historical cases, "I was just following orders" has not been exculpatory and, in fact, legally became blameworthy and punishable. The Nuremberg trials established the legal precedent that obedience to orders was not a legal excuse and the expectation that manifestly illegal and/or immoral orders ought to be disobeyed. In the case of the My Lai incident in Vietnam, the disobedience is recalled as morally virtuous; U.S. Army chief warrant officer Hugh Thompson landed his helicopter between civilians and the marauding U.S. soldiers, and others facilitated the evacuation of civilians to safety. Thompson's actions were rewarded with the Soldier's Medal.[6] In this case, disobedience against his own comrades was viewed as worthy of moral, social, and military recognition and approval.

William Shakespeare's play *Henry V* famously takes up the question of whether obedience to the king absolves the individual soldier of moral responsibility if the king's cause is not a just one. In a dialogue between the king (in disguise) and another character, Bates, the question of what kind of obedience is owed to the king and what agency and responsibility each soldier maintains for himself is explored. At the end, the soldiers agree that they are not responsible for whether the king's cause is just—that is the domain of the king—but they are each responsible for how they fight in battle. Another character, Williams, notes, " 'Tis certain, every man that dies ill, the ill upon his own head."[7] The play also explores the relationship between obedience and the possibility of maintaining jus in bello restrictions in war. At the siege of Harfleur, the king admonishes the town to surrender while his men are still within his control—the implication being that without that control and obedience, the rules of war cannot be guaranteed, and war crimes will likely follow. This raises the possibility that obedience is not absolute, but rather conditional. If it is conditional, upon what is it conditioned?

On the political side of things, in Plato's dialogue *Euthyphro,* the title character comes across to Socrates as arrogant, being so sure in his obedience to the gods that he is willing to take his own father to court for the death of a servant.[8] Euthyphro's actions seem to be a breach of the obedience and loyalty that a child owes to a parent, but he claims that his obedience to the gods and to justice more generally takes precedence over obedience and loyalty to his father. The lone individual exercising what they view as moral courage in the face of pressure from social forces is a common image of justified disobedience.

A similar dynamic is at work in Sophocles' play *Antigone* where the title character violates the decree of the ruler Creon not to bury the body of her brother, who was in rebellion against the city. This sets up a case of civil disobedience against the political community on the grounds of religious and family duty, which Antigone sees as a higher obligation. Creon sees this as an act of outright rebellion and disobedience and a threat to his political authority and that of the political community. We might ask: is Antigone simply prideful and arrogant, or is she a good example of justified civil disobedience? In addition to the issue of obedience is the related problem of conflicting loyalties that intersect with obedience.

The disobedient teenager, sometimes heroic and sometimes tragic, in rebellion against parents and authority is another common figure in popular culture. Romeo and Juliet arguably died for their disobedient love, causing great grief to their families and city. Civil disobedience of illegal acts against an unjust law or regime is seen as a form of political protest that can lead to political change, such as the acts of civil disobedience in the U.S. civil rights movement. Philosopher John Locke—a major intellectual forefather for the American Revolution—argues in his famous *Two Treatises of Government* that there is a right to rebellion, which in effect is a right to severe disobedience toward the state, even to the point of changing its government/leader: "Whensoever therefore the *legislative* shall transgress this fundamental role of society . . . by the breach of trust they forfeit the power the people had put into their hands . . . and it devolves to the people."[9]

Locke's argument follows Thomas Aquinas, who had argued that sedition against a manifestly unjust ruler was in fact sedition not by the ruled but rather by the ruler who had failed his responsibility to uphold and protect the common good.[10] If the ruler commanded something outside of his authority (often something that was against the authority of God), then the virtue of obedience requires that one is only obeying commands given by one within the scope of his proper authority. If the king commands something that is against the will of God, one is bound to obey God first, even if it means disobeying the king.

From the Bible to the idea of divine right of kings, there is a common theme in political philosophy making the case that the state is entitled to the obedience of its subjects and, later, its citizens. There is a moral obligation to obey political authority; the state expects this as the default position, such that any disobedience is punishable unless an exception such as civil disobedience or Locke's right to rebellion can be asserted.[11] In the Declaration of Independence, Thomas Jefferson and his coauthors begin with the idea that their rebellion must be justified: "When in the Course of human events, it becomes necessary for one people to dissolve the political bands . . . a decent respect to the opinions of mankind requires that they should declare the causes which impel them to the separation."[12] This statement is important as an explicit acknowledgment that this admission of disobedience required justification in a public way and by appeal to some notion of common values and practices held by the audience, by the political community of practice.

In the same way as the state, parents and the head of the family are viewed as entitled to this obedience as the proxies for political authority because the family is a mini-state.[13] Locke notes that children owe obedience to their parents in exchange for the goods of nourishment and education but that this obedience is not unconditional.[14] These examples all demonstrate that obedience is important, valued, and even laudatory in moral ways as the foundation of political obligation. On the other hand, the examples also show that there are times when disobedience is the right course of action, even to the point of going against one's own comrades and family and overthrowing the state.

WHY DISCUSS OBEDIENCE?

Even though obedience is a basic building block of many political communities, including the military, discussions of obedience are generally quite superficial and basic, avoiding the deeper philosophical questions:

- what exactly counts as obedience and disobedience?
- what makes these categories different than other qualities such as loyalty, honor, or deference?
- is there a moral obligation to be obedient or act in an obedient fashion?
- if there is, on what might that moral obligation rest?
- what are the implications of such a moral obligation?

This volume is designed to be an in-depth and nuanced philosophical treatment of obedience in the context of the professional military and the broader civilian political community, including citizenship.

Serious engagement with the kinds of questions around obedience, disobedience, and the shades in between requires more in-depth analysis and discussion of the conceptual landscape of obedience, especially in terms of its moral status and place within a system of moral—and in the case of the military, professional—obligations. For example, is the "slow roll" in carrying out an order by subordinates a kind of disobedience, a delayed or renegotiated obedience, or something else entirely? While obedience is also a legal issue, that is only part of the picture; it is the broader picture that this volume seeks to address—in terms of both the military and the larger political community.

One common treatment of obedience is addressed in religious contexts, such as Søren Kierkegaard's discussion in *Fear and Trembling* of Abraham's obedience to God in being willing to sacrifice Isaac. Aside from legal debates, obedience in the political sphere is often discussed in the context of social contract theory with such philosophers as Thomas Hobbes and John Locke, who see obedience as morally obligatory because the governed have consented to obedience in return for protection of their rights and escape from the state of nature. Discussions of civil disobedience and revolution further push the issue of how conditional this consent is and whether and under what circumstances it might be revoked or suspended for the purpose of political protest of unjust laws or regimes. In the military, the working assumption is of willing and immediate obedience, except in the extreme case of manifestly illegal orders; this is because of the oath that military members take upon entering the service, which legally binds them to the unconditional liability contract with the state and its representatives. They agree to act as the agent and servant of the state, even to the point of giving their lives if necessary. This is the unlimited legal contract and seems to point to a view of obedience that is much less conditional than the contract the citizen has with the state. The fact that members of the military are often both military members and citizens raises interesting questions about which mode of obedience ought to take precedence. Does the unlimited liability contract abrogate the social contract between the citizen or the state? Does it temporarily suspend it? These issues will be addressed in chapter 9 when we consider the dual identities and role of citizen soldiers.

Despite these treatments of obedience, there is little discussion of the exact nature of obedience, little attention to exactly where the line between obedience and disobedience is (or whether there is gray territory between the two), whether there is a moral (as opposed to legal) obligation to obey, and what such an obligation might be grounded in. In addition, little attention is given to the relations between obedience as a virtue and other virtues such as loyalty and discipline. Actions of principled disobedience tend to be treated as exceptions rooted in personal conscience or belief, as issues of personal individual liberty rather than as actions in relation to a moral community. Consider the conventional portrayals of Martin Luther King Jr., Gandhi, or Joan of Arc in this way—as outstanding, heroic examples of moral courage rather than being outside of normal human experience.

Obedience is a topic that has more recently been highlighted in popular and social media. Topics of discussion have included concern about too many requirements in military training leading to selective disobedience or nonobedience, Marine Corps members choosing which orders to follow, lying and candor in the military, and the March 2015 report *Lying to Ourselves: Dishonesty in the Army Profession*; these have all raised interesting issues about the role of following all orders.[15] These debates were also brought home as the media featured discussions about whether military members would waterboard or commit other war crimes if ordered to do so by the commander in chief. During the 2016 campaign, then-candidate Donald Trump asserted about military members, "They won't refuse. They're not going to refuse me. . . . If I say do it, they are going to do it."[16] On the civilian side, numerous discussions raised the issue of whether one should serve in the new administration if one thought they would be asked to do things that were ethically problematic.

These issues have been of perennial interest; after Nuremberg and again after the Vietnam War, there was increased interest in the question of obedience and disobedience in both military and political contexts. Questions about selective conscientious objection arose particularly regarding the Iraq War in 2003, with examples such as former Army lieutenant Ehren Watada refusing to deploy to Iraq on the grounds that the war was unjust (as opposed to the war in Afghanistan, where he had deployed). For many people in both the military community and the political communities more generally, questions of obedience and disobedience have more recently taken on an increased urgency. There has been more willingness by veterans and even active-duty servicemembers to be more vocal and partisan in political matters, raising questions about the military/civilian relationship and whether having a voice, especially a partisan one, in political affairs is a violation of the military's obligation to be the servant and agent of the state. One example is veterans and some active-duty military organizing on social media in favor of gun control, an explicitly partisan political position.

Bearing this broader context in mind, this book seeks to address the following questions: What is obedience? Is it a virtue, and if it is, why? What are the moral grounds of obedience? Why should military members and citizens be obedient? When ought they act in an obedient fashion? Are there times that one ought to not be obedient? Why? How should we think about obedience in contemporary political communities? The question of the nature and components of obedience is critical to discussing the moral obligations related to obedience as well as the practical issues and implications related to how we ought to think about obedience. This virtue is taken as a starting point in both political and military life but is often unexamined in any critical or deep way, avoiding the complexities and areas of ambiguity. Until we know what obedience is and how it operates, it will be difficult to make effective and convincing arguments about its moral import, limits, and implications for the military and political community more generally.

In addressing these questions, the book draws on arguments and materials from a variety of disciplines including classical studies, philosophy, history, international relations, literature, and military studies, with a particular focus on cases and examples to illustrate the conceptual points. While a major focus of the book is questions of obedience in the contemporary military context, many similar issues and considerations apply to other political communities—in particular, obedience as citizens in a contemporary nation-state. The question of how and whether a citizen ought to obey an unjust law or pledge obedience to a political leader who espouses and supports policies that they find morally objectionable has been and continues to be a feature of political life, whether one opposes abortion, universal healthcare, or more restrictive immigration policies. Further, members of the military have historically had a dual identity—as both citizens and military professionals—that must be accounted for. This can also shed light on the civil-military culture gap and on how obedience should be understood for civilians and the political community at large.

PRESUMPTION OF OBEDIENCE

In both military and political contexts, there is a presumption of obedience; therefore, it is important, at least in an initial way, to assess what the grounds for such a presumption might be and whether and why there is a moral obligation for obedience. Since Nuremberg at least, the argument for blind or unconditional obedience has been rejected as problematic; that leaves open the question of where the line ought to be drawn between obedience and disobedience. Recently, prominent military leaders have argued for "disciplined disobedience" as a critical skill for future wars, highlighting the question about when disobedience is required, effective, and moral.[17] The ideas of mission command and the strategic corporal before that seem to imply a different, more critical kind of obedience than the conventional military picture suggests.[18] In addition, there are serious ethical, political, and practical implications of our answers to these questions that must be engaged and considered. Deciding that the moral obligation to obedience is more limited and that the military member and citizen are justified in having more agency over when and whether they will obey will have serious implications for military training, education, culture, and effectiveness, as well as for the shape of our political interactions with agents of the state, such as police officers.

In his classic book on military professionalism, *The Soldier and the State*, Samuel Huntington argues that obedience (along with loyalty) is a core virtue for the military professional.[19] The military views obedience as the default position, and it is an idea that is identified with the military as well as the civilian citizenry. Just war theorist Michael Walzer notes that "no military force can function effectively without routine obedience, and it is the routine that is stressed. Soldiers are taught to obey even petty and foolish commands."[20] General Telford Taylor observes that "military service is based on obedience to orders passed down through the chains of command, and the success of military operations often depends on the speed and precision with which orders are executed. Especially in the lower ranks virtually unquestioning obedience to orders, other than those palpably vicious, is a necessary feature of military life."[21]

In this conventional view of the military, obedience (with the noted exception of orders that are manifestly illegal or immoral) is seen as essential to the warrior ethos; obedience is a moral virtue, and soldiers have an ethical obligation to obey. One of the oaths that enlisted personnel take directly references taking orders (understood as lawful orders) as a duty. Various oaths or expressions of military culture and virtue heavily reference the ideas of loyalty, mission, respect for leaders, and teamwork, even if obedience is not explicitly mentioned. In talking with military personnel even casually, one is struck by the importance assigned to issuing, taking, and following orders as an integral part of military life. On first glance, it seems that in the military, the idea that one has a legal and moral obligation to obey is clear.

In the movie *A Few Good Men*, the character of Colonel Jessup demonstrates the importance of this presumption; his character is designed to be the Platonic form of the military virtue of good order and discipline, which involves immediate and willing obedience to orders without question. If this virtue is eroded, he notes, people will get killed. It is just that simple for him. Kurtz in *Heart of Darkness* is designed to demonstrate what happens when one departs from the model of obedience and good order and discipline; dark human desires and sins produce chaos, death, and pain in both the ruled and the ruler. Obedience is designed to keep these forces at bay and allows for well-ordered society: "You need me on that wall, you want me on that wall," notes Colonel Jessup when his views on military obedience, good order, and discipline are challenged in court.

There may be good cultural and historical reasons for this presumption of obedience, rooted in practices of conscription and a largely illiterate military force that was likely to be resistant to discipline and required fear and physical punishment in order to maintain order and function. As we will discuss in chapter 9, military service was viewed in some circles as more akin to slavery or indentured servitude than as the service of free citizens for their country. The historical contexts that gave rise to many of these ideas have in fact now changed or at least been mitigated, so it will be important in our discussions to consider how an all-volunteer force that is literate and much more educated than in the past ought to change these understandings, practices, and assumptions.

There are also important practical and institutional reasons that obedience is seen as important and central to the military and its proper function. The military is hierarchical and communal in nature, functioning as a team and a group, particularly in combat. The quick and efficient processing and executing of orders are essential to combat effectiveness, esprit de corps, and trust among the combat group and likely save lives while allowing the mission to be accomplished within proper constraints. When people do not follow orders, question orders, or delay executing them, there can be disruptions and myriad other consequences, sometimes fatal ones. The 1944 Port Chicago mutiny, involving African American sailors who refused to load munitions onto ships after insufficient safety measures led to a fatal explosion that killed more than three hundred, is one example of this kind of breakdown on obedience and discipline having serious effects (namely the conviction of fifty persons sentenced to fifteen years of hard labor and dishonorable discharge).

All this said, we should note that if obedience is a core virtue or value, it may be more implicit than explicit. Obedience is not listed in any of the core values of the U.S. military branches; it is not listed in the commissioning oath for officers, nor for noncommissioned officers (NCOs), and is not a part of the officer's, NCO, or soldier's creeds or the warrior ethos statement. These are all viewed as critically important documents for the military ethos and identity, so the absence is striking. The enlistment oath for enlisted members of the military does articulate obedience to the orders of the commander in chief and officers.[22]

On the political side, civilians, even as children in school, pledge allegiance to the flag as the representation of the nation; are we to see this as a kind of obedience analogous to upholding and defending nation and Constitution in the military oaths? The naturalization oath taken by new citizens asserts in part, "I hereby declare, on oath, that I absolutely and entirely renounce and abjure all allegiance and fidelity to any foreign prince, potentate, state, or sovereignty, of whom or which I have heretofore been a subject or citizen; that I will support and defend the Constitution and laws of the United States of America against all enemies, foreign and domestic; that I will bear true faith and allegiance to the same."[23] This is remarkably similar to the oaths that military members and government officers (such as the president of the United States) take upon assuming office, so that supports the idea of an analogous concept and obligations.

DEFINING OBEDIENCE

In order to think through these issues clearly, we will need to examine exactly what obedience is, define it, and explore how it differs from other categories and concepts such as loyalty, discipline, and deference. To do this effectively, a dictionary definition will not suffice. Dictionary definitions typically get at how a word is commonly used by a society or other group, but we want to look deeper than that. We want to discern what the elements, nature, and essence of obedience are. What do all the things that we think of as obedience have in common? What are the important differences between types of obedience? What is it that makes obedience distinctive and different from other related ideas and concepts?

This kind of definition is critical because it provides a common and precise shared vocabulary that we can map onto the conceptual analysis in the book. The concepts and questions that this book pursues are complicated, and the point of a common and precise language is to help clarify and simplify matters so that the discussion can proceed with all parties roughly on the same page, using similar language to discuss similar concepts and then proceeding to think about the concrete implications and applications of the ideas under discussion. If we are talking and thinking at cross-purposes, using different terms and language, making progress will be much more frustrating and difficult. If we are working from a shared or overlapping understanding, there can be progress even if there is not consensus.

Once we have a working definition, some conceptual scaffolding, and a common vocabulary, then we can examine why obedience is so critical in the military and political life and what grounds or justifies that importance. Is obedience a virtue, a trait, or an action that is morally praiseworthy? Is it always so, or only under certain circumstances? What are those circumstances, and what about those circumstances renders it a virtue? Can it also be a vice and lead to immoral and destructive behavior?

CORE ARGUMENTS

Over the course of this book and our examination of obedience, three broad categories of arguments need to be considered, and it will be important to be clear at various points which of these arguments (or combination of arguments) we are appealing to. The strongest case for obedience will likely appeal to a combination of these arguments, while the weaker cases tend to appeal to one. Traditionally, arguments about obedience have been legal, which means that apart from legal sanction and punishment, there is no good reason to be obedient. Since Nuremberg and Vietnam, there have been attempts to combine legal and practical arguments, but if it turns out that legal sanctions are not enforced and the practical reasons change or no longer hold, the arguments for obedience are weakened. Both of these kinds of arguments are contingent upon empirical states of affairs in the world; they depend upon external motivations, sanctions, and incentives to make the case for obedience. The problem comes when these motivations are missing or inconsistently present or inconsistently enforced. If I am not home to enforce my rules, my children will likely fail to obey them. In the absence of a police presence, looting or other crimes may be more likely to happen, as citizens judge the likelihood of getting caught and/or punished is much lower.

First, there are pragmatic/practical/prudential arguments that address the concrete issues and implications of obedience. Generally, these might include considerations such as unit cohesion, combat effectiveness and efficiency, and the ability to control large groups of people who need to work together under severe stress, deprivation, and uncertainty. These kinds of arguments make the case that lack of obedience/disobedience creates practical problems; therefore, there are practical reasons to be obedient. For example, with respect to Vietnam, Richard Gabriel and Paul Savage argued that lack of leadership led to disobedience, which in turn was a critical factor in low unit cohesion and combat effectiveness.[24]

Second are moral and ethical arguments. These will include questions about the obligation to obedience (duty) and the moral grounds on which that rests. It also includes questions about the relation of obedience as a moral idea to the moral obligation of loyalty to the commander, military, state, or community of soldiers. Can I still be considered a moral person, a person of virtue, if I am disobedient to my mother, my commander, or the state? In relation to the military, there is a particular ideal moral virtue in relation to obedience based upon an oath or an understanding of professionalism/professional identity; taking an oath to serve changes the moral landscape and creates ethical obligations that did not exist prior to the speech act of the oath. Upon commissioning, the new second lieutenant has entered into a new moral (not just legal or practical) community of practice that includes an identity, professional obligations, and virtues that she was not bound to prior to taking that oath.

Third, there are legal arguments and obligations to be considered independently of the moral and practical arguments above. This includes the idea of the contract where the oaths of office taken are legally binding—the idea that one "signed up for this." In addition, there is the idea of the unlimited liability contract—the military member entering into a legal contract with the state that involves sacrifices and liability including possible injury, harm, and even death. Military members recognize that upon joining, many of the legal rights they enjoyed as a civilian (freedom of political speech, movement, dress, and appearance) are now restricted, and they are at the beck and call of the state.

I will make the case that the legal and practical arguments are important, but that what has been missing from the debate are the moral arguments for an obligation to obedience. Those arguments provide an internal motivation and consistency that enable and support what I call "critical obedience" even in the absence of external motivations or factors. The nature of the moral argument I make also allows us to address the critical issue that obedience is not simply an individual virtue, choice, or action but also has a collective aspect that must be considered. Returning to Antigone, her actions and their moral status must be considered within both an individual and a collective context, which is why my argument settles on the idea of negotiation. This approach allows us to account for individual actions but within a social and political context that imparts a different kind of meaning and import. Antigone is not merely engaging in the burial of her brother as a private action of a grieving sister; by doing so, she is engaging in an act of political protest, disloyalty, and crime for which she will be punished with death. The soldier who disobeys an order is not merely making an individual choice about what to do today but is engaging in an activity fraught with meaning that can generate a host of adverse consequences for himself and many others.

OVERVIEW OF THE CHAPTERS

The first half of the book is structured to move from the foundation of definitional work to thinking about the moral concepts involved in obedience, their grounds, and moral justifications. The second half of the book takes this theoretical account as foundational and then seeks to look at concrete and specific connections, implications, and arguments based upon that theoretical basis. As with the definition, the point of the theoretical account is to generate a common and shared conceptual understanding of obedience as a moral concept, which can then ground the arguments in the rest of the book. The theory is important, but it is in the service of the practical. The extensive use of examples throughout the book is designed to illustrate the conceptual points under discussion and give some concrete material to test these points.

Chapter 2 examines the nature and definition of obedience and sets the groundwork for the major questions and issues that will be addressed in the rest of the book. Chapter 3 considers whether and under what circumstances obedience is a virtue—that is, a moral character trait that one ought to cultivate—and whether the virtue is acting in an obedient way or being obedient as a general disposition. From there, chapter 4 will address the moral ground of the obligation to obedience, whether and under what circumstances there is a moral obligation to obedience, and what that might mean in military and political life.

In the second half of the book I consider some implications of this theoretical account. Chapter 5 looks at the relationship between disobedience and discipline to consider whether obedience is essential to maintaining good order and discipline. Chapter 6 looks at the relationship between obedience and loyalty, arguing that they are related to separate virtues and should be treated as such. Not every act of disobedience is an act of disloyalty; this argument has important implications for both military and political life. In chapters 7 and 8 I develop an account of how we should think about obedience, with an emphasis on the role of judgment, discretion, and obedience as a kind of negotiation. Chapter 9 considers how these ideas apply to citizens and especially servicemembers in their dual role as military member and citizen. The final chapter considers some implications of the arguments that I have made by looking at several important cases and considering the ideas of reasonable challenge and "critical obedience" that bring together the ideas in the book and offer a way forward.

The core claim of this book is that conventional ideas of obedience are not nuanced and granular enough to grapple with the range and complexity of obedience and disobedience in contemporary political and military contexts. We need an account that acknowledges things such as mission command in the military context and the ways in the political context in which citizens may exercise agency (via selective obedience or civil disobedience) to bring attention to and try and persuade their fellow citizens and political authorities to change laws or practices they consider unjust. Actions by groups such as Black Lives Matter or anti-abortion protests at clinics are examples of these kinds of actions in the political sphere. In both contexts, we need to think about the impact and role of social media and other public and communal modes of discourse, as well as how obedience and disobedience in a democratic republic cannot depend upon old assumptions and practices. The nature of the public context of both the political and military communities has changed significantly enough to warrant revised thinking and justifications.

Such an account is needed to deepen our discussion of obedience, disobedience, and the shades of gray in between. It is also needed to move the discussion of disobedience away from the idea of the prideful, arrogant individual such as Antigone or Euthyphro, sure of their own personal convictions, toward a more critical sense of disobedience as a reflection of the standards and commitments of a community of practice. Obedience is both individual and collective, and any account must take that seriously. Consider two examples. First, while the focus in *Antigone* is understandably on the title character, her sister Ismene is interesting as a study of a different kind of obedience. She tries to talk her sister out the of seditious actions, but when Antigone is caught and arrested, she confesses to participating and is charged with the same punishment as her sister. Was she disobedient? In what way, and toward whom?

Second, consider also the character of Fluellen in *Henry V* who often reminds the other characters (even the king) of the laws of war and functions as the voice of conscience of the community of practice. At the siege of Harfleur, he reminds his fellow soldiers of the historical "disciplines of war" regarding siege warfare, and when the boys in the baggage (who are noncombatants) are killed by the French, he is the voice of grief and injustice. Both of these characters are obedient, although perhaps not in the usual ways that we think of obedience, particularly in the military context.

KEY TERMS

In this book are several key terms that I may use in ways that depart from common meaning or that need clarification. First, I do not use *moral* and *ethical* as interchangeable, as is often the case in common discourse. *Moral* refers to the beliefs, commitments, and ideas of a person or group (including institutions such as the military or a nation-state) about what is good/bad or right/wrong. These are generally about issues more significant than table manners or etiquette, although sometimes these may overlap. *Ethical* refers to reflection upon, justifications for, or discussion of what is moral and immoral and why. This can include examination of specific moral claims (for example, "war is immoral"), or it can refer to a moral system or way of thinking about right/wrong like utilitarianism or the warrior ethos. *Ethical* generally refers to higher order concepts, justifications, or questions about why or how a particular moral belief, claim, or system is correct. Both of these terms are distinct from the term *legal*. To say abortion is wrong is to make a moral claim that may be at odds with its legal status. If I mount an argument to justify or defend my position, or you ask me questions or challenge my position with your own argument (not just a claim, but an argument with justification), then we are now engaged in ethics.

Second, the ideas of *obligation* and *duty* are related and often used together and sometimes interchangeably, but there are important differences. To say that I have a duty to do something is to say that it is legally or morally required (by law or moral principle) in reference to all moral persons and that if I failed to do that thing, I would be subject to legal or moral sanction because duties are due regardless of context or relationship. In the case of law, this might mean punishment, but in the case of moral obligation,

I would be judged to have done something immoral and possibly even risk being thought of as an immoral or unvirtuous person of bad moral character.

To say that I have an obligation to someone or am obliged to do something is more specific to a context or relationship, but I would still face sanction and could be viewed as an immoral person if I failed to carry out an obligation. To say that I have a moral obligation to care for my children is to say that I would be viewed as doing something immoral or morally wrong if I failed to care for them, even if there were no law requiring that I care for them or if such laws were not enforced. I have this obligation by virtue of my relationship with them and their vulnerable status; others would judge me as not being a moral person if I failed to attend to this duty, since I am bound by this relationship regardless of whether there are external pressures or sanctions for failure.

Obligation and duty both carry a level of being bound in certain ways that restrict agency and choice but not to the point of being coercive or avoiding responsibility. In order to be moral or virtuous, a person recognizes and freely consents to both duties owed to all and to certain obligations owed to certain persons in certain contexts for certain moral or legal reasons. They are expected to carry out duties and obligations consistently in order to be considered as having a virtuous or good character.

Finally, the term *military professionalism* is used throughout the book to refer to the norms, beliefs, and commitments of the members of the profession of arms.[25] While there is a debate about whether only officers are professionals or whether enlisted (especially NCOs) are included, I will assume it refers to all members of the military at least in the sense that they ought to aspire to be professionals. A profession is generally defined as a group that is entrusted by society to carry out certain actions (with specific permissions) for the common good. Professions typically have a body of knowledge or specific expertise and are self-regulating in terms of who is admitted to the profession and by what process, and whether and how members remain in the profession.

For our discussion, all of these aspects of a profession apply, with the norms and moral commitments that govern the profession of arms including the Uniform Code of Military Justice, the core values, principles, and ideas enshrined in the U.S. Constitution, just war tradition, and military history and tradition (including various oaths, codes, and the warrior ethos). There will be minor variations according to branch and function within the military, but military professionalism captures the overlap of norms, ideas, and commitments of this community of practice.

USING THIS BOOK

This book was conceived as a volume that will address important questions about obedience, disobedience, and related issues in ways that are designed to be as accessible as possible and that can be engaged by a general audience interested in a deeper treatment of these matters. The book is designed as a philosophical treatment of obedience, but this treatment is intended to be the basis for discussing practical and concrete implications of the philosophical account of obedience. Accordingly, endnotes and references to various scholarly debates have been kept to a minimum so as not to interfere with the line of argument in a concrete and applied context. While some readers may find the first few chapters to be more abstract than they might prefer, I would encourage a bit of patience. The conceptual work is necessary and foundational for the practical payoff in later chapters.

I envision this volume as one that might be used in small group contexts (university classrooms, professional military education, informal book groups) where the provided discussion questions could launch inquiry and exploration. These questions may also provide a useful starting point for individual reading and reflection, but it is important to note that they are only a guide. What is important is what readers take away from the text and the questions raised in terms of their own context and experiences, which can then spur further reflection and discussion. I hope that this volume can serve to generate a deeper and more wide-ranging discussion on the topic of obedience, which is necessary for us to be critically engaged and obedient citizens, whether civilian or military.

CHAPTER 2

THE NATURE OF OBEDIENCE

ON SATURDAYS, it is time for my sons to clean their room as a part of their weekly chores. Naturally, the room resembles a disaster zone. As usual, there is resistance and pushback. "Who is supposed to do what?" "He never does his share!" "I am not cleaning his side of the room." "Why can't we clean our room later?" "How clean does it have to be?" "Why do we have to clean it at all—after all, it is *our* room?" I remind them of the parameters of the task, of the consequences of failing to do the chore, as well as the reasons why this task is important for them and for our household. A command or order has been issued, and I await compliance while anticipating possible noncompliance. Will they obey? What counts as obeying? What will constitute disobedience? What will happen in the event they are disobedient?

Recall the earlier discussion of the film *A Few Good Men* and its treatment of obedience. The movie centers around the results of an ordered disciplinary action carried out on a Marine, who unexpectedly dies as a result. The film sets up with conflict between the obedience and loyalty the Marines owe to their superiors and their orders and the obligation that Marines have to protect the innocent as a part of their identity as Marines. The characters in the film wrestle with several critical questions: Who or what is

27

owed obedience in this case? What exactly counts as obedience here? Had the Marines not carried out the disciplinary action, would that have been disobedience? Are there other values besides obedience that ought to take precedence?

Both examples (and others already discussed in chapter 1) raise questions about the nature and definition of obedience and, by extension, disobedience or actions that might be short of full, conventional obedience. These examples also are useful material for probing the definition, nature, and limits of obedience, while challenging and reassessing our conventional understandings of the concept. In this chapter we will define obedience, discuss how it is distinct from related concepts such as respect, deference, and honor, and examine whether we are looking for people (whether in civilian or military communities of practice) to act obediently or whether we want them to be obedient, and why this difference might matter.

WHAT IS OBEDIENCE?

In any discussion, it is important know what is under discussion—what makes it distinct from other related ideas—to isolate constituent parts in order to generate stable meaning and impart reliable significance to the term so the discussion can advance. The task of this chapter is to engage in this process with the idea of obedience, to provide a clear and stable foundation for exploring various aspects and complexities in the rest of the book. "Surely," the reader might now be thinking, "it's not that hard; we can just look up the definition in any dictionary and move on from there." While some may see the attention to definition as merely semantic, we cannot effectively think about matters without conceptual clarity of what exactly the thing under discussion is. How many times have we been in that argument with a family member or partner, only to discover after several hours and lots of yelling that we were actually in agreement but were either using different terms or meant different things while using the same term?

Clarity and precision—both conceptual and linguistic—really do matter, especially in complex matters where there is disagreement.

The dictionary definition of any term tells us how the word is conventionally and commonly used in various contexts in a particular time, place, and culture. This, of course, is subject to lots of variation and is hardly suitable for philosophical or practical exploration where we want a relatively fixed meaning as a foundation. The word "gay," for example, was typically used in one fashion around the turn of the twentieth century (to mean happy, jovial), and by the end of that century was conventionally used to denote homosexual orientation; the dictionary definitions tracked and reflected this change in conventional use but did not tell us anything about the nature of being gay or gayness independent of social convention.

Accordingly, we are looking for what I call an "analytical" definition. This kind of definition is designed to get at not only the essential and necessary qualities without which x would not be x, but also those characteristics that are relatively stable and common across all of the instances of x—irrespective of time, space, culture, and context. This definition then would isolate the unique, distinctive, constitutive elements of x and exclude everything that is not x, even things that are related and may seem to bear a resemblance to or overlap with x.

In one of his early dialogues, *Laches*, the philosopher Plato (through the character of Socrates) takes up the issue of courage, providing one model for a search for the analytic definition.[1] Scholars often call the formula in the early dialogues the "What is F?" question where Socrates' partners in discussion, often considered experts or knowledgeable on the topic, provide a series of definitions—often conventional, rather like our dictionary definition—which Socrates then proceeds to problematize, critique, and question to try and attain this conceptual clarity. For example, Laches first defines courage: "He is a man of courage who does not run away, but remains at his post and fights against the enemy; there can be no mistake about that." Socrates then raises the objection that that is a description of a certain specific instance of courage (courage in combat), as opposed to the nature of courage that all kinds of courage would have in common.

Eventually, revised definitions are offered for discussion—courage as "the endurance of the soul" and "a certain kind of wisdom"—with the same process of dialogue, challenge, and revision to the definitions until Socrates' interlocutors get frustrated. The source of the frustration is usually some kind of impasse with an internal contradiction that they cannot resolve. In this case, they have ended up defining courage as a part of virtue without defining what virtue itself is, and so they are caught in circular reasoning. One of characters is the well-known general Nicias, who is presumed to be an expert in courage. This adds to the frustration and irony of the conversation, which ends with a promise to be continued the next day.

While many readers get frustrated with the lack of a clear and definitive definition at the end of these dialogues, Plato's point is that the practice of philosophy involves an ongoing process rather than a specific result. An important part of the process is breaking ideas into their elements and aspects, examining each critically to see if they are in fact essential and constitutive or contingent upon time, place, experience, context, or bias. His concern is to provide foundations for certain and objective knowledge on which other ideas and claims can be built—especially ethical and political claims relative to how we should live. While we might not necessarily endorse his project of objective knowledge, the precision of and critical thinking in this process are still valuable for producing clear and meaningful definitions and ideas for productive discussion on difficult topics.

COMMON APPROACHES TO OBEDIENCE

In that vein, let us begin with two common approaches to obedience and see how they suit what we are after. First is blind, unquestioning, and instant obedience—what I will call unreflective obedience. In this case we follow orders as they are given, without any real reflection upon whether we *should* follow them; we trust that they are valid and should be carried out, or we perhaps are in the habit of obedience, much as a well-trained dog is. The new recruit in basic training is generally expected to give this kind of obedience, as are young children, especially where physical safety is involved. "Hold my hand, we are crossing the street," is not up for discussion or deliberation by the child, and we would presume that the responsible parent knows better than the child what is safe. The training sequences in the Vietnam War film *Full Metal Jacket* capture well this kind of expectation in basic training in the military. Orders are given and followed, or else there are swift and severe consequences. Again we presume that the drill sergeants and other military members in charge of the training know best what is required in war and how to prepare recruits for that experience.

Second, there is obedience as a kind of passive nonresistance, which is not so much positive obedience as negative obedience or lack of disobedience. Here, the obedient action is the path of least resistance. In his book *The Things They Carried* author and Vietnam veteran Tim O'Brien describes his decision to go to the war in this vein. It was not so much that he chose to go to the war as that he lacked the courage to disobey the draft and flee across the border into Canada. For him, obedience was the path of least resistance, but he was by no means enthusiastic or even really willing.[2]

What is problematic is that neither of these cases involve authentic, sustained, and critical intention, deliberation, and decision to carry out the order, where the action is a voluntary or a truly willing one chosen by the agent in accordance with their values, priorities, and projects. In thinking about obedience, my argument is that more than an action matching the command is required. The Greek philosopher Aristotle distinguishes between actions that are voluntary, involuntary, and mixed on the basis of whether the agent—as opposed to outside forces—is the source of the action: "We have found, then, that we wish for the end, and deliberate and decide about things that promote it; hence the actions concerned with things that promote the end are in according with decision and are voluntary."[3] On this idea, obedience requires a wish (or desire), deliberation, and decision all directed toward a particular action, which is a more robust way of thinking about (obedient) actions than these two cases present. Insofar as these two cases reflect common intuitions about obedience, what they highlight as basic elements will not be enough.

Medieval philosopher and theologian Thomas Aquinas, who was heavily influenced by Aristotle, argued that there are three kinds of obedience: obedience sufficient for salvation (obedience to God), perfect obedience (to human commands that are lawful), and indiscriminate obedience (to everything, whether it is lawful or not).[4] For Aquinas, what makes a command appropriate to obey (lawful is the term that he uses) is whether the commander is commanding something within his authority. For example, if a king commands something that is against the will of God or in some other way outside his authority, it is not a lawful or binding command and need not be obeyed.[5] In a similar vein, he argues that sedition against an unjust ruler is not sedition on the part of the people but rather on the part of the ruler who is committing sedition by commanding or ruling in ways that fail to uphold justice and the common good. In human affairs, Aquinas is advocating perfect obedience, but that requires that it be within lawful boundaries.

What Aquinas contributes to our discussion of the nature of obedience is this idea that obedience has limits, which is at odds with the idea of unreflective or blind obedience discussed earlier. If obedience has limits, it will require some reflection (even rather minimal) in a given context to assess whether the command is lawful or whether obeying would be indiscriminate obedience.

This means that at the least, deliberation and decision are elements of obedience, not just action. We will return to this idea in our discussion of John Locke and David Hume in chapter 4 in relation to civil obedience and disobedience, but this point about reflection applies to both political and military contexts since it is central to the development of ideas of obedience and obligation.

Thus far, the common notions of obedience seem to be missing something about obedience related to actions being voluntary: desire, deliberation, decision. In both the *Full Metal Jacket* training and Tim O'Brien's example, one or more of these is missing. In the example of my sons cleaning their room, we clearly do not have unreflective obedience, and if they do obey, it is unlikely that it will be passive obedience. I might decide to apply coercive measures if I meet resistance, but if I have to coerce my sons, is their response really obedience? Based upon this discussion, it would seem that it is not. Obedience has to be more than an action that matches the command, so we need desire, deliberation, and decision followed by action.

DISTINCTIONS FROM RELATED IDEAS

Other related ideas, such as respect, loyalty, and deference or honor, may seem similar to obedience and may even be found in conjunction with it. We will discuss loyalty in some depth in chapter 6, so here we will look briefly at respect and deference or honor.

Respect

Given the import and seriousness of obedience and its frequent presence in hierarchical relationships, we might think that obedience requires respect. If I am bound to obey my father, that means that I must respect him, right? While this seems intuitive, examples of obedience without respect are fairly common; the obedience is often driven by threat of consequences or adverse sanctions, some kind of power that the issuer of the order holds over us. I might obey the speed limit posted on the highway not out of respect for the law, but because I do not want a speeding ticket. I might, in fact, think that this particular law is dumb and violates my rights and that I am a better judge of how fast I ought to drive. A teenager might obey school authorities to avoid punishment, even if he does not respect them at all (and in fact, may harbor resentment and disrespect for what he views as unjust and tyrannical practices). In this vein, Niccolò Machiavelli famously noted in relation to leaders that it is better to be feared than loved, since fear will motivate obedience where love may not or only inconsistently do so.[6]

We can clearly have obedience without respect, then. The problem here is that this kind of obedience is only effective as long as the external pressure or sanction is there and known to be consistently enforced. Returning to Aristotle, this obedience is not truly voluntary but rather is a mixed action where a significant portion of the agency and motivation (desire) for the obedience comes from something other than the agent. If we alter those external forces, would we still get the consistent and predictable obedience that the military and political communities think is important? Many a drill sergeant or parent of a teenager would likely answer negatively based upon experience.

What about the other way? Can one have respect without obedience? This seems less likely to be the case, since if I respect someone, I will be more motivated to obey them; there is trust and often a social connection to their projects and aims. That said, there could be exceptions where a person I respect is acting out of character, exercising bad judgment, or operating in ignorance relative to a particular action. I might generally respect my grandfather but might disobey his command to use a free and open WiFi network for a credit card purchase if I think he does not understand the implications of such an action given his ignorance about that technology. A friend who has gone through a bad breakup might ask me to join in a revenge plot against their former lover, but I would refuse because

I recognize that their emotional state is driving the decision and the consequences could be quite negative for both.

Again, while respect and obedience often overlap, they are different concepts. The important question is what we say about cases where there is respect but no obedience, which seem to involve a judgment on the part of the commanded about the intentions, knowledge, or capacity of the commander. We think there is a problem somewhere in the chain of motive or reasoning—that the commander is wrong and, therefore, we ought not obey. Agency seems to be important to obedience in a full and complete sense; where agency is missing, we will find obedience is lacking, even in cases where there is normally respect. Disobeying an illegal or immoral order in the military context or conducting civil disobedience in the political context are cases that fit this model of respect without obedience. If this premise is correct, it undermines the standard argument that disobedience is problematic because it reflects disrespect of the person giving the command.

Deference/Honor

Another category with overlap and confusion is deference or honor. Given the traditions and history of the military, especially in regard to ceremony and rank, we might compare military, and to a lesser degree political, leadership to aristocracy or royalty where deference is expected and given purely on the basis of office and rank. Such deference is often connected in important ways to the specific history, culture, tradition, and context of a particular role or office rooted in habits of display and behavior. This deference might overlap at times with obedience, but there are also important distinctions and differences. Deference is given solely on the basis of class, position, or rank and does not require any insight into the merits, knowledge, or experience of the person to whom it is given; there is simply a presumption of value, authority, and power. Tamler Sommers discusses this kind of deference as horizontal honor: "A defining feature of horizontal honor is that it's distributed equally to all group members. Another is that it is not tied to a specific action or achievement."[7]

Deference and honor go beyond obedience to show recognition of social or political position, as well as some agreement with or endorsement of the value of the office or person in question. When I curtsy to the queen or acknowledge the authority of a general officer with a salute, I am, in some way, giving endorsement to what they represent and the values inherent in the office, institution, or role that they inhabit. People in these kinds of positions are surrounded by daily habits, signs, and signals that reinforce to them and others the position and its accompanying power. This endorsement is given without its recipient necessarily doing anything to merit or deserve it beyond occupying the office or role. An incompetent and immoral general officer or a very lazy queen who shirks her duties is still accorded deference and honor, although they might not necessarily get respect.

Accordingly, one can give obedience without deference or honor in an analogous way as we discussed relative to respect. As a member of the military, I obey the commander in chief, even if I refuse to give deference or honor. I might not endorse the values the office represents (I might be a monarchist who would prefer a queen as head of the military), or I might not agree that the particular person ought to hold that office. Given that deference and honor seem stronger, more pervasive, and less related to critical assessment than respect is, the kind of obedience associated with deference will either be blind or passive obedience. In giving deference or honor, we only must acknowledge that a person holds an office or role; there is no need for more deliberation than that. It is much more immediate, given without reflection and where social pressure is strong, not necessarily reflecting our own desire, deliberation, and decision to do something in accordance with our own priorities and commitments.

Is this necessarily problematic? Given the nature of political and military life, one could argue that the less time for reflection and critique one has—the more immediate and predictable the response to the authority figure—the smoother things will run in periods of stress and time constraints. Even if deference and honor are not obedience, they are good practice for building the kinds of habits that obedience requires. While deference and the related idea of honor may often be confused for a sign of obedience and may require similar habits (showing respect, following orders, observing the chain of command), they are actually incompatible with the true, "critical" obedience we seek in military and political communities of practice because of their unreflective and uncritical nature. We will return to this argument in chapter 10.

PRESUMPTION IN FAVOR OF OBEDIENCE

Related to respect, deference, and honor is the notion of a presumption of obedience in both military and political circles. Obedience is often viewed as a character trait or virtue of the good/ moral person, soldier, or citizen. Samuel Huntington notes of the military man: "Consequently loyalty and obedience are the highest military virtues: 'the rule of obedience is simply the expression of that one among the military virtues upon which all the others depend.'"[8] This reflects the strength of this presumption, such that most of the discussion is not about the nature or reasons for the presumption but is rather about justifying relatively rare instances of disobedience and/or justifying the punishment and sanctions against disobedience. Such disobedience is often viewed as a threat to the state, the group, and/or the social order, and any justifications are usually narrow and rare, such as disobeying a manifestly illegal order in the military. I return to this here since it seems to be a critical part of the definition and nature of obedience. Obedience is generally an obligation owed to justified authority, and it carries individual as well as social weight so strong that it appears presumed rather than explicitly argued for. We will return to this issue again at different points in the book to see how and where it fits into our discussion, especially of critical obedience.

Another point to note here is that context may be significant: there may be differences between obedience in garrison and in combat mission contexts. A recent article that includes a list of things a senior rater in the military will look for seems to make clear that these suggestions are about impressing upon senior commanders that one is fully committed to the community and their interpretation of what counts as membership.[9] At first blush, this list is about helping people understand the subtle aspects of the military profession and community of practice that they have joined. This includes strictures such as not bringing pets and kids to unit events unless invited, wearing proper attire for more formal events, having the family involved in military communal life, and writing thank-you notes. Since every profession has its own norms, practices, and standards, such suggestions would no doubt be a helpful articulation for those new to the community.

However, upon closer inspection, most of the items on this list have little to do with the military profession as such and more to do with enforcing social (not moral) norms of a community—in particular, one oriented toward a garrison and not a combat context. To take Don Snider's distinction between the profession and the bureaucracy of the Army to heart, this list speaks to the bureaucracy rather than to the profession.[10] This is especially true of the points about whether one's spouse works, the behavior of children, and the level of their involvement in the life of the unit as a reflection on the values, capacities, and virtue of the soldier. Such things seem to be more about reinforcing a certain view of social organization and relationship, family, and community life that does not bear directly on the profession of arms as managers of violence in the interest of the state. The second kind of requirements appears most prevalent and prioritized in the garrison context, which seems more oriented toward the bureaucratic aspects of the military, raising interesting questions about why this is the case.

At this point, one might note that these suggestions are about showing that one is a full and committed member of the team and that following them would increase unit cohesion, teamwork, and esprit de corps, thus improving mission and combat effectiveness. In response to this point, the problem is that teamwork is about what you do, not about what you are. Teamwork is about how you do your job and how you carry out your responsibilities; whether you have an optional form of swag on your uniform, a spouse who shows up at events, or angelic progeny is more about who you are. It is about a certain identity based upon social norms that are policed by the senior members (as they were policed when they entered the community) and with being able to demonstrate that one is willing to be obedient through the exhibiting of outward signs rather than actions related to the profession.

Someone can come to work, be highly effective and committed to the aims of the team, and have good relationships and collegiality while engaged in work, but have other priorities, hobbies, and relationships outside the workplace, limiting engagement outside of duty hours as a matter of work/life balance and healthy professional boundaries. In the civilian context, the film *Office Space* offers a satirical look at the kind of social conformity at play, reflecting our discussion in both the civilian and military contexts. The main character is admonished by multiple supervisors because he forgot to put a specified cover on a document, while his girlfriend gets in trouble at her waitressing job because she has only the adequate level of decoration on her uniform. We can think of these kinds of conformity issues as similar to the issues in the garrison context articulated by the senior rater list.

Therefore, obedience in the garrison context may be more about maintaining control of individuals within a bureaucracy than obedience in the combat context, which is more about achieving a mission where obedience is a means to that end. Garrison obedience is about obedience as a habit, largely without critical thought and deliberation, to reinforce a social and military identity and allow for a well-functioning bureaucracy. Obedience in combat, on the other hand, is useful in that context to the degree that it does help mission effectiveness and allow a unit to operate as a team and is less useful an as end in itself. It is valued to the extent that it helps achieve the mission. To the degree that it fails to do this, it will be jettisoned or modified— often without much serious sanction and perhaps to praise. A familiar trope in literature and film is the soldier who is hopeless and disastrous in the garrison context but who performs well in combat precisely for the same reasons that she was unsuited in the other context. Combat is about action, about performance, not about identity.

One concern to be raised is that the line between the garrison and combat contexts is not always clean and clear; there may be areas of gray in between or movement between the two contexts. In addition, members of the military often move between the two, so we cannot think about obedience only in one context and not consider the other. Especially in the contemporary context, with multiple deployments in theater alternated with time in garrison, people more likely are regularly cycling back and forth between the two and need to be able to operate in both; accordingly, our definition and concept of obedience must take both (as well as the gray areas) into account.

Another concern could be the argument that the training and education that are part of the garrison context are about readiness and preparation for the potential combat context. This level of unity and social control is needed in order for people to effectively function as a team in combat. It is about showing that you can control yourself and your environment, which is necessary in combat; it is about demonstrating that you will bring your entire self to the fight. This returns us to the question of whether we want obedient action, or if we want something more—people that are obedient as a matter of habit, identity, and disposition.

ACTION OR DISPOSITION?

The garrison versus combat context pushes us to a deeper consideration of the nature of obedience and this distinction: is obedience an action, or is it a disposition? Is it enough to act obediently, or is there something more? Must one be obedient, and what exactly does that mean? Further, this requires a deeper assessment of the degree to which obedience does/should involve intention, deliberation, and decision. Is obedience a matter of doing or acting out what one is ordered or required to do, or a matter of character or disposition that one takes as a part of one's personality—that one ought to be obedient? This distinction requires deciding whether we are looking for soldiers to act in an obedient fashion—that is, to predictably follow orders—or whether we are looking for something more—that is, soldiers with an obedient disposition. The latter means that they will be much more likely to obey orders immediately and without deliberation because they are predisposed toward obedience. If soldiers with an obedient disposition are what we want, what are the implications for responsibility and accountability, since we might think such actions are not fully voluntary?

Huntington's view of obedience, instilled in the military through basic and other introductory training, is that it is automatic, unreflective, and unquestioning, unless some egregiously odd circumstance exists. In much military writing on this topic, this kind of obedience (especially for enlisted ranks) is presumed as a professional habit and disposition, but even discussion of it relative to the officer corps focuses on the exceptions being only in cases of manifestly illegal or immoral orders. The reason given for this presumption of obedience is the chaos of war, where we need military members to act predictably in concert as they are told. There is also a time issue; pausing to deliberate, reflect, discuss, and assess is a luxury that the chaos of combat does not afford. Events are unfolding too quickly, and any delay could be potentially fatal and/ or imperil the mission.

This view of obedience, which appears to remove the process of intention, deliberation, and decision from the idea of obedient action, is problematic for several reasons. First, being able to show intention (which often includes deliberation and decision) is necessary for attributing responsibility and punishment, whether moral or legal. Second, if predictable, habitual obedience is the desired outcome, practicing proper deliberation and decision is essential to that process. One can get regular obedience with external threats and sanctions, but only as long as those external forces are in effect. Having that process internally motivated is more reliable and efficient, since it will then produce obedience even in the absence of threats and sanctions. As we will argue later, we want two things. The first is appropriate obedience following Aquinas, which will require critical, reflective obedience to know when we should and should not obey. We also want intentional, voluntary, internally motivated obedience, which will be the most consistent form and will allow for reasonable and effective accountability and responsibility.

OBEDIENCE AND TRUST

What is the corollary in the civilian political realm? The same kind of time issues normally do not exist there, although the same interdependency and need to work together remain important, as do the dependability and predictability needed to have civil order and a functioning political system. We often take this for granted until it breaks down in cases of natural disasters (such as Hurricane Katrina) or social protests gone awry (such as the 1992 Los Angeles riots). In these cases, the problem is not just the threat and peril to property and law and order, but also the threat to the sense of trust between citizens living in community together. When this trust breaks down, much of the normal functioning of society we take for granted is imperiled. When I stop at a stop sign or light, I trust that others at that intersection will act in ways that are consistent with traffic laws and customs.

If they fail to or I cannot trust that they will, there can be serious consequences, such as traffic accidents or road rage.

Presumably both civic education and professional military education and training are designed to address these issues. When a person is called out, sanctioned, or counseled, is it for failing to do something or failing to be obedient—like having a "bad attitude," not demonstrating a commitment to the team, and interfering with unit cohesion? A critical issue is the intersection between obedience and unit cohesion or the ability of the combat or other group to effectively execute the mission. If trust is central to command and leadership (as many in the military claim) and supports unit cohesion, which version of obedience is necessary for that? Will obedience in action be enough?[11] Or do we really need people to *be* obedient as a character trait in order to trust them?

My argument is that people acting in an obedient fashion on a regular basis is enough for the purposes of both the civilian political and military contexts and maintains the agency we require for responsibility. If part of the concern is trust, we develop trust in someone by observing their actions and the extent to which their actions are consistent with their words—that is, their integrity. I cannot reliably know what people's internal dispositions are (they may lie, pretend, or seek to deceive). The demand for being obedient imposes an epistemological burden that is impractical in civilian political and military contexts where we may not be intimates with the people in question and thus have to base our judgments on a fairly small body of actions.

"Habitual" obedience seems necessary for the military to effectively function, but how does one keep it from collapsing over time into "blind" obedience? If military members do not regularly have a chance to develop moral judgment and discretion and to practice it (like they have the chance to practice obedience), how will they know and have the ability and aptitude to disobey or selectively obey/under-obey? This aptitude is required for Aquinas' perfect obedience and for the critical obedience I will argue for later in the book, so more fleshing out of the need for and nature of such moral and professional judgment is required.

To avoid the collapse of habitual into blind obedience, we need to make the case that habitual obedience can still involve intention, deliberation, and then decision even if the time frame is vastly shortened through repetition and practice. There seems to be an important difference between habitual and automatic, unthinking behavior. This is a critical piece to develop, given the role of military training; it's not that training gets you to not think about it, but rather to think about it much more quickly. For example, I learned to drive in college on a manual transmission. At first, it required much intention, deliberation, and decision (on a fairly slow timeline) in order to drive competently. I had to think about every movement and every nuance, coordinating everything in a way that felt unnatural. Over time, with more habituation, practice, and muscle memory, I could drive smoothly without giving it what I thought of as intentional and deliberate thought. It was more like the background music as I drove. However, I was still acting voluntarily—employing intention, deliberation, and decision, but I was so practiced at it that it could be in the back of my mind and other things could be in the forefront. When something happened on the road that was not routine, I would become aware that the act still involved intention, deliberation, and decision, as I had to re-engage more active thinking about my driving or responding in ways outside the muscle memory–worn track.

AGAINST DISPOSITION

There is a tendency to see obedient action (especially repeated over time) as a reflection of an obedient disposition or character, rather than as explicit, intentional, deliberate decisions and actions. In the military, as well as in political contexts, we appear to be training people to be obedient as a character trait because we want habitual and predictable obedience, particularly under conditions of stress and pressure. We have noted the extent to which obedience in garrison contexts appears oriented to the disposition regardless of the results—being obedient as a character trait and as a demonstration of loyalty to the commander. The implied argument is that obedience is a way of showing loyalty and building trust and unit cohesion and that it is really more about the person of the commander. Therefore, being disobedient is problematic because it disrupts that basic relationship and expectation of loyalty and, by extension, the relationship with the unit or other group. To be disobedient is to demonstrate a failure of loyalty and is a character flaw, as opposed to thinking about it in terms of the action and its impacts on the mission.

The case of generals or admirals (or other senior leaders) such as Gen. Douglas MacArthur who are disobedient to the president or other civilian leadership or who use their position as a platform for dissent illustrates this kind of problem. It is a case not simply of an officer dissenting or refusing to obey an order but rather of disloyalty and even a lack of patriotism since loyalty to the office of the president, if not the actual person who occupies it, seems important to demonstrate as a member of the military. Loyalty is a primary virtue that we expect members of the military to demonstrate along with obedience. Unsurprisingly, then, we assume they are related and intertwined.

However, this dispositional approach is problematic because of this focus on personal relationship and loyalty, as opposed to thinking in terms of action grounded in intention, deliberation, and decision. What is conducive to the military function is that people act in obedient ways for the right reasons and intentionally, since such agents will then repeat those actions appropriately, not just blindly, and can, therefore, be held accountable for them. The dark side of loyalty and obedience is clear from the war crimes literature and the stories of ethical violations, coverups, and nepotism that show up with alarming regularity in the news; a more critical approach to obedience is designed to avoid those and other problems. The "Fat Leonard" scandal in the U.S. Navy revolved around the role that personal relationships and loyalty played in facilitating large-scale corruption, stealing, and other immoral behaviors. Given the importance of relationships and interconnectedness to esprit de corps, unit cohesion, and combat effectiveness, this view is understandable but is to be resisted.

KEY QUESTIONS AND ANSWERS

Where do we find ourselves at this point in the discussion regarding obedience, its definition, and its key elements? So far, we have seen that obedience is different than respect and deference/honor, even if they appear to overlap and have commonalities. Obedience does share the association with other hierarchical relationships and includes judgments about justness or legitimacy of the authority or the course of action involved. We also noted the distinction between being obedient, which can be problematic, and engaging in obedient action. Finally, blind and passive obedience is problematic because of a lack of clear desire, deliberation, and decision; the conclusion is that obedience needs to be voluntary.

My working definition of obedience will be *the intentional and voluntary carrying out of orders or commands, given by a commander or other authority figure who represents legitimate political authority in action.* This is a pretty basic definition that can serve as a starting point, but it does generate some questions that we will take up as we move through the rest of the book, framing many of the critical issues we need to address in developing the account of authentic and critical obedience necessary for both the military and civilian political communities.

First, given the centrality of the commander to nearly any account of obedience, we need to consider the nature and role of this figure in the concept. Does obedience really require a commander? What kind of figure and justification of authority are required to generate obedience? Does it matter whether the power is legitimate? Can illegitimate commanders require obedience, or is obedience only required when the commander wields just or legitimate power? And how would the commanded know whether the commander had just or legitimate power, as opposed to just giving deference based upon their position/rank?

To return to Aquinas, it seems that such knowledge would be necessary—at least in a rudimentary way—to be able to assess whether the commander was issuing a lawful command or commanding within their authority. This is certainly true in the case of knowing whether the order is manifestly illegal or immoral, which is the current legal threshold in the military. In the event of a coup or other more dramatic political issue (such as a contested election), the military would have to know who the legitimate commander in chief is so they know whose orders carry weight and which they ought to follow.

Second, in what sense do we think of obedience as social versus individual? Does obedience assume some kind of social or community context? Can one be obedient to oneself? Must the object of obedience be an outside person/commander? Saying that one could be obedient to oneself seems odd, which suggests that obedience is an "other-regarding" virtue—that is, a moral trait that is directed toward or has as its object other persons or objects. This would require other persons with which to demonstrate the virtue, making it a social (as opposed to an individual) virtue.

In both the political and military realms, this means that obedience must be considered not as an individual matter between myself and the person who is issuing the command to me. It would mean that there is also a broader community that is impacted by my obedience or lack thereof, and as such obedience and disobedience have social meaning and impact apart from the specific individuals involved in the command. If a soldier disobeys a command, why is it a concern for anyone other than the soldier and her commander? What are these broader implications, and why do they matter? Exactly how serious are they?

Third, we must consider intention of the commanded, the one giving the command, and the community in which the command is embedded and occurs. Does the intent of the commander matter? What if the commander issues a command with malicious intent? Does that matter? What about the intention of the person to whom the command is given? Does the intent of the person commanded matter? Can I accidentally or unintentionally be obedient, or is intention necessary, and what kind and level of intention is necessary? For example, the idea of mission command seems to put a fair amount of stock in the idea of commander's intent and being able to discern that, but what about the intent of the person obeying? It is possible that one might end up carrying out their intent accidentally, inadvertently, or against one's own intentions through intervening events. Is that enough? In this chapter we have argued that intention, deliberation, and decision are necessary to have a voluntary action and that these things are therefore necessary for full, critical obedience. However, one might argue that this is too high of a bar to clear and that some level of intention and deliberation short of this is sufficient for our purposes, especially if it results in success of the mission or other political end.

Finally, does the outcome of the command (the action) matter? Can it trump other considerations? As long as I achieve the desired outcome of the commander, the intent of the order, does it matter how the commanded do it? Again, the mission command philosophy might be seen as an example of this last concern that takes a more outcome-oriented approach, although within the parameters of the commander's intent.[12] As long as the bedroom gets cleaned, does it matter how my sons accomplish this task? They are enterprising young men, so what if they subcontract out the task to local neighborhood kids for a share of their allowance? The work gets done, and they collect the money but then pay out part of it to their assistants. Is that obedience? What about in the case where they don't pay the assistants, but rather threaten them (extortion) in some way to gain the fruits of their labor? In both cases, the room presumably gets cleaned, and my aims are fulfilled in terms of having a clean household and the rest of the day to enjoy as family time.

This raises the question of whether it is only the outcome that really matters, which pushes against mission command a bit, showing the difficulties of interpretation with commander's intent. Do my sons need to share my intent in order to act in accordance with it? Often there will be elements of the commander's intent that are implicit, assumed, or unspoken that may be at odds with how the outcome is achieved. In this case, part of my intent in having my sons clean their room is for them to learn organization, tidiness, and the ability to work together as brothers in maintaining their space in accordance with my standards. Thus, it turns out that I have a particular intent (commander's intent) but that I also want them to have a particular intent (or range of intentions) in order for me to consider their actions obedient. Outsourcing the labor will not fulfill it; nor will extortion, which actually might be worse in my eyes than outright disobedience.

As these questions demonstrate, there are many degrees of complexity and aspects of the topic that we will need to consider, but now we have a serviceable definition and some basic ideas to use as a foundation for the discussion. In the next chapter, we consider whether and in what ways obedience is a virtue and part of a system of morality, as well as the extent to which obedience must be considered in the social context, not merely the individual one. If obedience is a virtue, what exactly does that mean, and why is it important?

CHAPTER 3

OBEDIENCE AS A VIRTUE

The King gave you a commission because he thought you knew when to disobey an order.
—AN OFFICER IN FREDERICK THE GREAT'S ARMY[1]

Integrity and instant obedience are the sine qua non of the military institution.
—SAM SARKESIAN[2]

MORAL STATUS OF OBEDIENCE

BENJAMIN FRANKLIN'S LIST OF VIRTUES included temperance, silence, order, resolution, frugality, industry, sincerity, justice, moderation, cleanliness, tranquility, chastity, and humility. He considered these moral traits valuable for happiness, success, and prosperity in his own time and context; they were early American core values, so to speak. How do these match the virtues we might think are important in our own political and military contexts? Would the lists have similar virtues? What is the connection between the virtues valued and the social and cultural context of a community? Does the context matter, or are virtues consistent across time, space, and culture?

In this chapter we turn to obedience and consider whether it is a virtue, what kind of virtue it might be, and how the context impacts the nature of the virtue. Both military and political communities of practice tend to view obedience as a good thing, as foundational for life, flourishing, and success in those communities. Here we begin to unpack exactly how and why it is a good thing by examining the moral status of obedience. What is a virtue, and what place do virtues occupy in a moral system? In particular, we will look at the virtue of obedience in the larger context of military professionalism to consider its place in a community of moral practice in the military, as well as to consider the corollary for citizens within the political community.

NATURE OF VIRTUE

To begin, we examine exactly what a virtue is and how it is important to the moral universe or community of practice in general; then we can apply that analysis to more specific political and military contexts. The term virtue often is connected to the ancient Greek word *arete* (excellence) and comes to be identified with moral excellence or good character. A person of good moral character then would typically be expected to exhibit certain virtues; for example, courage, temperance, charity, and justice might be examples of some classical virtues thought to be central to the moral life (the good life).

It is helpful to briefly examine Alasdair MacIntyre's genealogy of virtue in his book *After Virtue,* especially his analysis of virtue in terms of practice and traditions, beginning with the heroic Greek period. This account gives a sense of several different views of virtues historically but also moves the discussion into a contemporary context. MacIntyre first notes that in the past, stories, such as the epic *Iliad*, were the primary mode of moral education. Virtues are related to a particular role that an individual might inhabit within the community: "Courage is important, not simply as a quality of individuals, but the quality necessary to sustain a household and a community."[3] Virtues in the heroic context require a particular kind of person (identity) and a particular kind of social structure. Accordingly, in the *Iliad*, the role of the warrior is a central one, and individuals play out the virtues of that role (in the persons of Achilles and Hector); this illustrates the role that the warrior plays within the heroic Greek social structure where kinship is primary.

Three central elements form MacIntyre's view of virtues and their relation to the good life: a conception of what is required by the social role inhabited by the individual; a conception of virtues as qualities that allow an individual to fulfill this role; and the acknowledgment that the human condition is vulnerable and fragile to destiny and death, and that the virtuous person does not avoid this fact, but their moral actions are responsive to it.[4] The narrative form in heroic societies expresses this moral life of individuals in a collective social structure, which conveys certain ideas and commitments about the good life. In the *Iliad*, Achilles expresses the values of honor and the warrior role, where everything but victory and dominance over the enemy is secondary, except perhaps loyalty to certain members of his kinship of warriors. Hector, on the other hand, represents the value of loyalty and fidelity to the state, to family, and to the honor of a warrior who fights not for himself but for others. His death and the maltreatment of his body at the hands of Achilles represent a clash of two different roles (warrior and citizen soldier) and two different conceptions of the good life. Achilles wants victory and glory; Hector wants to be with his family and see Troy safe.

Moving on from the heroic period, Plato sought to give an account of virtue that was more unified into a single theory— where justice is the central idea, as opposed to the general state of confusion and incoherence that he saw in the discourse, with rival conceptions of the virtues. MacIntyre notes that by Plato's time, the understanding of the virtues was no longer tethered to a specific conception of a social role.[5] In particular, Plato was concerned with what it means to be a good citizen and a good man, which, in his view, are connected, given the social and political context of the *polis* or city-state as opposed to kinship as the formative collective commitment. It is not surprising that Plato's focus is the virtue of justice, which comes to be defined as each person in the state, and each part of the soul in the individual, attending to their assigned tasks and concerns and not interfering with those of others.

Following Plato's concern with the definition and nature of the virtues and their role in the good life, Aristotle distinguishes between virtues of *thought* (especially prudence, which is necessary for ethical deliberation) and virtues of *character*. In the *Nicomachean Ethics*, he notes that "excellence, then being of two kinds, intellectual and moral, intellectual excellence in the main owes both its birth and growth to teaching . . . while moral excellence comes about as the result of habit."[6] For Aristotle, virtues of character (moral excellence) are the source of virtuous action, which must be habitual and reflect the mean between excess and deficiency. For example, Aristotle notes of bravery (courage), "Hence whoever stands firm against the right things and fears the right things, for the right end, in the right way, at the right time and is correspondingly confident, is the brave person."[7] The brave person, then, is neither rash/reckless nor cowardly/fearing the wrong things; she does the thing that reflects the mean between excess and deficiency, taking into account the particulars of the context.

The standard example of the young soldier sacrificing himself on a grenade or by taking other offensive or diversionary actions to save the lives of his comrades and allow them to win the battle or be successful in their objective might seem excessive and rash at first. (Audie Murphy is the archetype of this character, but he is not the only example.) On closer inspection, the soldier judged this action necessary in the context to achieve the objectives, and the sacrifice did bring about the desired end without requiring more sacrifice or harm than necessary. It may be that other reasonable options had too high a cost or would not achieve the objective, so in the context—given the facts of the particular situation—the brave action is the mean between cowardice and rashness.

This kind of excellence requires correct choice of the virtuous thing expressed in action; this is achieved through practice, prudence, and experienced habit. The agent begins with desire leading to deliberation (prudence or practical reasoning) and ending with action based upon choice. The person with virtues of character will act in virtuous ways regularly and will learn from mistakes to become more regularly and habitually virtuous over time. Virtues, in this kind of view, are defined by social community, with the individual being embedded, nurtured, and educated within that context, looking to exemplars, practicing the virtues, and learning from moral mistakes to improve over time. The person who is honest will be able to develop practices of honesty by habit and by adjusting that habit in relation to people she sees as moral exemplars in her community. The stories about the reputed honesty of such presidents as George Washington and Abraham Lincoln are the kinds of exemplars held up to school children to emulate: "Be like Honest Abe!"

However, for this to work, we will also need virtue of thought or intellectual excellence. In the military context, I refer to this as professional judgment and discretion or prudence in the political context, allowing us to assess, deliberate, and decide, as well as to learn from failure and mistakes. The brave person needs prudence or professional judgment and discretion to assess how significant a threat is and how she should engage that threat to achieve her desired end. If the threat is such that it would make the achievement of the end impossible or at an unsustainable cost, it would not be brave to pursue it. It would be reckless and therefore not virtuous. In the typical war movie scenario, a character often discovers that other options are foreclosed or would have such high casualty rates or other disadvantages as to render them reckless or pointless relative to the goal, and that assessment (based upon prudence or professional judgment and discretion) informs the choice of means to achieve the end.

Given this overview of some important ways of thinking about virtues, what is the place of virtue in a moral system or universe? Two of the other major moral systems—deontology and consequentialism—focus on the idea of universal or general principles being the foundation of the moral life (duty), with the moral person being one who discerns and chooses actions consistent with such principles.[8] German philosopher Immanuel Kant argues that in order to have a good moral character (good will), one must act from a motivation of duty alone and must know what duty requires.[9] Dealing with the problem of moral disagreement about duty will require a universal moral principle based upon reason; for Kant this is the categorical imperative, "Act only according to that maxim whereby you can at the same time will that it should become a universal law."[10] This imperative connects and grounds the moral character (virtues) with a rational, universal principle.

While John Stuart Mill disagrees with Kant on the content of that universal moral principle, he agrees on the necessity of having one. His utilitarian principle of moral virtue is grounded in Aristotle's idea of happiness as the highest end of human activity; that which creates the greatest happiness for the greatest number of people is moral.[11] Once again we see that the understanding of virtues must be rooted in a universal moral principle rather than a role or communal conception of the good life.

A virtue approach of Aristotle and MacIntyre, on the other hand, focuses on character traits and the moral training and education necessary to develop these in action. A virtuous person will exhibit a variety of virtues regularly in action, as opposed to following universal principles about which action to engage in. The issue here is what grounds the virtues or how one decides between competing sets of virtues that define rival conceptions of the good life. Kant and Mill are both trying to address this problem of moral disagreement and incommensurability, but MacIntyre has another approach to engage this problem while still preserving a commitment to particularity and avoiding universality.

MacIntyre sees practice, and the history of the practice relative to a particular community, as the unifying concept of the nature and tradition of virtues. By practice, he means "any coherent and complex form of socially established cooperative human activity through which goods internal to that form of activity are realized in the course of trying to achieve those standards of excellence which are appropriate to [it]."[12] In his view, virtues are essential to this idea of practice and the way in which we achieve the goods internal to it. Of course, this raises the same problem that vexed Kant and Mill: how do we know what defines the good life and which virtues we ought to cultivate? MacIntyre responds that practices and their virtues are defined in terms of a particular community and tradition of which they are a part: "A living tradition then is an historically extended, socially embodied argument, and an argument precisely in part about the goods which constitute that tradition."[13] Instead of appealing to a universal principle outside the community to settle the question of what the good life is, that question will be settled through argument and negotiation within that community in reference to the practices and the virtues of that tradition. It is important to note that these practices and virtues are not static but can and do change over time. When I refer to a community of moral practice, it is MacIntyre's concept that I have in mind.

One more thing to note about MacIntyre's view is his distinction between virtues and the morality of laws and the need for both as part of his conception of practice within a living tradition.[14] One can morally fail the community in two ways: by being deficient in the necessary virtues (failing to be good enough) or by committing an offense against the laws of the community. MacIntyre stresses that these are not at all the same thing: "To do a positive wrong is not the same as to be defective in doing or being good." These are both problematic, but it is critical that they are problematic in different ways, not as two sides of the same coin. It is important to note the connection to prudence and judgment as the link between being good on one hand and not violating the norms/laws of the community on the other. This settles the question that Kant and Mill are using the universal principle to address by providing a standard for judgment to resolve moral disagreement.

The advantage of this account is that it addresses the issue of moral disagreement within the internal workings of the community of practice, which matches better with the two communities that this book is addressing. MacIntyre gives us a way to retain particularity and context, which are necessary to the account of obedience as negotiation. For an example outside of our two focus communities, consider higher education: what level of free speech on controversial matters makes for a good university? The standards of what constitutes acceptable and tolerable speech by public speakers at universities have arguably evolved over the past decade or so. This evolution has come from within the university system over concerns about accessibility and sense of belonging, safety for students (particularly from historically marginalized communities), and changing assessments of what kind of speech creates a hostile or threatening environment versus speech that is educationally useful and transformative for students. In addition, universities have considered their changing role as a community of moral practice within society. These changes and judgments, while being spurred by outside events, were made with respect to communal practices and traditions about what counts as a good university and what it ought to be in the larger society.

SOCIAL VIRTUE

Having discussed the definition and source of virtues, we can now turn to whether we are to think about virtues as individual or social. Why does this matter? Are virtues only about the development of individuals vis-à-vis their social role, or is there something more robust and complicated going on involving the social context? If virtues were social, what would a social virtue be? If virtues are primarily about the individual and his own development, even within a socially defined role, then the individual is primary and the social aspects are the background. If the virtues (at least some of them) are social, then the social context is primary and determinative; it conditions and limits the ways in which the virtues take shape, continue to develop, and are judged.

In the military context, there are norms relating to roles and their function in conjunction with other roles in a moral community of practice; there are also norms that go beyond just those roles to the community itself. One way to look at a virtue-based account is through the idea of core values. The military uses different versions of core values: the Army uses the seven values of loyalty, duty, respect, selfless service, honor, integrity, and personal courage (or LDRSHIP), while the Navy and Marine Corps use three—courage, honor, and commitment—as the touchstone and communal understanding of the values that each individual is expected to demonstrate.[15]

Ethicist Nikki Coleman notes that obedience is not on the list of virtues for forces in the United Kingdom, and the same is true for the U.S. military.[16] This is in contrast to Samuel Huntington, who notes obedience and loyalty as the most important military virtues, and to others who list obedience along with many of the virtues listed under core values.[17] Military writers Sam Sarkesian and Thomas Gannon include obedience along with other traditional core values (such as integrity and honesty), but it is not listed in *The Professional Soldier*, Morris Janowitz's classic discussion of military honor, in which he argues that honor and trust are the "wellspring of military ethics."[18] As a partial explanation of the absence, the core values movement in the U.S. military dates to the 1980s, after these authors were writing, but it is noteworthy. Considering the foundational role these earlier influential writers gave to obedience, why is it missing from the core values lists?

First, it may be that obedience is not itself a virtue but has some other moral status that provides the grounding for the actual virtues, like the core values. It may be that honor, selfless sacrifice, or loyalty as core values assume or require obedience in order to even be possible as virtues. Aristotle argued that friendship was necessary and a precondition to the moral life because it was with our friends that we practice the virtues, especially justice. Along these lines, obedience is not a virtue, but rather a precondition to certain virtues. In order to demonstrate selfless service, personal courage, or honor in the military, one must first demonstrate obedience, because that is the context in which those virtues can be demonstrated.

Second, it could be that obedience is part of military professionalism or of being a good citizen in a certain political context but is not a virtue in the traditional Aristotelian sense as the mark of the moral person. Saying that obedience is part of military professionalism but is not a virtue or core value would mean that obedience is only a virtue in the context of this specific role. There may be some idea or principle essential to good citizenship or military professionalism that, like the first argument, requires it. Some possibilities related to military professionalism that might require obedience are good order and discipline, self-regulating community of practice, civilian control of the military, or the agency role (acting on behalf of society).

Third, it is possible that obedience is not a virtue of individuals—like the other core values, which are designed to be virtues demonstrated by the individual—but rather is a social virtue to be demonstrated by a community of which the individual is only one part. This might be a virtue that individuals express through their social context but that is the mark of a good soldier or citizen, not of a good person. This would have to involve a pretty clear bifurcation between the individual as a moral agent and as a soldier or citizen, which we may find problematic if there is not overlap or integration to some degree.

In *Tribe: On Homecoming and Belonging*, war journalist Sebastian Junger makes the case for certain virtues associated with military and political life as social virtues, although he does not necessarily use that terminology. His claim is that our sense of "tribe" and community has broken down and that especially in the case of post-traumatic stress, the issue of veterans' homecoming is not so much the trauma of war but the lack of a meaningful return and re-entry process into civilian life and the political community.[19] He also argues that courage is a communal virtue and that cowardice (failure to show courage) is "another form of community betrayal" that is often punished by immediate death or severe stigmatization and expulsion.[20] Not only are you an immoral individual if you failed to show this virtue, but also you failed and betrayed the community in doing so. Consider the plot of the film *The Four Feathers* and how the main character's fiancée essentially rejects and publicly shames him because of his cowardice. If we agree with the view that courage is a communal virtue and not simply a matter of an individual and his or her own fear, then we must ask who the community or audience is.

On the one hand, the community could be the other warriors or soldiers in one's unit or group. Junger seems to have this in mind in his discussion of the military reaction to deserter Bowe Bergdahl, who was captured by the Taliban; the military views his walking off as an act of cowardice and a betrayal of his fellow soldiers, in part because of the increase in attacks on U.S. forces during the search for him.[21] On this line of thinking, failure to be courageous is to let the other members of your unit or group down; this is a rejection of the central values of unit cohesion, loyalty, and the bond between soldiers and is a literal rejection of community. The basic job of the tribe is to protect the tribe and its members from harm, and courage as a social virtue is designed to do this. You are a moral individual as a member of the group to the extent that you do this.

On the other hand, we might have a broader notion of tribe and community in mind. In *The Four Feathers* and the film *300* (which portrays Spartans at the battle of Thermopylae), the women are the enforcers of this standard. The Spartan queen quotes the famous dictum, "Come back with your shield or on it," which lays out the choice between an honorable return (based upon communal standards and tradition) or death. This causes us to consider whether cowardice is just a betrayal of other warriors and soldiers or if it is also a betrayal of the larger community, even the members who do not wield violence on behalf of the community. Is it also the beneficiaries who are betrayed? In this case, where the existence of the tribe is at stake, this seems more straightforward as it impacts everyone, but in other cases of elective war or colonial wars, this idea is more complex.

In either case, we are faced with a question about how the actions of an individual can also involve obligations to and moral implications for the larger community, however that is defined. This is also the case with the virtue of loyalty, which is other-regarding in the sense that it directly involves others; one must have an object of loyalty in a way that is different than courage. Are there other virtues that also have this individual and communal aspect? It might be that obedience, like courage, is a social virtue and that we can see lack of obedience as communal betrayal. If this is the case, is disobedience betrayal of the military community/audience, or is it also a betrayal of the broader community? If obedience turns out to be a social virtue, it will change how we think about the moral grounding of that virtue and the implications of its violation beyond the commanded and commander, which we will take up in the next chapter.

Obedience does require a social context—at the very least, it requires a commander and one who is commanded—but more often the command is not restricted to one individual but is given to a group. Further, the commander (whether in a military or political context) is giving orders not on his or her own behalf but as a representative or agent of the state or other political entity. Both these points indicate more of a social virtue than an individual one, even in a social context; you are a good member of the community and secondarily a good person to the extent that you display this virtue. We may even find that we attribute much less value to obedience as an individual virtue while seeing its value as a social one.

Now we can return to the question of whether the core values are really virtues. If they were individual virtues even in relation to a specific social role, the core values would be sufficient. However, it seems clear that the core values alone are not enough, which is why the virtues articulated in other creeds and statements will not be enough either; we need something more robust to determine the social virtues of the military professional on one hand and the citizen on the other. Lists of virtues may be elements in that account, but something more is needed to ground them in the vein of MacIntyre's idea of practice and living tradition.

MILITARY PROFESSIONALISM

Building upon MacIntyre's conception of virtue as requiring a practice and tradition to be embedded, we now turn to military professionalism as a way to understand the practice and tradition of the military. Anthony Hartle's account of military professionalism attempts to flesh out in some depth both the virtues that define this practice and the more general grounding principles. He considers what the virtues of the military professional are, as well as the relationship between those virtues of character and military professionalism. I argue that military professionalism is a broader normative structure within which these virtues could live, but it can also handle changes to these virtues. For example, the problem of masculinity and the warrior ethos within the profession has proven challenging with the integration of women and those of homosexual and transsexual identities. The role of a particular version of warrior-ness and of masculinity as defining the military professional is at least up for debate. A recent blog piece by the pseudonymous Angry Staff Officer rejecting the warrior identity came under substantial fire from those who insist that the traditional version of the Spartan, masculine warrior must be preserved.[22] Hartle tries to lay out in a coherent way the different virtues and moral commitments that he sees as comprising the professional military ethic (military professionalism), but we soon see that there are a great many things on his list. He begins with values such as the rule of law, human rights as an individual liberty that he sees as deriving from the U.S. Constitution, and the commitment made to uphold and defend that by servicemembers. It also includes the officer/commissioning/enlistment oaths that define what it means to serve in this community of moral practice. In this vein he discusses a great many of these obligations (including obedience) as falling under the virtues of duty, honor, and country, which he takes to show a shared conception of military professionalism.

Hartle also includes the laws of war and the Uniform Code of Military Justice, which he sees as enshrining moral (not just legal) concepts such as individual rights and the avoidance/minimization of harm, as well as the welfare of the individual soldier, in that superiors ought to extend an ethics of care and to not waste life and resources unnecessarily. Both these ideas connect to the concern in just war about proportionality and reasonable chance of success as part of what justifies the use of military force by the political community. Finally, he notes the principle of civilian control of the military, which highlights the military as professional agents of the state who do not act in their own interest and on their own behalf.

While we have already discussed some of these ideas, they go beyond the basic concepts of military professionalism as articulated by Samuel Huntington and others. Huntington argues that obedience is critical (along with loyalty) to military professionalism. In his view, it is designed to further the objective of the superior, whose professionalism and competence must be presumed. The military hierarchy is based upon the presumption of these two things.[23] He thinks that questions about obedience and conflicts with respect to this arise in two contexts: obedience versus competence, and obedience versus values (moral, personal, and legal). Unless there is a serious and clear issue with the second, Huntington argues that the presumption of competence on the first would require obedience as a matter of professionalism.

In a similar vein, philosopher Michael Wheeler, in his discussion on loyalty, asks what the paradigmatic case of obedience is and argues that it is quick order under fire in combat, which is also what Huntington and others seem to have in mind.[24] Military ethicist Martin Cook more recently has argued that dutiful obedience to valid constitutional authority is at the root of the military profession, but I would note this is really obedience to a community, not to one specific commander, since he or she commands not on his or her own behalf but as an agent of that constitutional authority and political community.[25] Cook's view connects us back to something like the deeper and more complex account offered by Hartle, especially rooting obligations of military professionalism in constitutional values.

If Hartle and Cook are right, they have given us a working outline of some rules/principles and traditions that comprise military professionalism (at least in the U.S. context). However, it is not clear that these accounts address (or intend to address) how we know when they are wrong, at odds with the aims of the profession, and need change. How do we know what things can bear change without destroying the moral community of practice, the profession of arms? What we notice here is that there are many aspects to the professional military ethic, and while many of them intersect, there will be times when the elements are at odds and/or in conflict. We need to streamline this conception more consistently with MacIntyre's framework so that we can then consider how obedience fits into it. The military profession needs to be seen as a community of moral practice, which implies that it functions as a tradition à la MacIntyre. The advantage of this approach is that it will generate a way for us to organize and prioritize the extensive list of the elements that authors such as Huntington and Hartle provide in trying to define military professionalism. The practices and tradition (which are indexed to the nature of the community involved) then become the lenses through which we understand, assess, and, if necessary, change elements of military professionalism.

COMMANDED AND COMMANDER

My argument in this book is that obedience is not solely about the traditional picture of the commander and the subordinate and the link to personal loyalty and respect. In opposition to the classical view put forward by Huntington and others, one might wonder: Without personal knowledge of the commander and their aims, how is obedience not simply deference rather than a sign of respect or a virtue in itself? We have already noted the problems with thinking of obedience in terms of or requiring deference, since it departs from a more intentional, critical obedience that is necessary and desirable. In addition, if both persons are professionals, should not the presumption of professionalism and competence be reciprocal and not just one-way? This question may get to the issue of authority in the military, of which obedience is designed to be one demonstration. If that is the case, we will need to consider whether authority is only one-directional and what the implications for that are in both the military and political communities. It may be possible that there are different kinds of authority to be considered, which would provide an alternate and more nuanced view of obedience as something that is negotiated by members of the community of practice, as we will discuss in chapter 8.

To be a virtue, obedience must have reference to the common (or at least the community) good on one hand and to professionalism and the professional community (the profession of arms) as touchstones on the other. Another way to see this is that obedience is subject to at least some of the just war criteria in order to be binding—for example, just cause, legitimate authority, proportionality, and reasonable chance of success. This pushes against the dispositional view of obedience discussed earlier and more toward the habit of obedient actions as justified in the circumstance, and by moral considerations such as (and judgments about) military professionalism and the just war criteria. In addition, if obedience is a social virtue, the norms, practices, and tradition of the military and political communities of practice put boundaries on how we understand obedience.

To illustrate this point, in Shakespeare's *Henry V*, the issue of the agency of the individual soldier and obedience arises in the context of personal obedience to the king removing any sin or responsibility for the war and its cause, except that of fighting badly. The king is responsible for the cause of the war, and "our obedience to the King wipes the crime of it out of us." This is in stark contrast to more contemporary views that see the soldier as the agent of the state, apart from the ruler who occupies the position; the obedience is not personally to the ruler, but rather to the political community.

Michael Walzer echoes this theme in arguing that this agency role with respect to the state limits the responsibility of the soldier to jus in bello matters; however, the soldier never fully cedes moral agency to the state but rather retains some individual agency and responsibility.[26] As with Shakespeare, the individual soldier is still responsible for how he or she fights. A soldier who commits a war crime or abandons comrades is still liable and responsible for those actions apart from the question of whether the conflict is objectively justified according to the jus ad bellum considerations. Even if Tim O'Brien thinks that the Vietnam War is unjust, he is still responsible and has agency relative to following the laws and rules of war and should be held to account for these things, as Lt. William Calley and his troops arguably were at My Lai.

In this vein, philosopher Malham Wakin argues that obedience is central to the military function but that competence and character are intertwined, echoing Sir John Hackett's point about not being able to be immoral and a good soldier, sailor, or airman, and that an overemphasis on obedience can be a danger in that it puts a strain on integrity.[27] This connects to the earlier point that there are moral elements that condition the requirement for obedience. Martin Cook argues that intellectual independence is a hallmark of military professionalism.[28] If this is true, there are further implications for the presumption of professionalism and competence that Huntington highlights as undergirding the presumption in favor of obedience; it is a more complicated picture than the traditional one that Huntington suggests. Intellectual independence (what I am calling a requirement to use judgment and discretion—to be critical) would suggest that the presumption of knowledge and professionalism cannot be maintained, that obedience cannot be deference. This means that the military professional does and must retain some level of moral agency; the critical question will be exactly how much agency is retained and under what circumstances it is to be exercised. The military still needs to function, and to the degree that we agree with Wakin that obedience is central to that function, there are tensions and complications in the exercise of individual moral agency that must be addressed.

OBEDIENCE AND JUS IN BELLO

The argument that soldiers are agents of the state with limited responsibility is important, since it is the obedience to higher command authority in the military organization that morally grounds the commitment to jus in bello and makes it practically possible. It is only a reasonable expectation of obedience within a chain of command and control that guarantees responsibility for jus in bello. Recall King Henry's threat to the French at the siege of Harfleur about what will happen if he loses control of his troops: "Therefore, you men of Harfleur, Take pity of your town and of your people, Whiles yet my soldiers are in my command, Whiles yet the cool and temperate wind of grace O'erblows the filthy and contagious clouds Of heady murder, spoil and villainy."[29]

Revisionists of just war thinking such as philosopher Jeff McMahan, who try to undermine attempts to limit responsibility to this realm only (and seek to broaden it to include jus ad bellum as well), also unsurprisingly advocate select disobedience or rejecting and questioning the presumption of obedience.[30] McMahan rejects both the agency argument and the division of moral labor, claiming the members of the military are not only responsible for the requirements of jus in bello but also morally culpable for acting if the cause of the war (jus ad bellum) is not just: "A person is morally liable to attack in war by virtue of being morally responsible for a wrong that is sufficiently serious to constitute a just cause for war, or by being morally responsible for an unjust threat in the context of war."[31] In his view, this is not a judgment that resides with the state; each individual citizen (military or civilian) must also judge and consider their actions in light of the justice of the war. This shows how important the linkage of just war thinking and obedience is, even for those who disagree with Walzer.

McMahan's view is at odds with the presumption in favor of general obedience, even at the higher levels. The conventional presumption of obedience is tied to a certain view of agency that is quite limited; one must be obedient, and the more junior (and enlisted) you are, the more obedience is presumed as necessary. The higher up the chain of command (and the higher the rank of officer) one is, the more agency one is presumed to have and the weaker the presumption of obedience is. Those who have less agency have less responsibility, and their higher obligation to obedience transfers the responsibility to the one with more agency. If obedience is a conditional virtue and obligation, then it is dependent upon the level of agency that the person has. This idea seems opposed to what McMahan and the revisionists are arguing; they place a high level of agency upon the average soldier who is responsible for both jus in bello and jus ad bellum considerations, as well as the burden of disobedience if he judges the cause is unjust.

At stake in this debate is the question of individual versus collective responsibility for actions in war as well as for the war itself. This is a question about who has agency in which realms, how much agency they have, and what they ought to be held responsible for as a result of that agency. This parallels the tensions that Richard Dagger discusses in assessing the problem of autonomy versus civic virtue in the political realm.[32] He argues that the idea of civic virtue demands looking outward and promoting the common good, which reinforces the connection between virtue and some conception of the good (and the good life) in the role of the citizen. On the other hand, the idea of autonomy (stemming from the philosophy of Immanuel Kant) prizes the agency and judgment of the individual with reference to rational, universal principles or ideas, independent from history, context, and community.

For Dagger and his idea of civic virtue, which is similar in the military to acting as an agent of the state, virtue is a role-related concept, the disposition to be willing to act in accordance with a specific role and its norms. He notes, "Virtues are valuable because they promote the good of the community or society, not because they directly promote the good of the individual." For McMahan, taking up this role does not change the agency or obligation of the individual to act in ways that are consistent with moral principles such as autonomy, even in war. Unlike Walzer, MacIntyre, and Dagger, he denies that there are different moral realms with unique or specific moral considerations: there is only the moral agent in every situation with the same obligations.

WHAT KIND OF OBEDIENCE IS A VIRTUE?

Given this discussion, we need to consider what kind of obedience is a virtue and how that fits with integrity, the more individual virtue that concerns McMahan and others. Integrity may be an individual moral virtue, but in both military and political communities of practice, it is a trait rooted in the norms of community practice and tradition. For the military community, that includes professionalism. If we follow Aristotle, in order for obedience to be a virtue, it must involve deliberation (prudence), choice, and action; it cannot be instant and unreflective, even if it is habitual. In the case of obedience, like courage, it also must be a social and not an individual virtue and cannot be reducible to loyalty, respect, or deference. This will rule out both the blind, unreflective obedience and the passive obedience discussed earlier and will require a more critical and nuanced approach than is typical in classic discussions of the virtue.

The objection could be made that such a critical approach is fine in the civilian political context but is simply incompatible with or unsustainable in warfare. In that realm, it is a luxury that cannot be afforded. In response, I would observe that moral responsibility must apply to both realms for both the moral and practical reasons that we have already discussed. Blind and passive obedience is simply too dangerous and undermines the moral authority of war, which is, at its basis, an act of the political community. Therefore, many of the moral distinctions and concerns that apply in the civilian political community also apply in war.

Since, according to Walzer, combatants have generally consented to being treated as objects of war but noncombatants may not have, routine obedience is necessary and encouraged, but "soldiers can never be transformed into mere instruments of war."[33] If this is true, soldiers maintain some moral agency, which means that obedience must be limited. The question then becomes how and when that obedience is limited and how these limits can be maintained while preserving the command and disciplined control of troops. Therefore, it must be the case that unreflective obedience is not a virtue and may in fact be a vice and counterproductive to the military function. Only a certain kind of obedience—within the bounds of military professionalism and consistent with the military function and community of practice, chosen through deliberation and acted upon—can be a virtue. If it does not involve deliberation and choice, it is not voluntary and thus has an element of coercion.[34]

A final consideration is whether it is obedience as a virtue in itself that matters in the military and the political community, or if it is the results that obedience produces that matter. Is obedience only a virtue insofar as it produces results, a means to another end—that is, only a practical, not a moral, virtue? Obedience is supposed to produce teamwork, unit cohesion, combat effectiveness, victory, political progress—is it still a virtue if it fails to produce these, or is it an impediment to these things? This returns us to the distinction between obedience in the garrison context as opposed to the combat context. The garrison context seems to value obedience as a virtue in and of itself, regardless of results, while combat contexts appear to value obedience as a practical virtue that produces results. When it fails to do so (as we will see in chapter 8), it fades as a virtue relative to the military.

What about the civilian political context? Surely a disposition to be obedient is something that we want in good citizens. Returning to Dagger and his discussion of civic virtues, we would have to ask first whether and/or to what degree obedience is important to the role of citizens, and second, whether and/or to what degree obedience supports the common good. In general, we might say that in both cases, the answer is affirmative until it isn't. Recalling Aquinas' concern about perfect versus indiscriminate obedience, the disposition to obedience simply goes too far. We need enough of the autonomy and agency that McMahan and others argue for to provide for reflective, critical obedience here as well. We will see this in later discussions of conscientious objection to the draft during Vietnam and other cases of civil disobedience. Disobedience is necessary at times to raise public consciousness in order to effect political changes that cannot be gained through other conventional, legal channels when those channels are controlled by authorities failing to use their power in the interest of the common good.

In the civilian political realm, too, we ought to obey when the cause and authority are just, and we must be able to discern whether and when this is the case. This judgment is conditioned by the fact that there are limits placed on autonomy and agency by the practices and tradition of military professionalism and the political community in question, but it still must be made to ensure that we avoid blind, unreflective obedience on one hand and passive obedience on the other. Dark moments of our political life (such as the internment of Japanese Americans in World War II, for example) have been occasioned by an absence of critical obedience.

Having discussed in depth the nature of obedience as a virtue, a social virtue bounded by the practices and traditions of the communities in question, we now turn to the second part of MacIntyre's schema, the question of moral obligation and the law. When is failing to be obedient not just a matter of failing to be a good, virtuous person but in fact a violation against the community? In the next chapter, we consider whether and under what circumstances the virtue of obedience generates a more general obligation to obey.

CHAPTER 4

MORAL GROUNDING OF OBEDIENCE

Civil disobedience is a political act in the sense that it is an act justified by moral principles which define a conception of civil society and the public good.

—JOHN RAWLS[1]

I authorize and give my right of governing myself to this man . . . on the condition that thou give up thy right to him and authorize all his actions in a like manner.

—THOMAS HOBBES[2]

TWO QUESTIONS

WHEN DETERMINING WHAT GROUNDS the moral obligation to obedience, we need to look at cases where it fails to happen—for example, the draft and antiwar protests in the United States in the 1960s. The case *United States v. Sisson* took up the question of conscientious objection to the Vietnam War on secular moral grounds, which is the same argument that Tim O'Brien considers in *The Things They Carried* about escaping to Canada to avoid the draft. In both cases, the individuals involved had personal moral qualms and principled objections to following the law, but they also understood their choice within the political and social framework of their communities and disputes about what was fair and just—not just questions about obedience to the law. Should they agree to go fight—on their nation's behalf—in a war that they believed was morally unjust, not just on personal grounds but also relative to the norms and values of their political community? Fighting in such a war would seem to endorse immorality and to actively contribute to the pain, suffering, and death such immorality would inevitably produce.

Similarly, in Ted Shine's play *Contribution*, one of the main characters takes part in the civil rights movement in the South in the 1960s—alongside her grandson, who is participating in lunch counter sit-ins—by poisoning certain prominent racist leaders in their town: "I helped y'all integrate—in my own fashion. . . . I gave him peace! Sent him to meet his maker! Tore his very guts out with my secret spice seasoning."[3] And recall that Antigone goes against the decrees of the leader Creon to bury one of her brothers, a rebel against the state, which leads to her execution.

Are these characters behaving selfishly, acting on their own personal judgment, or are they breaking the law and in doing so trying to make a larger point to their communities? Like the instances of conscientious objection to war, these cases have a public aspect and therefore are not simply a matter of personal judgment but rather of taking a stand on public, shared political principles with some intent to persuade the members of the communities to change things. If we can think about disobedience in this way, then is obedience not also a public act, not merely a matter of personal individual judgment, but enacted in the social and public context for reasons other than just the personal? Our discussion of obedience as a social virtue from the last chapter appears to lend credence to this view, but more consideration is necessary to make this case.

The epigraph by political philosopher John Rawls highlights the connection between obedience (or lack of it) and certain moral principles and conceptions that are not simply personal moral judgment. While the examples of civil disobedience discussed above involve illegal actions by individuals, as acts of civil disobedience they raise questions about when, whether, and why the moral obligation to obey (in this case, the law) is binding and ought to be followed. There may be times when that obligation is not binding or gives way to a higher obligation, and one ought to disobey for moral reasons.

In this chapter, we turn to a deeper account of the moral status of obligation, beyond the previous question of whether obedience is a moral virtue and how that might be the case. Turning to MacIntyre's second consideration of the morality of law, we consider the role of obedience in a broader moral system and communities of practice, addressing several questions: What is the moral grounding of obedience? What generates the obligation to obey, and why is it not a universal or unconditional obligation? These questions are important if we want to make the claim that obedience is more than a virtue, more than just about being good. If we want to say that obedience is also an obligation, that we will think you are harming the community if you fail to be obedient, we need to consider what exactly it is that generates an obligation—that moves obedience from just a virtue to something more.

In addressing these questions, I will argue that obedience is not understood as unconditional but is rooted (in both the military and political communities) in justice and the common good. This will include the just war thinking considerations of just cause and legitimate authority, as well as proportionality and reasonable chance of success in relation to the mission or the political aim. Just cause means that the end or the goal is rooted in justice and the defense of rights or some other important principle of justice. Legitimate authority means that the person exercising authority has been given this authority by the members of the community (military or political) and exercises it with their permission, on their behalf, and within the norms and parameters of that community of practice. Proportionality refers to the idea that the good or end to be achieved should outweigh the risks or the harms necessary to bring that end about and is connected to reasonable chance of success, which is a judgment about the obstacles and resources the community brings to the mission or end.[4] This line of argument sets the stage and is a necessary first step for the arguments about moral and professional judgment and discretion (chapter 7) and obedience as negotiation (chapter 8) later on. The fact that obedience is to be grounded in a specific way is important to understanding when it is a binding obligation and when it should be resisted. Part of the foundation for this line of argument will be the idea of the promise or oath that one takes when entering a new moral community with its own practices and traditions as creating new moral obligations, a new moral context. It is this point that will be pivotal in helping us think through the obligation to obey, since it provides the normative structure and limitations of that obligation.

COMMON GOOD

First, it is important that the goals and authority behind the command to obey are consistent with principles of justice, especially that of the common good, in order to have binding moral force and not be simply a matter of virtue. Consider what it means to say that someone has an obligation to do x. Generally, in moral accounts, this means two things: that one is required by moral law, principle, or virtue to do x, and that if one fails to do x, this failure is blameworthy and may adversely reflect on both the action in question and the moral character of the agent. For example, philosopher Immanuel Kant argues that duty (often interchangeable with obligation) is a recognition of the necessity or binding nature of an action out of respect for the moral law.[5] To say that I have an obligation, a duty to tell the truth, is to say that I recognize it is required by a moral law or principle and that the principle in question is binding on me and applies to me as a moral agent. It also means that if I fail to carry out this duty or obligation, I am doing something immoral, violating moral principles, and am subject to moral sanction from others, which may include adverse judgments about my moral character or virtue.

For example, if I am speeding in a school zone on the first day of school, we might think that I am not a virtuous person and that I am not exhibiting an important moral characteristic—prudence or care. However, if I have a moral obligation to uphold public safety or care for the children in my community, then my failure here is not just a matter of my own individual virtue; rather, I have failed by violating the norms and values of the community. It is not just that I am not a virtuous person, but I also have violated the laws and norms that I am obliged to uphold as a member of that community of practice. These are the two ways that MacIntyre highlighted that we can fail as moral agents and members of a community; both are important pieces to the picture, but the second is a stronger moral claim upon members of the community.

Some philosophers argue that there is no prima facie general obligation to obey laws as such, even if there are good moral and practical reasons for obeying a specific law. For example, philosopher Richard Wolff argues that adhering to such a general moral obligation would be to violate our own autonomy/principle of autonomy (which is our primary obligation) to obey simply because someone has authority over us. We can do as we are ordered, but not because we are so ordered. Blind obedience is problematic in this view, but recognition of authority is not if we still reserve judgment about whether to obey on grounds other than authority alone.

Richard Dagger disagrees with Wolff and thinks there is a general obligation to obey grounded on a principle of fair play.[6] He claims that Wolff fails to see the social dimensions of autonomy and that "a more positive way to secure cooperation is to cultivate the desire to do one's part in the cooperative endeavor."[7] This desire fosters civic virtue, acting for the common good even if it is personally painful, rather than just focusing on autonomy and the individual in isolation over and against the state.

Second, we turn to Aquinas to consider if the virtue of obedience is a different kind of virtue that carries specific obligations that other virtues do not; if so, it would help us understand how obedience goes beyond being a virtue to being a moral obligation. Aquinas makes a distinction between specific virtues and general virtues, asking whether obedience is a special virtue.[8] He argues that it is and that therefore disobedience is a special sin. This is because obedience is a virtue oriented toward the common good and therefore related to justice and the other virtues. If obedience is just about following a rule, then it is not a special but a general virtue—as such, obedience is a part of justice. This connection to justice will prove critical in helping bridge from virtue to obligation.

Accordingly, we see this distinction illustrated in the actions of Antigone. She is a threat to masculinity and the political order as well as to the personal power of Creon, because she is arguing for a view of justice at odds with what he is representing and trying to maintain. In the same way, the grandmother in *Contribution* is a threat to law and order, rooted in Southern white supremacy where the conception of justice involves the white person *as* the law. In both cases, specific actions (burial, giving poisoned food) are not just actions of the individuals involved but actions against the state and the conception of justice contained in those systems.

The point in both cases, however, is that the law or the action of the state (which in effect functions as the law) is being disputed as being valid, just, and in the interests of the common good. Philosophy of law scholar Kenneth Kipnis observes about civil disobedience that "where it is reasonable to believe that the law is invalid, the provision of some legal protection for conscientious violators will help . . . to settle the questions of validity and insure that the laws measure up to our standards of fairness and justice."[9] Erwin Griswold in the 1968 dissent to *United States v. Sisson* registers a common concern to this kind of civil disobedience—if people were able to disobey with impunity, then disobedience becomes legitimate and rejects conscience alone as a basis for disobeying civil government.[10] Legal philosopher Ronald Dworkin rejects this view, noting, "Society 'cannot endure' if it tolerates all disobedience: it does not follow, however, nor is there evidence, that it will collapse if it tolerates some."[11]

While we can agree that there is a general obligation to obey the law and other legitimate authorities, we can also acknowledge that there will be times when the validity or justice of the law or command will be contested. There are times when judges and dissenters, when Antigone and Creon, disagree on matters of validity and justice based upon judgments about important moral and legal principles. We will need to have recourse to communal ideas of justice and the common good in order to settle these matters. Laws or commands that do not reflect justice undermine part of the very reason for the obligation to obey, even if you think that obedience is still a virtue.

MORAL OBLIGATION TO OBEY

Given the foundation of thinking about the general obligation to obey in terms of justice, especially just cause and legitimate authority, we now turn to some more specific arguments to further ground the moral obligation to obey. The point here is to consider which of these views will make the most sense for the two communities of practice that we are considering in this book as a way to think about the moral obligation to obey.

First, we might think that obedience is the price or part of the consent with the state for certain protections in the social contract.[12] Under social contract theory, philosopher Thomas Hobbes argued that in entering the social contract with one another, we agreed to surrender most of our rights to the state in return for protection; we do so and maintain this obedience, even in the face of abuses by the state, out of fear of having to return to the state of nature (a hypothetical state of war and chaos).[13] Fear motivates and justifies the obedience to the state. It is important to note that for Hobbes, the contract is between members of society, and therefore we agree with one another that we have an obligation of obedience to the ruler, but the ruler is not party to this agreement. The obligation to obedience is generated "when men agree amongst themselves to submit to some man, or assembly of men, voluntarily, on confidence to be protected by him against all others."[14]

Philosopher John Locke, following the natural law accounts of Thomas Aquinas, agrees with Hobbes on the fact of the social contract as the basis for the obligation to obey, but he has a very different view of human nature and the motivations for this agreement.[15] For Locke, the contract is between the rulers and the people, not between the people as it is for Hobbes. Therefore, this consent for Locke is conditional upon the state fulfilling the terms of the contract by providing protection of life, liberty, and property; if these protections are not provided, the people have a right to rebel and to replace the government with one that will perform those duties. Accordingly, there is a general obligation to obedience—surrendering part of one's liberty to enforce the natural law to the state, which can do it more efficiently—so that the state can perform these duties. What both these views make clear is that the kind of obedience needed rests on some level of agreement and consent and is not based purely on fear of punishment or coercion; the obedience must be freely given and entered into.

This argument is part of a more general understanding of consent and authority. Locke argues that children owe obedience to their parents in exchange for the good of nourishment and education; it is not unconditional.[16] In the case of leaving the state of nature to enter into a political community, men agree to submit to the ruler on the condition that he will protect them/their property from others. The agreement to obey the ruler is conditional on this being done. Otherwise, why submit and give up some portion of one's natural rights? Since this obedience is conditional, it can be revoked: "Whenever, therefore, the legislative shall transgress this fundamental rule of society . . . by this breach of trust they forfeit the power the people had put into their hands . . . and it devolves to the people."[17] We can see this right to rebellion argument reflected in the opening lines of the Declaration of Independence: "When in the Course of human events, it becomes necessary for one people to dissolve the Political Bands. . . . a decent respect to the opinions of mankind requires that they should declare the causes which impel them to the separation."

Second, we might say, following philosophers David Hume and Thomas Aquinas, that obedience is necessary to support the virtue of justice.[18] In order to have justice in war and justice in the state, there must be a general, although conditional, obligation to obedience, since obedience is what secures the possibility of justice. For Hume, an obligation to obedience is the mark of the virtuous person, since the virtuous person would also be committed to justice as a moral virtue or requirement: "All men . . . are sensible, that they owe obedience to government merely on the account of the public interest; and at the same time, that human nature is so subject to frailties and passions, as many easily pervert this institution, and change their governors into tyrants and public enemies."[19] Like Locke, however, this obligation has limits: "There is evidently no other principle than interest; and if interest first produces obedience to government, the obligation to obedience must cease, whenever the interest ceases, in any great degree, and in any considerable number of instances." Thus, obedience is necessary in order to have justice, and moral people have an interest in and obligation to justice. However, if obedience fails to secure or uphold communal justice, then the obligation ceases to be binding, as obedience is a means to that end. It is not the end itself.

Third, returning to the more specific topic of the military, one argument for the moral grounding of obedience is that the commander/the state has a right to command reasonable obedience from subordinates/citizens. Obedience is necessary for good order when large groups of people are to work together in a predictable and organized fashion under conditions of stress; it is a necessary check on self-interest and emotion. Further, obedience is necessary to efficiently do this work toward a particular aim or mission accomplishment, whether in the military or political communities of practice. Returning to *Henry V* and the question of obedience to the king—even if his cause is not just—we see this idea of the ruler depending upon the obedience of his soldiers to fight the war. In exchange for this obedience (which, as we have discussed, is a limitation on their agency as political actors), they are only personally responsible for their individual conduct in war (jus in bello), which is within their control and agency, not the moral status of the war itself (jus ad bellum), which is not.

POSSIBLE GROUNDS FOR MORAL OBLIGATION

What have we established thus far with regard to the moral grounding of obedience? To this point, we have effectively ruled out the idea that it is the person commanding and the recognition of their authority alone that provide a moral justification for obedience. It also cannot be personal loyalty, respect, or deference or because this person is an authority per se. In addition, we have established that there must be just cause and legitimate authority, and that those things must be connected to a broader conception of justice that involves the common good and consent. Beyond these general ideas that ground the moral obligation to obey, what are some more specific issues, especially in terms of the military context, that we ought to consider?

First, we could look to utility/usefulness, more narrowly conceived as proportionality and reasonable chance of success. What grounds the obligation to obey is its ability to get things done, to achieve the mission or end within the parameters of justice. This would mean that obedience is obligatory to the extent that it is effective in getting things done and is conditional upon that. Results, and only results, matter. Would this, then, make obedience a contextual, situational obligation? Does this mean that obedience must be considered on a strictly case-by-case basis? In addition, how is one to judge in advance what the results of obeying are likely to be? Or does the requirement for usefulness or results mean that we can only judge whether an act of obedience is justified after the fact? This could put agents in a position in which obedience is a gamble that will be justified later by results.

This view has epistemic problems to overcome in order to be viable and practical. How would one make the judgment about the likelihood of proportionality and reasonable chance of success such that one could decide whether to obey (in advance)? For example, should you participate as a uniformed member of the military in the Iraq War, where obedience would be justified if you thought the results would bear out that obedience as valid and consistent with justice? If you think there are weapons of mass destruction, if you think the war is just, then you should obey. However, what happens if you are wrong? What counts as a reasonable epistemic justification at the time? To address these questions, we also must account for limited knowledge (the government may have information that I do not have), as well as attempts at deception on the part of the government or self-deception on my own part.

Second, we could ground the obligation in the nature of the military community of practice (including ideas of military professionalism), which then generates the obligation to obey. Obedience would have to be a distinctive virtue and requirement of membership in this community; without obedience, one cannot be a full member of the moral community of practice. The idea of obedience to civilian authority for all members of the military and the specific obligation of enlisted personnel to obey superior orders (articulated in their oath) would both seem to support this particular line of argument. Such obligations to obedience are central to being a military professional. One cannot be so without it; the community requires it. If this is this case, it is only as a member of the community of practice that one has an obligation to obey. What happens in the case of overlapping communities of practice when the demands of obedience come into conflict? For example, in chapter 9 we will discuss the dual role that servicemembers occupy as members of a military community of practice as well as a political community of practice as citizens. What happens in the case of a conflict between these two? How does one decide?

Third, we could look to the various oaths and legal contract with the American people as the grounding of the obligation. In taking oaths of office and enlistment/commissioning oaths, one could argue that the military member enters into a contract with the American people and the larger political community. On this view, there is something morally significant about oath taking and promising as a speech act that would be enough to alter the moral landscape and generate a new set of moral (not just legal) obligations. One might wonder if uttering words in a particular context is enough to create a new moral situation or obligation. This would also connect to the idea of the unlimited liability contract that Nikki Coleman and Martin Cook discussed as the basis for the obligation to sacrifice up to and including one's life for the state, if necessary.[20] In order for this argument to work to ground the moral obligation to obey, these cannot simply be legal contracts; they would need to imply some moral obligation associated with the contracts.

For example, Walzer's account argues that soldiers have consented to be treated as objects of war, on account of their status as dangerous people, as posing threats in ways that noncombatants simply do not and have not consented to.[21] As a result, they can be targeted (and killed) and be held responsible in certain ways that noncombatants cannot. Is it the oath that we think of as the source of this consent? As such, obedience is a moral obligation to ensure that the soldier is not acting on her own behalf or in her own name, but as an agent and on behalf of the state. As we have noted, it could be the case that the obligation to obedience is a necessary ethical condition for jus in bello restrictions in just war thinking. One can only have the separation of jus in bello and jus ad bellum considerations, the moral equality of combatants and noncombatant immunity, if we can—for the most part—count on obedience as a basic commitment and moral obligation that soldiers have consent to take up.[22]

Finally, it could be that there is a general obligation to be obedient as a moral agent unless there are contravening concerns. Obedience is the virtue of the moral person generally, regardless of military or political context. Why might there be a general obligation here? Hume connected this specifically to the question of justice, but we could make a broader argument that obedience is simply one of the constellations of virtues that defines a good person. This argument is easier to make if we think a good person is also a good citizen or is social in nature, such that there are some virtues that are not just about the betterment of the individual and their pursuit of the good life, but rather about the pursuit of the good life in community with others.

GROUNDING OF THE MORAL OBLIGATION

Taking into account the range of these options, I do not think the oath and legal contract alone are sufficient to generate a moral obligation to obey in either the military or the political context. The problem with locating the obligation with oaths connected only to a legal contract (and not to a broader moral context) is that it assumes that the law cannot be wrong. In addition, the moral obligation would only extend to specific elements that are in the oaths and the law, which as we saw in the last chapter were only a small part of military professionalism. Obedience exists within a much broader context of practice and tradition, so we need a moral, not just legal, justification. This also covers instances when the law or legal authorities are wrong.

My argument is that the moral obligation to obey must be grounded in the oath and the related moral and legal contract, conceived in a specific, broader way. We need to think of taking the oath as a speech act involving entrance into a moral community of practice, which changes one's moral obligations or involves taking up new ones. If this is the case, it would provide grounding for moral as well as legal commitments to that community and its members, creating a reasonable presumption of obedience, except in certain cases where obedience would be at odds with the various elements of justice.

Let us begin with the oath as a speech act. Philosopher John Searle coined the term to denote a mode of speech that also involved action as an internal part of that speech.[23] A speech act is not just words; it also accomplishes action using those words. Nothing beyond the speech itself was required for it to be an action. We might think of certain cases—taking marriage vows, judges pronouncing people as guilty or divorced, revoking or invoking parental rights—where the speech itself is the act. An oath or promise in many situations falls into this category, but in our discussion, we are interested in the speech act as an action with moral implications, as creating or imposing new moral obligations.

In his account of promise making and whether it implied a new moral obligation, David Hume noted that a promise is a resolution to do a certain thing. If the promise were all there were to it, it would not create any new obligation.[24] However, "They are the conventions of men, which create a new motive . . . experience has taught us, that human affairs wou'd be conducted much more for mutual advantage were there certain *symbols or signs* instituted. . . . whoever uses them is immediately bound by his interest to execute his engagements and must never expect to be trusted any more, if he refuse to perform what he promis'd." The promise or oath alone does not create a new moral obligation, but it creates a new motive (grounded in interest) to keep our promises: "Afterwards a sentiment of morals concurs with his interest, and becomes a new obligation upon mankind."[25]

For Hume, a form of words along with an intention creates certain changes, which seems mysterious if we think of promising as creating a new natural obligation. Rather, he argues that promising is a social convention we enter into from interest as a motive; this motive is what creates a new obligation, but an artificial one rooted in interest. If Hume is right, a new promise creates a new moral obligation; in the case of the military or political oath of office, this means that a new moral situation or obligation is created. To return to MacIntyre, I am arguing that the oath or promise (especially in the military case) is the mechanism for entrance into a new community of moral practice (the profession, the political community), which then involves new moral obligations that are not just private in nature but are rooted in the public interest. This brings together the argument about the importance of justice (including just cause, legitimate authority, proportionality, and reasonable chance of success) with the oath or promise as the entrance point for the community of practice. Both are necessary. Without the oath, it is hard to see why a given individual ought to be bounded by the moral obligations related to the practices and traditions of a given community; membership in the community without an account of consent and agreement to that membership is not enough to generate moral obligation.

What about being born into a political community of practice rather than taking an oath of citizenship? We periodically affirm (for example, by reciting the Pledge of Allegiance, showing deference to the flag on patriotic occasions, voting when we turn eighteen, paying taxes) or participate in the political community in ways that are a more implicit reaffirmation of an unspoken promise or one that was made on our behalf and that we take up at adulthood. Consider the difficulty involved in renouncing citizenship as evidence of the strength of these implicit promises and agreements when it comes to citizenship (or, in many countries, the difficulty in entering the political community as a citizen if one has not been born there).

How does this argument track in the real world? Do members of the military and citizens really see their moral obligations to their community of practice as being rooted in an oath or promise? Do they recognize that taking that oath changes the moral landscape for them? For members of the military, this connection is highly internalized and is expressed quite clearly and explicitly in public declarations on various issues, especially in terms of whether they owe moral obligations to the president (as a person). We regularly hear from members of the military that they understand they take an oath to uphold and defend the Constitution, to protect the political community and its ideals; they are clear that this does not require personal loyalty or a moral obligation to a particular person or political agenda or party. These ideas are very much a part of the values of military professionalism and are regularly articulated as internalized by the members of the community.

The case for this connection in the political community and for citizens may be weaker, since there is not always an explicit oath that defines the pivotal moral moment. However, the conflicts and high passions around the ritual enactments of patriotic activities suggests that citizens take seriously the ideas that their obligation to the state is not merely legal or pragmatic but has deep moral roots and carries moral obligations. The ritual reaffirmations of the implicit promise or oath to the nation and their importance and gravity in public life speak to this.

This all indicates the presumption of obedience is based not solely on the individual act of taking an oath but rather on the kind of community of practice in question and its aim and/or function. How does this work? In these cases, the oath as a speech act marks entrance into the community and into a new set of moral obligations (not just legal ones) that creates the obligation to obey as part of the practices and traditions that define that particular community. In the same way, the promises that are part of a marriage ceremony (whether religious or civil) alone do not give rise to a set of new moral obligations; they only do so within the communal practice and traditions of marriage in a given culture or society. Two children saying the marriage vows looks like a wedding ceremony and bears many of the same outward and verbal signs of one, but in our societal context we understand marriage as between two consenting adults for a variety of motives (love, partnership, raising children). Children acting out the vows do not obtain the benefits of the vows and are not under the usual moral obligations of them.

However, this obligation to obedience is widely recognized as conditional, so what are the exceptions, and what do they tell us about this moral grounding? Approaching from a slightly different angle, the debate about conscientious objection (selective or general) seems to recognize the limits on this obligation to obedience when it is in violation of the oath or some other normative (legal or moral) standards. Selective conscientious objection is different from conventional conscientious objection, which involves objecting to participating in a given war on the grounds that one is philosophically or religiously opposed to war in general.[26] In selective conscientious objection, the person is not opposed to war in general but rather is opposed to participating in a particular conflict on the grounds that it is morally problematic. This amounts to the idea that individuals à la Jeff McMahan can and should decide whether a particular war is just (in the jus ad bellum sense) and not leave that judgment to the state, as the conventional just war approach would have it.

I do think that this presumption is based not solely on the individual act itself but also on the kind of community of practice in question and its aim/function. Some level of obedience is seen as a communal or social virtue necessary in general to the function of both the military and political communities, so any exceptions to obedience must also be connected to the function of the community. That is, disobedience in a particular case is necessary to the mission or goal (proportionality and reasonable chance of success) or rooted in communal values that obedience would actually undermine. Selective conscientious objection could be viewed in this light, since those making such an appeal are referencing values of justice and other aspects of military professionalism to make their case. Consider the case of Lt. Ehren Watada, who refused to deploy to Iraq (having been to Afghanistan and being willing to return) on the grounds that the war there was unjust.[27] His appeal was not simply a matter of personal preference or opinion but was rooted in the shared values of his communities of practice.

At this point, we consider two objections that apply more broadly to the argument of conditional obedience, not just to selective conscientious objection. First is the concern that such an approach, especially within the military, will create confusion and chaos, undermining good order and discipline within the communities of practice. If each person is allowed to make judgments about justice and related matters, everyone will come to different, incompatible conclusions, creating moral conflict. Second, one might object that if we allow conditional obedience based upon the judgments of individuals, the military and political community will be unable to rely on obedience, which makes waging war (or engaging in other political activities) more difficult for the state. Obedience cannot be a mere matter of contextual choice or preference; it must be a habit and general obligation for the community of practice to function and for its members to flourish.

To answer these objections, we will require an account that addresses the concern about the connection between disobedience and discipline, as well as an account of how judgments can be rooted in not just personal but also shared values and norms within a community of practice, which provides some fairly predictable limits and parameters for judgment and action. This is necessary to avoid the extremes of blind obedience and random obedience based only on personal judgment or whim in any given situation.

To conclude this discussion, the most plausible case for the grounding of the moral obligation is a combination of relational and pragmatic justifications. Any grounding of moral obligation to obey must be rooted in the conceptions of justice and related concerns (like the just war criteria) that are part of the norms, practices, and traditions of the community of moral practice in question. These questions of justice are not abstract concerns but also involve impacts (both short and long term) of the actions and policies that obedience will be carrying out. This is the pragmatic piece: What are the ends and the means to be used to achieve them? However, we must also consider the relational aspect. How does a person come to be a member of the community of practice, and how does that impact the specific moral obligations (including to obedience) that must be borne? We can now unite Hume's account of promising as a point of entrance into the community of moral practice with MacIntyre's idea of community as defined by practice and tradition and requiring both virtue and stronger lawlike obligations. These two strands together give us a coherent account of why and how there is a moral obligation for obedience within the military and political communities of practice.

However, any understanding of obedience runs into difficulties unless it is rooted in an assumption of military professionalism (or shared political and moral values) of both parties and the relationship between the two, as well as an understanding of the mission (or an end, in the case of the political community) and its execution. Any obligation to obedience can only be conditional, and it is a communal virtue, not about the commander or leader except insofar as he or she is a member or agent of that community. If this is correct, we can set up the argument for the second half of this book as a negotiation based upon considerations of the intersection of proportionality and reasonable chance of success with the values of the military profession and obligations (or political community of practice) entailed in that normative framework understood through the concepts of Hume's and MacIntyre's accounts.

Obedience, therefore, is about the commander as a representative of the military and political community; the oath as entrance into a new moral community with specific and new obligations that did not apply before; the community's normative standards of military professionalism or shared political and moral values; and the achievement of mission accomplishment or achievement of ends as its mandate. Any obligation to obey must be grounded in the conjunction of these elements, which will have to be adjusted for the civil and political community perspective (probably including a weaker obligation to obey). We want the weakest obligation to obedience that is still compatible with these elements to permit the least violation of rights and maximum autonomy of each citizen.

In the case of a lawful order in the military, to target combatants in a conflict that contributes to a justified military end, we would expect to see all four of the above criteria fulfilled if carried out by recognized military professionals. If, on the other hand, members of the military were ordered to round up and imprison or kill members of their own populace with a certain characteristic (religious affiliation, red hair, truck drivers) for criticizing certain political policies or persons, we can see that one or more of the criteria would not be fulfilled. In this kind of case, we have legitimate grounds for questioning obedience and possibly for disobedient action since the conditions of the moral obligation to obey have not been met. This is what it means to say that the moral obligation to obey is a conditional one. However, it does not mean that anything goes or that each individual may state and act upon any personal preference, belief, or whim.

IMPLICATIONS

This line of argument means that there is a conditional moral obligation to obedience, but that obedience is much more complicated than the conventional unthinking or automatic obedience of Huntington or the passive obedience of O'Brien. We have begun to lay out the nature and bounds of what I will call "critical obedience" as the kind of obedience that is morally and practically sustainable and justifiable. The commander must be a representative—that is, a legitimate authority and be acting in the interest of the common good—on behalf of a community of moral practice with norms and traditions that members entered into by means of consent, promise, or oath. This consent can be implicit provided there are occasions to reaffirm the commitment periodically to demonstrate that we are not dealing with passive obedience.

In addition, the acts of obedience commanded must be consistent with the achievement of political or military objectives required by the common good and consistent with moral norms/limitations such as proportionality and reasonable chance of success in service of a just end or just cause. These ideas all connect back broadly to Aquinas, Locke, and Hume and their conceptions of justice and public interest as providing a foundational justification to accept and act upon authority. This argument does cede some points made by such autonomy advocates as Wolff and McMahan that one cannot submit to authority merely because it is an authority; there must be some further judgment that agrees with the content of the command. This requires a reason or reasons outside the authority itself for justification. Where I depart from the autonomy advocates and agree with Dagger and Walzer is that there is a collective and communal aspect to the virtue of obedience (it is a social virtue) where the social context (practice and tradition in a moral community) limits autonomy in important ways.

This account requires that we think about obedience as a communal or social relationship between members of a community of practice, bounded and restrained by the normative standards and moral ideas of that community. Since it is a social virtue and produces moral obligations to the community of practice, there is a kind of reciprocity involved that is in tension with the ideas of blind and passive obedience that have defined more traditional accounts of obedience. The moral considerations rooted in the communities of practice provide the necessary limitations on the obligation to obedience, but they also define how autonomy will be manifested in deciding whether and how to obey. The member of the military or the citizen does not have autonomy over everything; they have autonomy over certain things within their sphere of control and influence. In return for this limitation, they can then be held morally accountable only for those things.

In addition, because of the nature of the moral obligation to the community itself (and not merely individual members of that community, such as the commander), obedience cannot be a case of simple individual conscience but must be rooted in the community of practice and its norms and values. If there are changes or challenges to the communal understanding of obedience or problems (disobedience), those actions are not just those of one agent but an appeal to a broader community. This appeal must be to a set of principles that would be recognized by the community as a means to influence or change elements that fail to measure up to principles of justice, fairness, or public interest.

The treatment of the African American community in the play *Contribution* is an affront not just to the citizens targeted but also to important shared ideals of the political community—equality, dignity of each person to be recognized as a human with basic rights, and freedom from arbitrary treatment/violations. Antigone's public defiance of Creon and her willingness to accept the sanction for her action, as demonstrated in her speeches justifying her actions to members of her community, also appeal to a shared sense of commitments to religious and family values that she sees Creon as trying to abrogate in the name of loyalty to the state. Lieutenant Watada's objection to being deployed to war in Iraq was made in the court of public political opinion in the United States, and he invoked aspects of justice and military professionalism in making his case. In all of these examples, the appeal is made not merely to personal belief, preference, or whim but in terms of shared norms and values within a specific community with shared practices and traditions. In this way, these cases demonstrate the understanding of obedience (and when the obligation to obey is not morally binding) highlighted in this chapter.

In the next section of the book, we will see in more specific detail how this idea of obedience and disobedience plays out within these communities of practice by examining the problem of disobedience and its relation to the issue of discipline. Can an account of conditional obedience be reconciled with good order, discipline, and an effective community of practice? Or do the earlier objections about chaos and disorder—which is Creon's charge against Antigone—hold enough power to undermine the idea of conditional obedience?

CHAPTER 5

DISOBEDIENCE AND DISCIPLINE

An order is an objective reality only in garrison life. In battle it is annulled by the enemy, who issues a contrary order. In addition, an order is only an order if it is obeyed.... Too much happens between the issuing of the order and its reception. Besides, war has a good way of teaching us to disobey. If the order had always been obeyed, to the letter, the entire French army would have been massacred before August 1915.

—Jean Norton Cru[1]

Thus discipline produces subjected and practised bodies, "docile" bodies.

—Michel Foucault[2]

TURNING TO DISOBEDIENCE

Pilot Hugh Thompson landed his helicopter between Lt. William Calley's troops and the noncombatants they were in the process of killing in the village of My Lai with the intent of stopping the killing. Was that disobedience? If it was, was it also a rupture in discipline? Did it undermine good order in the military sense? Rosa Parks sitting in the front of the bus was clearly an act of civil disobedience, as were the lunch counter sit-ins during the civil rights movement, but did those actions undermine good order and discipline in the political community of the United States?

In this chapter we turn to the nature of disobedience and its partner, discipline, particularly in the military. "Good order and discipline" is an important legal category, especially in the military, but it also forms part of the normative foundation of the profession of arms, at least in indirect ways. The Air Force Officer's Guide observes, "Military discipline is intelligent, willing, and positive obedience to the will of the leader."[3] General George Washington observed that "discipline is often called 'the soul of an army,' " and others argue that it must involve "absolute, conditioned obedience to authority even in the midst of chaos, when military members' natural tendencies would be to the opposite of what is demanded."[4] The thinking here is that military necessity requires sufficient authority on the part of the command to punish any behavior that might threaten good order and discipline. The link to punishment is an important part of the concept of discipline in both the military and political communities of practice, which we will return to throughout this chapter. A core question will be whether discipline requires punishment (or at least the threat of it) in order to be effective, in either a political or a military context, and what that means in terms of the nature of discipline as a moral category. If the core of discipline is, in fact, the threat of punishment, that changes its place in a moral (but not legal) account.

More than any other view, philosopher Michel Foucault's account is responsible for drawing the connection between discipline and punishment, arguing that in the modern era, the first is the foundation for the second. Foucault starts his work by thinking about the connections between discipline and punishment in the military context, and his paradigmatic ideas of discipline begin with the soldier in a professional military. He notes that "the right to punish, therefore, is an aspect of the sovereign's right to make war on his enemies."[5] As ideas of punishment evolved and changed over time, it became much less about society being the primary object of the punishment than about the disciplining of a particular individual: "The body and soul, as principles of behavior, form the element that is now proposed for punitive intervention."[6] Now punishment is about the control and manipulation of the individual and their body in the interests of society, but this is done away from the eyes and participation of that society.

For Foucault, " 'Discipline' may be identified neither with an institution nor with an apparatus; it is a type of power"[7] that is about control of bodies in a larger social context: "Discipline is no longer simply the art of distributing bodies, of extracting time from them and accumulating it, but of composing forces in order to obtain an efficient machine."[8] If we think about the idea of the machine, we can see the interest Foucault would have in the military; each member of the military has an important role to play in the overall working of the military as a whole. This is ostensibly why obedience is so important. Without obedience, there is no control of bodies; discipline backed by the threat of punishment secures this control. This same control is important (although perhaps to a lesser degree and in less explicit ways) in the civilian political context as well.

At this point we might wonder why the focus is on external discipline as opposed to self-discipline. Doesn't it make more sense to focus on individuals developing their own discipline as opposed to the state (or its proxies) having to impose discipline with a system of punishment and other sanctions? In the military case, the threats of punishment and discipline are very visible and secured by a clear and explicit power relationship. In the civilian context, the discipline seems less visible and less explicitly enforced by a power relationship except in certain kinds of cases; for Foucault, the invisibility of this power makes it stronger since it is internalized and, as such, does not rely as much on the direct control and demonstration

of power. Despite the emphasis on self-discipline in martial culture, we find that such discipline is habituated through and paired
with the more explicit external discipline. In the civilian political
context, there is greater reliance on more subtle and indirect forms
of discipline, which suggests a larger role for self-discipline. As we
shall see, this conclusion seems rather counterintuitive.

Foucault establishes that discipline is necessary and effective,
but might we go further and insist that discipline is a virtue? Legal
theorist Mark Osiel takes up this question in the military context in
relation to obeying orders. If discipline is a virtue, it would seem to
have both individual (self-discipline) and social or other-regarding
aspects. Osiel quotes from the Powell Report: "Discipline—a state
of mind which leads to the willingness to obey an order no matter
how unpleasant or dangerous—is not a characteristic of a civilian
community."[9] I will disagree that discipline is entirely missing from
civilian communities, but it is clear that a certain kind of discipline connected with following orders in adverse circumstances is
characteristic of the military context. We think of members of the
military as being asked to do unpleasant, dangerous, and difficult
things that the rest of us do not want to do. But is discipline a
virtue or one of the conditions of other virtues, like obedience?

In response, I would say that self-discipline is a virtue, but
virtues cannot be externally enforced with threat of punishment.
A virtue must be chosen and voluntary—which, given the coercive
role of punishment in external discipline, undermines the case for
it being a virtue. It is certainly necessary for other virtues and for
military professionalism; it is a precondition for virtue but is not
a virtue itself.

THE PROBLEM OF DISOBEDIENCE

As we can see from the above characterizations, obedience is
designed to support and facilitate good order and discipline, which
in turn is often supposed to be central to combat effectiveness.
Discipline and obedience are important because they are seen as

essential to accomplishing a mission or achieving political aims. If this argument holds, disobedience should undermine discipline. And yet Gen. Mark A. Milley, USA, recently extolled "disciplined disobedience," and earlier in the book we noted the quote about being an officer meaning knowing when to disobey orders.[10] So which of these characterizations is correct?

One consideration is whether we are talking about combat contexts (or other in extremis situations) or the garrison context and everyday civilian life. It is possible that some level of disobedience is desirable and necessary in combat and civilian political life, especially if it adds to military effectiveness, mission success, or political goals, but it is more problematic in a garrison military context. Disciplined disobedience seems central to the mission command philosophy as well as to raising consciousness about and changing issues of law and justice in the political community. This suggests that the question is not about disobedience itself, but rather about what kinds of disobedience are consistent with combat effectiveness, good order, and discipline and with political aims such as justice and democratic participation.

This brings us to the question of how to define disobedience. We typically think of disobedience as a direct refusal to follow orders, commands, or laws, but are there other forms of disobedience that need consideration? Are such actions that depart from following orders without explicitly refusing to really disobedience, or are they something else? Is disobedience a straight refusal, or might it include, say, not carrying out the content of the order without a straight refusal? What about slow walking and delaying implementation? Or carrying out the action but not fulfilling the commander's intent? Or fulfilling the commander's intent but in a different way?

In this chapter we will answer these questions by exploring and delineating the nature of disobedience, as opposed to obedience and categories of less than obedience that do not rise to the level of explicit disobedience that generally produces legal and moral sanctions. We will then be in a better position to consider the exact link with discipline and the conditions under which disobedience and related categories undermine discipline. These kinds of cases will be problematic in both military and civilian communities of practice; behavior that does not meet the definition of obedience but does not adversely impact discipline will be tolerable in the interest of developing moral and practical judgment and achieving justice.

WHY GIVE AN ORDER?

To ground this discussion, we need to consider what is involved in, and the intention of, giving an order. Toward this end, we will consider a hypothetical situation in a few different forms: I am driving by the local elementary school, which has a speed limit of fifteen miles an hour when children are present and twenty-five miles an hour at other times. We can see this law as a command— as an order to be obeyed in the interest of public safety. I have already argued that orders or commands must be reasonable and rooted in just cause for them to be morally binding; this seems to be a good example of an order or command that is both reasonable and has an intent or end that is rooted in considerations of justice for the community.

However, in another version of the hypothetical situation, things become more complicated. What if the placement of this school zone is adjacent to areas with speed limits of thirty-five to forty miles per hour, making it difficult to slow to the zone speed in time, and if it is in an area with little police presence? What if this school zone is well known for not being policed, and the children in the school are advised of this fact, along with being trained in strategies for avoiding speeding traffic? Here, the reason for the order is the same, but the difference is the degree to which the order is likely to be obeyed.

We might observe that commanders or other authority figures should not issue an order that they know will be disobeyed, noting it would be a sign that the commander did not really mean it. We might consider why there would be a posted school zone speed limit in the second version of the scenario, given that it would be unlikely to be obeyed. Why would a commander issue an order he knows will be disobeyed? How does he "know" it will be disobeyed? Does that mean that the commander ought to only give an order he "knows" will be obeyed? And how does he "know"? This line of questioning leads to a prior question about what the point of giving an order is. What are the status and aim of an order? The answer might seem obvious: to get others to do something! When I order my kids to clean their room, it should be obvious that the point of that is to get them to clean their room.

Is it really that obvious? If it were, it would not matter whether the order is likely to be obeyed, nor would it matter what the commander "knows" about the likelihood of obedience. This issue might only be a practical consideration and ought to have nothing to do with the moral status of the order itself. On any given Saturday I know full well that my order to clean the room could be disobeyed. However, I still give the order, and if it is not obeyed, maternal sanctions ensue. Disobedience is always a possibility—hence the need for giving the order. Otherwise, it is just a suggestion that I think is likely to be followed, and I do not need the power of the order (with its intimation of possible punishment and moral obligation). This odd line of questioning suggests that the giving of an order occurs where there is a reasonable chance of disobedience or lack of compliance, which accounts for the role of discipline and sanctions (punishments) that typically accompany commands and orders, as opposed to a suggestion or request.

Let's consider some possible reasons why one might give an order. First, one issues an order to give instructions about what is to be done. This seems simple and straightforward; it is simply the act of communicating what one would like done. I order my sons to clean their room; the private is ordered to mop the floor or make her bed in the barracks. Is this a suggestion, or is it something more? I might be simply giving my children a suggestion about home maintenance, but it seems more accurate to say that I am communicating either a demand or an expectation that their room will be clean. Is there a difference between a demand and an expectation? An expectation can be disappointed or not met without the kinds of sanctions and consequences that would come with the disappointment or failure to meet a demand. If the floor is not mopped, we would expect sanctions and punishment to be visited upon the private.

Second, maybe an order is not primarily about the action but is given to indicate the will and intent of the commander, which cannot be communicated in any other way. It may be that the commander's intent has been communicated in other ways that did not produce the required or intended results. The idea of commander's intent from the mission command philosophy seems to back up this idea—that the order is about carrying out an intent with respect to mission and that there may be more than one way to accomplish this. This would leave more discretion to the person carrying out the order, provided the mission is accomplished in line with that intent. The important thing is that an order is a means to communicate intent and bring about the desired results.

Third, it is possible an order gives an opportunity to test and show loyalty through obedience. In this instance, the order has little or nothing to do with the content of the order itself but is rather about showing respect to the commander and his or her authority. An outsider might think that some of the orders that are given in military life (especially in a garrison context) have little to do with an objective or task and are more oriented to practicing and proving obedience and a narrow kind of relatively unreflective loyalty to a person or community of practice. In the garrison context, with its emphasis on the community of practice and developing certain kinds of habits, the order may not seem to make any sense or be connected to a mission but rather is a test. Whether one follows the order is a test to demonstrate loyalty to the one giving the command.

A variation of this argument may apply, except that it is not about loyalty but about deference to the authority involved and an acceptance or endorsement of their power. While power and authority are not entirely the same, both are central and present considerations in the military and political communities of practice. In the military case, Foucault noted that one wields the power of war and of the state, which is one of the most profound forms of power possible, as it is rooted in the power of life and death. Clearly, deference plays a large role in the rituals and ceremonies of the military community, as well as in the political community in a different form. Obeying orders could be seen as a way to demonstrate deference to power and authority, as well as a way to reinforce power and authority by those giving the order. If the order is not obeyed, it would cast doubt on the ability of the authority to command deference or inspire loyalty.

Fourth, it might be that the intent is to get something done that would not be accomplished in the absence of the order. There are two aspects here: to do something that people would not think to do on their own or would not be inclined to do without an order. For my sons, the order to clean their room falls under the second aspect, as they do not want to do it. Otherwise I wouldn't have to issue the order. I don't have to command them to eat candy, open their birthday presents, or play in the pool; they want to do these things and will do them without commands.

Would my children not think of cleaning their room on their own? There have been some odd instances when they just decide they are going to do so—as a game or a bet or to try and earn extra money from me. The problem, then, is that this is something they would think to do on their own, but not necessarily when I want it to be done. To avoid various problems and to advance certain ends (such as my sanity or a sense of order), there needs to be predictability to when they clean their room. Accordingly, the order is issued on Saturday morning when other cleaning tasks are happening and before other things can happen. They do not necessarily see the broader picture of what I have planned for the day and where a clean house fits into that plan.

In a similar way, the platoon leader whose platoon is part of a larger military operation may understand her job and its role in a small area with other nearby combat groups but may not understand the place in the larger strategic landscape, nor the importance of the timing of her actions relative to that larger picture. Military leaders who are coordinating the larger movements of an army need to be able to depend upon her doing her part at the time and exactly in the way it is ordered (as they will need for all the other combat elements they are coordinating).

With these options in mind, we can return to our original question: What is the intent of the practice of giving and following orders? As we have seen, the distinction between the garrison and combat situations matters to some degree, since the answer is different. In the case of combat, the aim is the accomplishment of some end related to the mission. In a garrison context, the aim is sometimes the above, but many things do not fall into this category—being instead about loyalty and fidelity to the commander and building a demonstrable and predictable habit of obedience. Another difference between these two contexts may also be the distinction between discipline and power or authority. One can have authority without the ability to punish; one may depend upon persuasion or emotional or moral appeals to exercise the authority. The difference here appears to be that discipline requires at least the threat of punishment, reinforced by actual punishment if needed. However, would good leaders produce discipline without punishment, whereas bad leaders would have to rely upon discipline backed by punishment? The answer appears to center less on the establishment and maintenance of power and authority and more on that the purpose of an order is to communicate and fulfill the commander's intent, to do a thing in a certain way and time that the one commanded has reasons not to do on his own.

LINK BETWEEN OBEDIENCE AND DISCIPLINE

We now return to the link between obedience and discipline and whether one is necessary for the other. We start by considering whether there is a link between various activities in military training that are designed to instill and practice discipline and obedience. The first thing that often comes to mind is the drilling, the focus on standardized appearance (uniformity in many senses of the word), standardized behavior, and the like, which are designed to render human thought, appearance, and behavior more predictable. Presumably, the reason for this is to habituate servicemembers to think and act in predictable, consistent, and uniform ways when under fire that will facilitate mission success by allowing each body to act as a part of the machine of the military. Obedience is a habit of discipline that facilitates this.

To buttress this view, consider Richard Gabriel and Paul Savage's classic work on Vietnam, *Crisis in Command: Mismanagement in the Army*, which noted that many of the problems they saw with the performance of the Army during Vietnam (fragging, drug use, lack of discipline, and bad unit cohesion) could be boiled down to bad leadership among the officer corps.[11] In their view, the officers failed to lead, show character, or take risks, and they generally seemed unconcerned with their men; this led to the issues highlighted above, which then impacted unit cohesion and ultimately mission effectiveness. Bad leaders created circumstances in which there was bad or nonexistent discipline, which led to various types of disobedience, impacting the combat mission. This shows one explicit link between discipline and obedience, as well as the problems created by lack of discipline, which eventually manifested in lack of obedience.

This brings me to my eldest son. He begins the week by being manifestly disobedient to his father, which then has various ripple effects within the family unit. Surely if there had been better discipline, this kind of disobedience would not occur; this all seems very clear and straightforward. Good discipline is necessary for obedience, which is necessary for mission effectiveness or attaining political ends. Foucault, as we have noted, saw a link between discipline and control in various contexts; the control of bodies creates certain kinds of habits in relation to political and social structures. Obedience is an important habit in schools, penal institutions, and the military.[12] Is discipline a practice and habit formation for obedience, with such a clear connection that one cannot have obedience without discipline? Are those who demonstrate better discipline in fact more obedient?

Not necessarily. It is possible that discipline makes a certain kind of obedience (habituated, perhaps somewhat uncritical) more likely or easier, in the same way that other kinds of habituations make other actions more likely or easier. If I am in the habit of eating healthy, then certain kinds of actions (eating vegetables, smaller portions) are more likely or easier for me to carry out, compared to others who are not so habituated. This could explain why some people are obedient: they are in the habit of it. However, what if there are people who are obedient not out of discipline or general habit, but because they have made a moral judgment about the value of the command, the commander, and/or the context and impact of obedience in that particular situation?

In addition, we should consider that those disposed to be disciplined also happen to be more disposed to be obedient, and there is really no causal link of habit or discipline. This brings me back to my sons. My eldest is quite disciplined and likes structure but vastly prefers if he is in charge of said structure and discipline; therefore, he demonstrates disobedience on certain occasions. My youngest is impulsive and rather undisciplined, though he is happy to inform on others who are breaking the rules; however, he is by far the more obedient of the two children by nature. He prefers following the rules, and we cannot necessarily trace this to discipline and habit or to judgments about the justness of the commands.

Examples such as this raise the question about the connection between these two values and return us to the distinction between combat and garrison contexts. The conventional view of the importance and centrality of obedience as a military virtue is that under fire, lack of obedience can get people killed. One must obey in combat or deployment situations, because in those contexts there is not time, as Han Solo put it once in *Star Wars*, "to discuss this in committee." This suggests that in garrison contexts, there is more flexibility in terms of obedience and more room for discussion and negotiation. Is it the case that in combat/deployment situations, the cost of disobedience is higher, and obedience is more critical?

In garrison contexts, more bureaucracy and micromanaging of bodies and actions occur. Is the appearance of obedience here more important because of how disobedience looks relative to civilian minders, especially in terms of reputations, career promotions, and procurement issues? Of primary importance in this context is the appearance of obedience and, secondarily, the sense of predictability and control that comes with that, unlike in combat, where the reality of predictability matters more than the outward appearance of obedience. As a mother, this may be like wanting my kids to behave when we go to church so others will think well of me and trust me in other matters, not because there will really be any adverse consequences if my children misbehave.

In combat, there are more fluid circumstances where the individual has to interpret how an order is to be carried out given conditions on the ground. War is not predictable or controllable in the ways that we might expect of civilian life or even in a garrison context, so it would make sense that we make allowances here for some disobedience or under-/selective obedience. However, this point appears at odds with the conventional idea that obedience is so important under fire to keep people from harm and to achieve the mission. At the very least, there seems to be an interesting tension, and that idea may turn out to be problematic.

Obedience cannot just be grounded in the notion that a command was given, and the commander has legitimate authority over me. In combat, results matter a great deal. If disobedience leads to good results, it might be forgiven or tolerated, if not approved. If this is the case, this raises other questions about the grounds for the moral obligation to obedience in the military. It cannot be an absolute or even a general obligation; it is a conditional obligation, and it is conditional in important ways on moral considerations such as reasonable chance of success and proportionality.

The question is whether we are willing to say that one ought to be obedient, unless disobedience produces a greater good, and whether we are willing to give individual members of the military the discretion to decide this. We might be willing to give this kind of discretion to elite units or persons but not to the average enlisted member of the military. It is an interesting question: to whom are we willing to give such power, under what circumstances, and for what reasons, and what do we expect (in terms of selection, training, and accountability) in exchange for that power? The most plausible view is for the general population of the military, the assumption and obligation should be obedience, noting that narrow exceptions will be made.

Also of concern to this argument is the degree to which predictability is important and when it might actually be counterproductive to the mission. Troops could be given more discretion or leeway with regard to obedience in more extreme situations and less in garrison situations, where the adverse impacts of disobedience seem much less serious. There is a relationship between risk and obedience. On one hand, obedience is designed to mitigate the risk of "rogue" behavior and allow for smooth, relatively predictable behavior within a large organization in complex circumstances. On the other hand, we seem to be willing for this expectation to be more conditional and flexible in more extreme circumstances, especially where some kind of "greater good" might be achieved. Somehow, the risk here is worth it. However, if that is true, the same logic could be applied in garrison contexts. Surely there are also greater goods to be achieved by suspending or making more flexible the obligation to obey. In this context, we might allow this only to the degree that obedience contributes to discipline, and if it does not, it can be suspended.

Now we can examine the link between obedience and discipline in the civilian context. The link is less overt, although there are forms of self-discipline in citizens that are helpful to the flourishing of the political community; when this self-discipline fails, the state has to step in with external discipline. Police use of force is one example of this, and it becomes quite problematic at times when it is used in violation of norms of justice or in cases where self-discipline on the part of the citizen was present and therefore an intervention was not justified. The police using lethal violence against a law-abiding citizen who matches a profile of someone who is breaking the law might be one example, but so would examples of "driving while black" and similar racial profiling. The kinds of disobedience that are tolerated tend to be those that do not undermine basic order and discipline within the society (the basic law and order needed for society to function) and that are connected to shared and recognizable political and moral principles. If appeals to those principles in the interests of community are successful, the disobedience is tolerated or excused, although sometimes not until well after the fact. When it is not successful or the appeals fail, the disobedience will be punished or sanctioned. In both cases, the kind of appeal and the results of the disobedience seem to matter a great deal to how much latitude can be expected, just as in the military contexts we considered.

NATURE OF DISOBEDIENCE

At this point, we can think more definitively about what counts as disobedience as opposed to other categories of action. I want to consider that obedience is not an either/or proposition but exists in a range of intention and action. Outright refusal to follow an order seems a clear case of disobedience, but beyond that, things get murky. My Lai offers several helpful examples. Some of Lieutenant Calley's men turned their backs and refused to participate in the killing, while U.S. Army pilot Hugh Thompson put his helicopter down between the troops and the Vietnamese villagers and threatened to fire on Calley's troops if they continued the massacre.[13] Thompson was eventually recognized with the Soldier's Medal, but at the time his actions appeared at the very least disloyal, if not disobedient. Those who turned their backs and did not participate also seem guilty of disobedience, but not by directly saying no or explicitly refusing Calley's orders to his face as we might think of the standard model of disobedience. Additionally, we want to consider whether these actions are disobedience, whether this is a case where both obedience and discipline broke down, or whether it was just disobedience.

On the civilian side, cases such as the Ferguson, Missouri, protests and law enforcement responses or the Los Angeles riots, which seem to involve cases of civil disobedience (in certain cases quite flagrant and explicit), also seem to create a breakdown in political discipline fairly immediately. These kinds of events might be contrasted to Rosa Parks' civil disobedience or the lunch counter sit-in protests that were civil disobedience but did not result in immediate and clear breakdown in political discipline; those being disobedient were arrested, and civil order was not impacted.

To help us think about the nature of disobedience as a concept, I want to sketch out one possible taxonomy of disobedience and obedience. It is important to note that I think of these categories as porous and more as on a range or continuum than as hard and fast conceptual categories with clear boundaries. To begin, the highest level of disobedience would be the classic case of flagrantly refusing to obey orders (and asserting this fact directly and often publicly). A lesser form of disobedience is intentionally not carrying out orders, even if the person disobeying does not publicly declare their intent with words. However, there may be actions that do not fit either of these ideas of disobedience but that also do not involve intentional obedience to orders. These actions—the slow walk, avoidance, "forgetting" to implement orders, passive resistance, or acts of subtle sabotage such that it is impossible to carry out orders—will be called nonobedience, since intentions may be murky or hard to establish, but the fact is that the orders are not carried out in a timely manner according to the commander's intent, although the reasons or excuses for this may vary.

In a second category, nonobedience by other means, the person intends to carry out the orders, but through incompetence, ignorance, or events beyond their control, the orders are in fact not carried out; the objective/mission in the commander's intent is not fulfilled. For example, I intend to carry out the commander's intent and take the expected steps to bring the action about, but a strong earthquake occurs at a crucial time, and the action is not completed. Perhaps related to this would be actions to be counted as less than obedience. I intend to obey and bring about the commander's intent, but the effects of severe ignorance or incompetence on my part thwart the action, or it comes about in a way that is at odds with the commander's intent. Here my intention is to obey, but my deliberation, choice, and/or action interfere with full obedience.

In the category of obedience, we can start with obedience by other means: the order is carried out and fulfills the commander's intent through other means, even problematic ones. Obedience and adherence to commander's intent occur, but the choice of means is somehow morally, legally, or practically problematic. One could also have accidental obedience; there is no intent to obey, perhaps even an intent to disobey, but the effect that was commanded ends up happening despite lack of intent. Beyond these categories would be full obedience, which requires intent to obey, deliberation, and decision followed by action that comes from the agent (and not outside forces or due to coercion) that carries out the intent of the command, and this may include having certain desired effects. Full obedience will mean that my sons intend to clean their room on Saturday in accordance with my explicit instructions and implied expectations (which are consistent week to week); they deliberate between options and choose a course of action that will bring about a clean room. In addition, full obedience requires that it is their own intentional action that brings about fulfillment of the commander's intent, not through the actions of others or my coercion.

Given this taxonomy, we can consider a combat example to see how this works in practice. Keith Nightingale observes that on D-Day in 1944, "Disobedience that day began to be a shared virtue."[14] In one example, two junior U.S. naval officers kept their tanks on board their ships after noting the 100 percent failure of tank launches around them, instead continuing toward shore with their loads while looking for opportunities where the tanks were needed and could be better launched. There was no communication with superiors on the matter; they just acted. In another case, U.S. Army Rangers disobeyed their given orders and engaged the Germans, which resulted in an opportunity for Allied forces on the beach to proceed to their objectives. In both of these cases, Nightingale notes that decisive disobedience created success at Normandy.[15] In light of the taxonomy above, these actions were disobedience, although not the flagrant, public refusal of orders that we usually think of, because they were intentional and deliberate.

In these cases, discipline did not break down, and they might arguably be instances of a much broader interpretation of commander's intent (victory in battle) being carried out by other means. Accordingly, these examples represent disobedience to a particular set of orders but could represent obedience to the broader strategic intent behind those orders. Those who disobeyed turned out to be right, their actions contributed to the success of the military mission, and there was no breakdown or adverse impact on discipline, so the actions and results were viewed favorably. A critical element in these two examples (and other similar combat examples) is that those disobeying had an insight or information that was relevant to the situation that others did not have, and that making a decision on the spot—exercising judgment—was necessary to exploit an opportunity or turn events.

We can also reconsider the My Lai example, which seems to involve lesser forms of disobedience as well as various forms of nonobedience. Thompson's actions were closest to disobedience, as were those of the soldiers who turned their backs and refused at a certain point to participate. This is also a case where those who were disobedient and nonobedient were proved to be on the right side of matters—in this case on moral and legal grounds, since war crimes were in progress. The difference with this case is the question of the extent to which disobedience and nonobedience undermined discipline. From Lieutenant Calley's point of view, these actions most certainly did undermine discipline; from a broader idea of military discipline within the profession of arms (and not just the military unit or action involved), the actions arguably upheld military discipline in the broader sense.

We should further consider how forms of disobedience other than outright refusal might actually support good order, discipline, and military effectiveness, especially in relation to mission accomplishment. For this to work, prudence or practical reasoning—the ability to innovate, take advantage of changing circumstances on the ground, or see things that others cannot/will not see because of habit and the force of groupthink—will be required. We can see this at work in both of the D-Day examples as well as in the My Lai case. These elements of habit and groupthink are serious dangers to considering obedience as a virtue, which is why I advocate for "critical obedience."[16] We will discuss this idea in more depth later, but it bears significant relation to General Milley's idea of "disciplined disobedience." He argues that with such disobedience, one must be right (in terms of the outcome justifying your actions) and willing to take the consequences. This is similar to John Rawls' discussion of civil disobedience and is based upon the idea that disobedience is designed (at least in part) to persuade the other members of the community of practice that the law in question is wrong and violates important and communally helpful values and moral principles. The D-Day examples fit Milley's concept, while the analysis of My Lai fits as an example of Rawls' view.

If we return to the Vietnam War question of draft refusal and the actions of protestors and Tim O'Brien's decision not to flee to Canada, thereby passively deciding to go to war, we can see the range of disobedience and nonobedience but can also see that what looks like obedience (O'Brien's actions) might not be quite what it seems. From the outside, the draft protestors were engaged in full disobedience, and O'Brien seems to engage in obedience. His obedience—if it can be called that—is at best passive obedience and at worst a form of nonobedience, since he did not decide to go to war. What O'Brien intended and did decide to do was not to flee to Canada and protest the draft, which had the side effect of him ending up in the war in Vietnam.

MISSION ACCOMPLISHMENT OR BUILDING THE COMMUNITY

Returning to the consideration of what it means to give an order, if the intent (or primary intent) is to accomplish something, then informed and critical selective disobedience is not necessarily a problem, provided the disobedience turns out to be right and does not undermine discipline. If obedience is about building habits and demonstrating loyalty to and membership within a community, disobedience can be problematic for those efforts and may also undermine discipline. The difficulty is that in many military and civilian political contexts, obedience is really about both. To the degree that we can disentangle the first way of thinking about obedience from the second, or at least minimize the influence of the second view, we will be able to develop a stronger foundation for "critical obedience."

We have spent a fair amount of time in this chapter on military discipline and obedience, but returning to my disagreement with the claim in the Powell Report, civilian discipline and obedience will look a bit different. I have already noted that the civilian political context seems to rely more on self-discipline, since the connection to power and authority is more diffuse and complicated than the direct line that we see in the military. In addition, there are also less effective punishment and sanctions regimes in the civilian realm; there are fewer regular inspections or other bureaucratic mechanisms to maintain discipline over bodies except in prisons, schools, hospitals, and the military.[17] Further, enforcement even in these contexts is more selective and random; therefore, more disobedience, nonobedience, or less than obedience is and must be tolerated.

Civilian discipline outside of the four institutions noted above will take the form of public activities related to citizenship. Voting, following legitimate laws, assembling and protesting peacefully, practicing free speech, and freely exercising religion are all situations where bodies are controlled, and the power and authority of the state are used to bring citizens into machine-like coordination and achieve political aims. In this context, the state will take up enforcement of boundaries such as the difference between persuasion and incitement in regard to free speech, who may vote and under what conditions, or what laws are enforced, how this enforcement happens, and who is subject to this enforcement. Civil good order and discipline are still maintained through obedience, so discipline as a virtue is still practiced, albeit more indirectly and diffusely than in the military context. While punishment and the threat of it remain present, they are (for most citizens) less visible and explicit than in the military and less necessary to maintain civil discipline, which may be why—following Ronald Dworkin's views—more disobedience and related behaviors can and are tolerated.

For example, taking a knee during the national anthem at a sports or other public event was designed to be a more respectful option than sitting during the anthem; it was designed to be more persuasive to a broader audience to take seriously the objections around systemic racism and policing issues about which the protesters want to raise consciousness and motivate action.[18] While these protests have been quite controversial, the enforcement of civil discipline has been restricted to competing free speech, counterprotests, and economic boycotts. The police and courts have not been brought in to enforce a particular view, and by all accounts the protests have persuaded some members of the political community and have certainly raised consciousness about the issues of racial justice and policing in the United States.

Civil disobedience discussions such as Rawls' may be helpful in thinking about the nature of civil discipline and its relation to obedience because they direct us to thinking about obedience and disobedience as social, communal virtues rather than as a one-to-one relationship between the commander and the commanded. In order to be successful in civil disobedience contexts (such as with Milley's disciplined disobedience), one must persuade others to one's cause, appeal to communal and shared values and virtues, demonstrate reasonable last resort, and use restraint (proportionality). Martin Luther King Jr.'s choice to use nonviolence as part of a strategy of persuasion during the civil rights movement, especially relative to moderate and liberal whites, was designed both to raise consciousness and persuade members of the political community with an explicit appeal to shared moral and political values.

These examples of the use of civil disobedience as a part of a communal appeal to shared ideas and principles to persuade members of one's own community are important as we consider more deeply what disobedience and related actions could look like in a military context. As we will see, there is at least one model of this kind of disobedience that is workable—that is, does not undermine discipline—in a military context: the United Kingdom's reasonable challenge model.

CHAPTER 6

ON LOYALTY AND OBEDIENCE

Animals are reliable, many full of love, true in their affections, predictable in their actions, grateful and loyal. Difficult standards for people to live up to.

—Alfred A. Montapert[1]

A cause is good, not only for me, but for mankind, in so far as it is essentially a loyalty to loyalty, that is, an aid and a furtherance of loyalty in my fellows. It is an evil cause in so far as, despite the loyalty that it arouses in me, it is destructive of loyalty in the world of my fellows.

—Josiah Royce[2]

CATS AND DOGS

ALL ALONG THE VICTORIAN HOUSE–LINED STREETS in Newport, Rhode Island, the flags on each porch attest to the loyalties of the inhabitants. Nearly all fly the American flag, along with another flag to show allegiance to another communal group (the nations of Australia and New Zealand, the U.S. Marine Corps and Navy, the New England Patriots or the Boston Red Sox, with a few outliers in rebellious loyalty—the Confederacy, the Army, or the Seattle Seahawks). Each house publicly announces various loyalties with the simple display of flags, and the consistency and diversity of loyalties are remarkable to observe.

The story of Hachikō the loyal dog, who waited in the same place every day for nine years for his master (who had died) to return, seems to embody the virtue of loyalty. However, is this also a story about obedience? What is the intersection and/or overlap between loyalty and obedience? We often think of dogs as both loyal and obedient. Well-trained dogs obey our commands and do what we ask. Cats, not so much! Dogs seem to want to please us and protect us, and they show a certain kind of preference and partiality toward their owners that we think of as loyalty. There are many stories about other dogs (especially, though not exclusively) facing grave risks to save or protect their owners, and the story of Hachikō seems an extreme version of this. Hachikō faces exposure and makes himself vulnerable consistently over a long period of time to demonstrate his commitment to and bond with his master. While not facing death in a burning building or the risk of harm in nature that other animals face in showing loyalty (in one situation or context), Hachikō's behavior shows loyalty and commitment over an extended time without the reward of reciprocity.

The thought of loyalty in the public imagination might invoke the mafia, where a supreme virtue is loyalty to the family, understood in the extended sense of the crime family. Loyalties to sports teams can range from the bandwagon fans in a championship year to the intense loyalty of those who root for their team throughout losses over the course of decades. Businesses go to great lengths to develop brand loyalty with their customers, since this produces longer term profits and reduces the amount of money that needs to be spent on advertising to lure new customers. The country song "Stand by Your Man" extols female fidelity as a virtue and has entered the public lexicon to advocate for loyalty even in the face of male infidelity. Loyalty can even extend to those who are willing to kill or be killed for the object of their loyalty, with religious martyrs and suicide bombers being two examples of note.

However, would we consider any of these examples also to be cases of obedience? Marriage involves taking an oath, as does joining the mafia; these are perhaps the clearest examples of the intersection of obedience and loyalty. Some of the other examples do not involve explicit oaths but may include public affirmation of the commitment and some idea of obedience to higher authority, as in the case of religious martyrs or suicide bombers. Obedience and loyalty are both social and other-regarding virtues, which seem to relate at least in part to public roles and contexts. Therefore, overlap and connections between the two would not be surprising, especially in the military and political communities of practice.

In *Henry V*, the famous St. Crispin's Day speech before the battle of Agincourt reflects this nexus of obedience and loyalty: "He today that sheds his blood with me Shall be my brother; be he ne'er so vile."[3] Henry extolls a "royal fellowship of death" where the act of obedience of fighting for the king produces an ongoing relation of loyalty; this loyalty is not a one-time event, unlike the act of obedience. A key difference between loyalty and obedience is that loyalty is viewed as involving reciprocity and endurance across time. Loyalty as a virtue is about a shared life with commitments, values, and projects in common that crosses time and, in this case, space and social class.

In this chapter we consider the relationship between these virtues and how thinking about loyalty can clarify obedience, sorting out the differences between the two. We have already argued that obedience is not about a personal relationship with the individual doing the commanding but rather is about the community he or she represents and the obligation to it. One reason that obedience and loyalty are often confused is that loyalty can involve personal relationships and commitments in ways that obedience does not. This nexus is particularly morally problematic in the military, where notions of loyalty can contribute to toxic cultures and lead to war crimes and atrocities. The challenge here will be to develop an account of loyalty that is separate from obedience but that also maintains the critical stance that is necessary for an ethical account of both obedience and loyalty.

Such an account is vital to help set up the ideas of judgment and discretion that are foundational for negotiation and also to accurately come to terms with patriotism relative to the dual roles we will discuss in chapter 9 as well as setting up "critical obedience" in chapter 10. Loyalty can be problematic in many of the same ways as obedience can be, so similar approaches to setting the limits and conditions on loyalty are necessary as well. This chapter sets out what those limits will need to look like while considering the proper relationship between obedience and loyalty in military and political communities of practice—particularly whether one can be obedient without being loyal and, more importantly, whether one can be loyal without being obedient. Loyal disobedience, as it turns out, will be a building block in the second half of this book.

WHAT IS LOYALTY?

I have argued that loyalty "involves privileging the moral claims of some people, groups, or ideas over others on the grounds of relationship, membership, or other particularity."[4] In addition, loyalty is not just simple habits of attachment but involves ongoing obligations and duties that are expected to be reciprocal, at least to a degree. I am loyal to my siblings, have ongoing obligations and concerns with respect to them, and have a reasonable expectation that they will do the same. When this does not happen, we tend to think something is problematic; this is a sign of a dysfunctional family. Stephen Nathanson reflects a similar idea in his consideration of patriotism as a kind of loyalty: "The word 'loyalty' in this context also draws our attention to a certain constancy in these attitudes. We know that we can count on someone who is loyal, and because it is important that we able to rely on people, we tend to regard loyalty as a virtue."[5]

The Army core value description of loyalty describes it as "bear[ing] true faith and allegiance to the U.S. Constitution, the Army, your unit, and other Soldiers. Bearing true faith and allegiance is a matter of believing in and devoting yourself to something or someone. A loyal Soldier is one who supports the leadership and stands up for fellow Soldiers. By wearing the uniform of the U.S. Army, you are expressing your loyalty. And by doing your share, you show your loyalty to your unit."[6]

On the issue of political loyalty, eighteenth-century philosopher David Hume is a bit more critical, observing "that strict adherence to any general rules, and the rigid loyalty to particular persons and families, on which some people set so high a value, are virtues that hold less of reason, than of bigotry and superstition."[7] This raises the issue of emotion, as opposed to reason, that marks an important difference between obedience and loyalty; loyalty involves some level of emotional attachment to or concern for the object of the loyalty. The connection to emotion, specifically the role that it plays in empathy, will be the danger in loyalty and will also provide the necessary piece for ethical loyalty.

In addition to these definitions, we need to consider the various degrees of loyalty. Consider sports teams: on one end of the spectrum, there is intense loyalty that is more like fanaticism and seems to defy all rationality, with a high degree of intense emotion, while on the other end is the very tepid and barely registered loyalty that might be maintained as long as one's friends are fans and the team is winning. There are also more moderate forms of loyalty that occupy various points along the range between these two extremes. I am loyal to my favorite television show or series and have strong opinions on the character and plot lines, but I am not going to kill anyone who likes a different show. Often, the differences in degree of loyalty manifest themselves in actions but also in emotions and emotional intensity.

Of course, loyalty is not that simple, as we often have multiple and conflicting loyalties, even in a given context or situation. In the military, the classic example would be the problem of whistle-blowing on one's own comrades in the case of war crimes. Here one has obligations of loyalty to peers, to commanders/leaders, to the Constitution, to the institution of the military or the community of practice, to the core values or other normative structures of military professionalism, to friends and family, and to fellow citizens. Reporting war crimes up your chain of command is to be loyal to the Constitution, to principles of justice that you take to be a part of military professionalism and for which the institution of the military stands, and to your fellow citizens. On the other hand, doing so requires disloyalty to those within your immediate combat group or unit, and often to your direct chain of command, especially if they do not want the crime reported or think that nothing is wrong with the actions involved. This example is a classic case of what Stephen Nathanson considers in relation to patriotism: what is the supreme loyalty, and how do we sort out which loyalties take precedence, especially in the case of a conflict between our patriotic loyalty and some other moral commitment.[8]

In addition, there is the problem that loyalties can come into conflict with more general moral or religious commitments. In discussing patriotism as such a form of loyalty, Nathanson notes an important distinction between loyalty based in personal relationship—espoused by Alasdair MacIntyre—and that based upon a criterion or value outside of relationships—espoused by Anthony Hartle.[9] MacIntyre's account locates loyalty and other virtues in terms of the personal relationships within a historically rooted and understood community. One is loyal to their country because it is *theirs*; that is the foundation of loyalty. According to MacIntyre, loyalty involves "regard founded upon a particular historical relationship of association between the person exhibiting the regard and the relevant person, institution or group."[10] Note that there is an important difference from obedience, which does not necessarily require this kind of connection or relationship, since I may not necessarily know the person who is issuing an order, especially in the military context.

Hartle's account in contrast sees patriotism in terms of "loyalty to national institutions and symbolism because and in so far as they represent values that are primary objects of allegiance."[11] For Hartle, American patriotism is distinctive in that it is based upon moral values, which for him solves the problem of loyalty coming into conflict with more general moral or religious commitments; since loyalty is based upon values, there should not be conflicts. We are loyal to the United States because it stands for certain values and holds certain moral commitments that we also share, independent of the fact that we were born into or are members of the society as citizens. This independence is an important feature for thinking about loyalty, since it introduces the critical element that is more difficult in MacIntyre's view. How can one be critical of a community of practice that one owes loyalty to simply by virtue of being a member of that historically rooted and understood community?

This distinction between the personal connectedness and criteria- or value-based loyalty is important in considering the basis, justification, and grounding of loyalty in the same way that we considered the foundations of obedience. We also need to consider the possibility of some common ground between the two accounts, whether there are times when loyalties might be to one or the other and times when they are to both. For native-born citizens, patriotism might be an example of the second, as well as religious or cultural traditions that one acquires by virtue of family and geography.

To illustrate this tension, we can look at Hector and Achilles. As a member and representative of Troy, Hector was committed to his community, its moral norms, and the laws of war. Achilles, meanwhile, is oriented toward his own glory, his narrow tribal loyalties, and specific relationships with fellow warriors. Hector seems to recognize and respect (on some level) the loyalties of

Achilles and is willing to honor them. Achilles, on the other hand, seems motivated by self-interest and a desire for revenge and honor, rather than by respect for Hector or other Trojans as fellow warriors. Further, Achilles commits an act of warrior disrespect in desecrating Hector's body and forcing Hector's family to come begging for its return; respect for and return of enemy bodies are a basic moral obligation that was expected to be reciprocal. Here we have two different visions of loyalty—a narrow tribal one and a broader value-oriented one—that will be important to consider as we move toward an account of ethical loyalty.

DARK SIDE OF LOYALTY

While Achilles' loyalty to his Myrmidons and to his cousin Patroclus might be the exemplar of military loyalty, especially because of its contribution to combat effectiveness, we can see how limited this loyalty is and the adverse consequences of this narrowness. Hector, on the other hand, shows loyalty to his family and political community in ways that are appropriate and expected, but without foreclosing the possibility of wider loyalties to fellow warriors outside of Troy, to Helen (even though she is effectively an outsider and foreigner to whom it would be understandable if he did not show loyalty), and even to his brother Paris when circumstances would suggest such loyalty was not justified. It will be important later to consider what marks the difference between these two kinds of loyalty.

The narrow tribal conception of loyalty rooted in a limited sense of community and reciprocity is also what we see in the atrocity literature. In examining the role of military culture in the Canadian deployment in Somalia (in particular the role in atrocities and war crimes), where Canadian paratroopers tortured and killed a Somali teenager, Donna Winslow discovered a similar dynamic; she argues that highly intense unit cohesion can be divisive. Undue loyalty to the group can lead members to work at cross-purposes to the overall goals of the mission or the larger institution.[12]

Others have argued that bonding was so strong that covering up for, defense of, and devotion to one's buddy was expected. This can lead to stonewalling and covering up or preventing individuals from speaking out about inappropriate behavior: "If he [the group leader] incites his group to racist behavior they'll follow, even if they don't agree, because they won't distinguish themselves from the group. Because the group is all you've got. If you're in battle, no one else is looking out for you."[13] Participation in hazing rituals seems extreme and even cruel to outsiders, but to the soldiers, they are demonstrating their readiness to participate in the group regardless of personal cost; that is loyalty.

Another dynamic within the Canadian airborne regiment was the shared sense of elitism—that they were a cut above the ordinary infantry soldier and that the other soldiers were inferior. This led to them protecting their own against the military hierarchy as well as against demands for investigations by civilian authorities. In addition, there are differing loyalties within the military. The senior officers may be perceived as having more loyalty to the institutional values and not enough loyalty to the people involved, while the junior officers may be perceived as being loyal to their primary group at the expense of the larger institutional concerns and values. The issues raised by the 2003 abuse of detainees at Abu Ghraib prison in Iraq showed the working of group loyalty without loyalty to the larger values and institutions and the consequences of such loyalties.

The Canadian forces had a tradition of strong unit cohesion, teamwork, and loyalty as part of their group identity, and their actions reflected the desire to preserve this. This dynamic is surely not a unique one in military culture and therefore highlights the broader dangers of loyalty. If individuals will preserve their participation or connection to the group identity since it is so connected to their own self-perceptions, we will need to consider what is to be done in terms of training and moral education to deal with this dynamic, while not sacrificing the benefits of the virtue.

We see a similar dynamic of loyalty in the documentary *Kill Team* as well as the film *A Few Good Men*, discussed earlier. In *Kill Team*, one of the main characters is essentially held hostage by members of his own platoon who have committed war crimes when he tries to do the right thing and report them. Both examples highlight the tension between being loyal to a leader and to the members of one's combat group above all else, even when there is a conflict with moral principles or even other military values. In the case of *A Few Good Men*, the issue is obedience mixed with loyalty; the men think they have orders to perform a disciplinary action, which then results in the death of one of their own. The loyalty to the immediate combat group in both cases exercises a coercive effect on the individuals and compromises their moral judgments to the point where there is a serious conflict.

In addition to war crimes and atrocities, we can see this problem through the tendency toward the criminalization of the enemy, which is a result of undermining the moral equality of combatants. This features prominently in asymmetric conflicts and the views of just war revisionists such as Jeff McMahan. The moral equality of combatants is the view in just-war thinking that combatants on both sides of a conflict may be fighting in good faith—that is, they believe that the cause of their nation or political community is just. This connects to the idea that soldiers are responsible only for their conduct in war (jus in bello) and not for the war itself (jus ad bellum).

Those who are critical of the moral equality of combatants argue that only one side can be objectively just relative to jus ad bellum, and so this equality is morally problematic and ought not to be part of how we think about war. If the combatant in question is fighting in an unjust war for an unjust cause, we cannot say that their actions in combat are morally justified. In fact, McMahan and others would say they are culpable for actions that are not justified and not morally permissible and are therefore morally wrong and perhaps criminal according to international law of war. (McMahan does not want to go that far, drawing a bright line between moral and legal.) This means that if we think that the other side does not have a just cause, we are entitled to treat them as criminals rather than as enemy combatants with equal moral and legal standing to ourselves.

While there is a conceptual argument here, there are also important practical considerations on the battlefield that we can already see in the conduct of asymmetric conflicts from Afghanistan to Iraq and Israel. In any conflict, the temptation exists to cast the enemy as criminals. The rush to view the enemy as "other" and to form a narrow group loyalty are common features of war. This is the feature that the moral equality of combatants is supposed to slow down and limit to some degree by restricting moral responsibility. If this feature is eliminated, there is no reason to treat enemy soldiers as fellow soldiers entitled to a certain minimal level of respect, decent treatment, and return to their country at the cessation of hostilities. Instead, they will be (and already are in some conflicts where the moral equality of combatants is rejected) treated as criminals with few restraints on mistreatment. Once again, the narrow loyalties to one's own side and cause as just outweigh other broader considerations of loyalty and moral principles.

If we turn to the political community, we can see similar considerations at play in debates about immigration and the policing of certain minority communities. In both cases, there are elements of the population who are treated as having an unjust cause or reason for their actions—as having committed a crime and therefore being justifiably subject to harsher criminal treatment different from that of others. In addition, the partisan political loyalties since at least 2016 and arguably even earlier have produced a toxic public culture where debate and deliberation are difficult, compromise (the heart of political craft) is a crime, and one's political opponents are cast as enemies and criminals. The judgment that others do not have a just cause or justification for their actions moves us to criminalization and the adverse treatment that comes with that status, which is rooted in a narrow sense of loyalty and its accompanying obligations.

However, there is another piece to the narrowness of loyalty: empathy. We have already noted the roles that emotion and emotional attachment play in the idea of loyalty; we are loyal to those that we have emotional connections and attachments to, and absence of these will also be reflected in an absence of loyalty. In the kind of loyalty that Achilles displays, we also see a lack of emotional connection and attachment to (and emotional hostility toward) those who are outside his narrow sphere of loyalty. On the other hand, Hector—with his broader sphere of loyalty—also seems to have a broader sense of empathy beyond his immediate family and political community. He seems to have empathy for not only Helen but also for some of the Greeks, at least insofar as he observes the conventions that go with the practices of war, many of which are rooted in something like the moral equality of combatants. Such empathy cannot simply be a matter of personal relationship and attachment (MacIntyre) but is instead rooted in some recognition of common humanity, warrior class, or other values (loyalty to one's country). This empathy and ability to empathize, even in a general and abstract way, are important elements in a broader sense of loyalty, which will end up featuring elements of personal attachment but also must include a recognition of moral value as well.

ETHICAL LOYALTY

The above examples demonstrate that ethical loyalty must involve empathy to move beyond the narrow Achilles model. Empathy is important in order to expand loyalties and moral commitment to those outside one's direct sphere, to expand one's conception of loyalty. Being able to identify at least on some level with the experiences of others through moral imagination—which engages the emotions without being a slave to them—is critical to a more ethical form of loyalty. This returns us to Nathanson's argument about patriotism needing to be bounded by more general moral principles in order to provide a check on the narrow loyalty, especially of the more intense type, that can produce immoral and dangerous behavior.

What does the broader view entail? Loyalty seems to be a virtue of partiality, which involves putting the demands or projects of another ahead of other competing demands and projects.[14] George Fletcher raises the helpful idea of minimum versus maximum loyalty, which addresses the degree to which we identify or endorse these projects, values, and commitments when we are loyal. In the case of minimum loyalty, we may only endorse or identify with the projects and commitments of the object of loyalty insofar as it is necessary to maintain loyalty. If I am loyal to the president, that need not mean that I agree with every policy position he takes, but rather that I minimally endorse and identify with his office and the values and history that it represents. Maximum loyalty will clearly require a more robust identification with and endorsement of these things; presumably these are not mutually exclusive categories but comprise a range of endorsement and agreement.

For the purposes of ethical loyalty, I argue for more than minimum commitment but in general not as much as maximum loyalty, which could compromise the critical aspect that we want to develop. It would be possible, however unlikely, to have maximum loyalty, but we have to have critically reflected upon this commitment and subjected it to scrutiny in advance of making it, and it should in principle be open to revision.

Philosopher Josiah Royce wants to take a much broader, more abstract view in which the critical factor is loyalty to the idea of loyalty (or the virtue of loyalty). He cites the Japanese samurai as an example of the appropriate blend of individualism and communal commitment: "He never accepted what he took to be tyranny. He had his chiefs; but as an individual he was proud to serve them. He often used his own highly trained judgment regarding the applications of the complex code of honor under which he was reared. . . . And yet he was also a man of the world, a warrior, an avenger of insults to his honor; and above all, he was loyal."[15]

In a more contemporary context, both these views suggest that something like just cause might have a connection to loyalty. In the case of loyalty, we have argued that there is a partiality, a preference (whether conceived minimally or maximally) for the values, projects, and commitments of the object of loyalty. In both the military and political cases, it is possible that to have an ethical (broader sense) of loyalty, there must be some level of endorsement of the projects and values of that community in a way that is analogous to the idea of just cause. Just cause asks us to think about whether the end, aim, or purpose of the conflict is moral. Is the project, aim, or commitment moral? Does it reflect the important communal moral values? Achilles, for example, could be said to have the most minimal (if any) loyalty to the just cause of the Trojan War and Agamemnon; he is there for his glory and loyalty to his Myrmidons. On the other hand, Hector clearly has a high degree of commitment to Priam and his just cause (the defense of Troy) that requires him to sacrifice himself and his family on behalf of this cause. It is important to note that his loyalty and commitment are not uncritical and blind; he seems aware of the ambiguities and tensions involved (reflected in his interactions with his wife) but endorses the cause anyway.

Both Fletcher's and Royce's views allow for some distance and moderating influence on the emotions that one might have relative to a narrow sphere of loyalty, while at the same time allowing for the empathetic space necessary to develop other (even if they are weak and mild) emotions and emotional attachments. Ethical loyalty does not mean that the emotional attachments and commitments one has to the object of loyalty disappear or are not relevant; rather, empathetic space is made to consider whether emotions and perspectives outside that narrow sphere are morally relevant to the question of which loyalties are important and how we are to judge them when they come into conflict. I have strong loyalties and commitments to my family members, and they are strongly rooted in my emotional identification with and attachment to them because of a shared history, values, and commitments. However, that does not justify considering only their concerns without having to consider those of persons who are not members of my family. I may not reasonably be able to weigh the concerns of others as strongly as those of my family, but I ought to make empathetic space for the emotions and perspectives of others to be considered, heard, and felt.

LOYALTY AND TRUST

With a clearer sense of the nature and complexity of loyalty, we can now turn to another important element in loyalty, especially ethical loyalty, and that is trust. We have already noted that part of the concern about loyalty is that we need to be able to depend upon other people in both political and military communities. This question of interdependence and working together motivated the justification for obedience, which does seem important to ideas of loyalty in the military. Recall that Huntington mentions them together as the two core virtues in the military, and we have seen how loyalty is part and parcel of many of our communal identities. Naval thinker William Sims notes loyalty and initiative as his two core values that make up the military character.[16] In the military, loyalty is viewed as critical because of its role in building esprit de corps, unit cohesion, and combat effectiveness. Bound up in those three elements and connecting them is the idea of trust, so we now turn to that specific connection with loyalty.

Philosopher Michael Wheeler argues that the kind of loyalty that is imperative in the military cannot be uncritical, blind loyalty but a particular kind inspired by a recognition of trust and integrity, not fear, which makes it different from obedience.[17] Loyalty, like courage, is a communal virtue and is reciprocal in ways that obedience is not, since obedience is one-directional. According to

Wheeler, what generates true, ethical loyalty is a recognition of something that creates this sense of trust. This could be a trust in the competence of the leader, but it can also be related to empathy of the sense of moral character in the leader. This would support Hartle's argument about loyalty being connected to a recognition of something of value in the object of loyalty rather than just being about the relationship or personal connection. We have personal connections with lots of people, but that connection alone is not sufficient to generate loyalty.

In addition, there is a temporal element here. While obedience is related to a discrete and specific moment and event in time, loyalty needs to be built over a period of time along with the trust that fuels it. Soldiers will observe of a leader they are loyal to, "I would follow him into hell," but it is helpful to think about exactly what that means. For many, it conveys that they trust this leader to preserve their life, to lead them well even in very difficult circumstances. Why would they trust them so intensely? It is because their past experiences with the competence, character, performance, and leadership of this individual lead them to think risking themselves with the person is a reasonable gamble. They have shown in the past that they are reliable and have demonstrated shared values and commitment, which suggest trust and loyalty are justified. The best, most virtuous loyalty seems to involve both of the aspects discussed by MacIntyre and Hartle. For our purposes there is a connection, often with emotional aspects, to a historically rooted and understood community, but concurrently there is a sense that the values of the community are ones that one has endorsed in some way to be a member of the community.

We can see the importance of loyalty and trust in discussions of moral injury, which generally involve a sense of betrayal about something important and breaking of trust as a violation of the virtue and expectation of loyalty. Nancy Sherman and Jonathan Shay, who coined the term "moral injury," both define it in terms of this value and role relative to loyalty.[18] Shay argues that the betrayal of martial honor and respect by Agamemnon produces the rage of Achilles, which he argues is in fact moral injury.[19] There is expectation of reciprocity, the maintenance of bonds designed to create and maintain a relationship over time and within a community of practice and identity. When these bonds and expectations are broken, so too is the trust that is a part of loyalty, which then is experienced as betrayal and, in some cases, moral injury. While disobedience is frowned upon, it is not viewed as a breach of trust in the same way that disloyalty is, which would also explain the more significant emotional responses to it. This may be one reason why treason is viewed as worse than disobedience; it is a betrayal of expected bonds of trust and loyalty to a community.

Given the complexities and requirements of ethical loyalty and the desire to avoid both blind loyalty and obedience, we now need to sort out the exact relationship between loyalty and obedience. Obedience can be viewed by some as a chance to practice and demonstrate loyalty, while disobedience may be viewed as disloyalty to the commander/leader as well as the broader community. Obedience is also concerned with an action relative to a particular end or mission, where loyalty is more about character and commitments over the long term within a communal context. As we have shown, there are also multiple and often competing loyalties, whereas obedience is more singular and discrete as an event and so is unlikely to have internal conflicts.

OBEDIENCE WITHOUT LOYALTY (DISLOYAL/ALOYAL)

To begin, let us consider the question of whether one can be obedient without being loyal. This is important because we want to determine whether it is possible for these to be conceptually independent of one another or whether a connection between them is necessary. Based on our discussions so far, it seems intuitive that they are connected or have at least some overlap, and both are important virtues in the military and political communities of practice; both build trust, reliability, and predictability within groups of people aiming for concerted actions and ends.

Obedience without loyalty does seem possible; there is a certain kind of obedience that comes from fear or self-interest. My students obey (mostly) the commands that I give in class and in the course syllabus because they must do so to be successful in the course. This is obedience in a transactional sense, which may involve fear, self-interest, or a judgment of the costs and benefits. Outside of the class, it is not clear that there is a relationship that would command preferential treatment or prioritizing my moral concerns above others. Accordingly, we have obedience, but not necessarily loyalty.

Someone in a foreign country may obey the laws of the country out of fear of punishment or a sense of being a good guest without necessarily having any sense of loyalty to either the historically rooted community or the values and ideas that community espouses. This is an example of obedience without any of the connections and emotional aspects that we think of as being part of obedience. In both of these cases, there is a temporary arrangement or transaction that motivates the obedience but is not of sufficient duration to build or motivate loyalty. In addition, the personal connection or relationship is limited, which inhibits the development of loyalty.

Despite a longer-term relationship, many of the orders that one might be given in the garrison context are oriented in this way as well. These are cases where one may not even understand, much less agree with or endorse, the reasons for the order; the point here is to build the habit and practice of obedience on both the individual and collective levels. This kind of obedience would be especially true for the new member of the community, when there has not been time for loyalty and trust to develop that might motivate the obedience. The obedience here is transactional, not relational. Many forms of toxic or bad leadership will also fall into this category of obedience without loyalty or trust. Lieutenant

Calley's troops followed his orders, but contemporaneous accounts make it clear that he was not considered a good leader and likely did not command the loyalty of many of his men. In these kinds of contexts, people obey for reasons other than loyalty; it is also noteworthy that we see an absence of trust, underlining the connection between the two concepts.

Accordingly, there is some conceptual distinction between this kind of obedience and loyalty; they do not necessarily have to go together. If this argument is right, it further undermines the arguments raised earlier about obedience being a demonstration of loyalty to the commander or the state, since the obedience can happen independent from and in the absence of loyalty. In the case of fully willing, critical obedience, the person might be obeying (at least in part) because of loyalty and trust in the qualities or office of the person giving the order, but this is not necessarily the case for all kinds of obedience. Therefore, obedience cannot be the foundation of loyalty, even if it overlaps with it in certain circumstances.

LOYAL DISOBEDIENCE

Now let us consider the relationship between obedience and loyalty from the other direction: can one be loyal without being obedient? Might we consider cats to be loyal even though one might not think of them as obedient (or selectively obedient at the very best)? Further, can disobedience actually be an expression of loyalty? Those engaged in acts of civil disobedience or other forms of political protest often argue that their actions and criticism of their political community are evidence of their loyalty; if they weren't loyal, they would not care enough to undertake such changes. This was the argument of those involved in the civil rights movement in the United States; the participants viewed their actions as returning or recalling their fellow citizens to the core values of the nation and its history. In fact, it is the disruption of the expectation of emotional attachment and preference for the object of loyalty that brings attention to the reason for the disobedience and creates conflict that must be addressed.

The conventional view of loyalty involves obedience, so on the face of it, loyalty without obedience and loyal disobedience seem problematic and are tougher, less intuitive cases to make. It would seem if I am loyal to my mother, then I would obey her. If I am loyal to my mother, there are shared historical and communal connections, understandings, and emotional bonds between us. She presumably wants to communicate something to me that she wants accomplished to the point that this is not a request but an order. Loyalty means that I can be committed to and concerned with many of the same projects and concerns that she is and have taken up a moral position that I will prioritize those over competing ones, even my own. All of these things would seem to push us toward the view that if I am loyal, my obedience should be viewed as presumptive or at the very least highly probable. That is the point: we want to be able to depend on people in deep ways and over a long period of time, and loyalty facilitates that in ways that obedience alone does not.

On closer examination, I might argue I am disobeying her because she is giving a bad order (to harm my father, let's say only for the sake of argument!) or is asking me to do something that sacrifices shared moral commitments. The order may be bad because it violates the moral commitments of our relationship or, even more likely, the broader moral commitments of our family community. Here disobedience will involve making choices among competing loyalties and also using my own judgment and discretion about which ones take priority. It is possible that I have to be disobedient in order to be loyal, especially since loyalty is an ongoing commitment or disposition, not just one action. This is a way to maintain and be true to those commitments, as in the cases of civil disobedience referenced earlier.

This line of argument makes clearer why MacIntyre's view alone will not suffice for an ethical conception of loyalty. Loyalty cannot just be about the personal connections to a historically rooted and understood community (or members of it); there must be some reference to values or reason for the loyalty outside of these relational concerns. In this case, loyalty is unjustified despite the fact that she is my mother, because she is commanding me to do something that violates moral values important to our relationship. Part of my loyalty to my mother rests upon trust that she is the kind of person I want to be loyal to—independent of our relationship. In order to have ethical loyalty to my mother, I will require both the relational aspect alongside the values orientation to be in alignment.

If this is correct, here is an important distinction between loyalty and obedience. Loyalty is relational and multidirectional and has to do with the moral world and obligations of the object of loyalty. Loyalty is about relationship and the moral claims of the person or thing I am in relationship with, as well as the historical communities and relationships we participate in. Obedience is about actions and not about relationship per se. Obedience involves a command to do something; loyalty is more about being in relationship and community and valuing moral claims.

In addition, the consequences for disloyalty, unlike disobedience, do not seem to be punishment in a conventional way but rather a lack of trust between people and within communities. This lack of trust has other consequences, but they are more indirect and subtle. Obedience, on the other hand, is oriented toward either action or a disposition to engage in certain actions; it involves a hierarchy with legal and moral obligations with specific and direct sanctions related to the efficiency and the smooth running of a community of practice. If a soldier disobeys a lawful, valid order, there will be direct consequences aimed at maintaining discipline and other norms within the military community of practice. If I am viewed as disloyal by my mother, there will be emotional and social sanctions from her and perhaps other members of my family and community. I might incur their anger; they might ostracize me and try to get others to do the same. She might cut me out of her will or exclude me from family events and community.

Similarly, civil disobedience can be seen, both by the protester and the larger society, as an act of political loyalty. The acts of civil disobedience involved in the civil rights movement, the antiwar protests of the Vietnam era, or the National Football League kneeling protests could be viewed as disobedience, which was loyalty in the sense of affirming and calling the political community toward the larger values and political/moral commitments. They were, following John Rawls, designed to persuade other citizens to endorse and act upon a different view than that endorsed by the state (law) at that point.

Returning to the military context, the aim is to have military members who are not just obedient but also ethically loyal, and that includes demonstrating the other virtues of military professionalism. Military professionalism requires loyalty to more than just the members of one's immediate professional circle; it requires obedience and loyalty to the profession and the values and norms embodied in that community. As Hartle points out, that means loyalty to the criteria of justice within the bounds of this community of practice. This reverses the usual argument that the values and norms of the community are bound by general and universal considerations of justice or limited by the demands of justice. The implication is that judgments about the norms and values are to be leveled by those within the community, as opposed to from external critics.

Therefore, in order to have ethical obedience and loyalty as virtues, they must be conditional and bounded by the moral norms of at least the community of practice. However, it is not as simple as saying it is the community of practice. There will be times when the moral community norms need to be changed and revised, but this needs to happen from within the community of practice in order to be authentic and to result in sustainable changes that become a part of the internalized identity of the community. We do need a wider and more critical sense of both loyalty and obedience in the service of justice and the common good, but these things cannot be coercively imposed from the outside. If they are, then loyalty and obedience are not the result of deliberation and choice and therefore are not virtues.

While arguable, one might see conflict in the military profession around the integration of women in combat roles and the inclusion of persons of non-cisgender sexual identities into the military more broadly as reflecting the difference between change imposed from the outside and change motivated and owned by the military profession as a whole. Significant portions of the profession hold the view that a certain vision of masculinity and related combat performance is essential to the military norms and values of the profession and therefore reject these integrations. Compare that to the changes in uniform or acceptability of beards or body art that were motivated from within the profession and, while controversial and subject to energetic internal discussion, were not greeted with the same level of animus as the integration changes. The difference is that in one case, the discussion about norms and values happened within the profession as a largely internal matter, while in the other case, the discussion was imposed from the outside and in many ways highlighted a basic and unresolved dispute within the profession about its nature. Former secretary of defense James Mattis' comments to the effect that "the jury is still out" on women in combat roles reflect this ongoing negotiation and conflict in the military profession.[20]

Ethical obedience and loyalty as virtues within communities of practice will require the exercise of judgment and discretion about moral claims and commitments; what "moral" means here is not a person's individual morality, but rather ethical norms in the context of military professionalism and that community of practice, as well as within the political community of practice. As with civil disobedience, any such actions must appeal to those standards in an attempt to persuade members of the community of practice to change course. This will necessitate more attention to and education in the exercise of professional judgment and discretion within the ethical frame of the communities of practice so that, like other essential skills and habits of mind, this is practiced and well developed.[21] This will be the topic for the next chapter and the foundation for the arguments that follow.

CHAPTER 7

THE ROLE OF JUDGMENT AND DISCRETION

On rare occasions in our history, the leader on the ground, at the crux of a fleeting moment on the battlefield, has decided to disobey his instructions for what he judges as the greater good of the unit and the larger task at hand.

—KEITH NIGHTINGALE[1]

[A] subordinate needs to understand that they have the freedom and they are empowered to disobey a specific order, a specified task, in order to accomplish a purpose. Now, that takes a lot of judgment . . . it can't just be willy-nilly disobedience. This has got to be disciplined disobedience to achieve the higher purpose.

—GEN. MARK MILLEY, USA[2]

AGENCY AND THE ROLE OF JUDGMENT AND DISCRETION

STANISLAS PETROV, dubbed "The Man Who Saved the World," was a lieutenant colonel in the Soviet Air Defense Forces in September 1983 when the new air defense system indicated with high certainty

that up to five U.S. intercontinental ballistic missiles were incoming. Despite this information, he hesitated. He did not immediately
inform his superiors, as military protocol at the time would have
advised; instead, he waited. As it turns out, the message was a
malfunction in the relatively new system and not an actual notice
of incoming U.S. missiles. When pressed on why he did what he
did, Petrov said he "instinctively" knew that the message was not
right.[3] He also noted that it was his civilian training that led to
his decision—that if others had been there that day and followed
orders as soldiers were trained to, the authorities would have been
called without question. Whether Petrov avoided a major escalation
is a matter of some dispute, but this example is a clear case of using
judgment and discretion (in this case, professional judgment and
discretion in a military community of practice) to make the right
decision, even if it was not the decision that would be have been
indicated and that did not necessarily please his superiors. As it
turned out, however, he was correct.

If the arguments in the last few chapters about the important
role of critical obedience and loyalty, as well as disciplined, loyal
disobedience, are correct, we will need an account of judgment and
discretion (including professional judgment and discretion within
the military) to ground such decisions and ensure that assessments
are not based on bias, prejudice, whim, emotion, or some other
arbitrary factor. Concerns about unrestricted and unconditional
disobedience as detrimental to discipline and good order in the
military and combat effectiveness are well documented and would
impact the ability of the state to depend upon certain behavior
that they arguably have a right to expect from military members
and citizens. As with just war thinking, it is important to carve
out space for moral judgments without creating chaos and justifying every whim or disagreement.

The Petrov case can be seen as an example of one decision that
worked—that is, it turned out to be right. On the other hand,
there are examples that did not work, often because someone

did not have the full picture. In the buildup to the Normandy invasion in 1944, Gen. George S. Patton (who had been removed from command for slapping a soldier) was assigned to head up the so-called ghost army at Pas de Calais to give the Germans the impression that he would be leading the invasion there. Patton was reportedly not happy with his assignment, but what if he or someone in his command had chosen to be disobedient? This would have been especially problematic if the disobedience happened and the person being disobedient did not know the intention or the function of the ghost army in the larger strategic plan for D-Day. That would be a case where a decision was made to be disobedient, perhaps for good reasons invoking professional judgment and discretion, but ignorance of the larger plan made the decision wrong. This would be likely in both military and political communities of practice where leaders may have access to information (perhaps classified) that other members of the community do not.

At stake here is the question of individual agency and action, how one gets to that action and exercise of agency through deliberation and decision, and how one is held responsible for those. The issue is that of the action originating with and being in the control of the agent. Aristotle distinguishes in his *Nicomachean Ethics* between voluntary, involuntary, and mixed actions, where the difference is the level of agency, deliberation, and decision that the agent exercised in the situation.[4] For Aristotle, choice—which needed to include desire, deliberation, and decision—was required for us to consider the agent virtuous and responsible for a given action. When this is the case, an action is voluntary and can be assessed as virtuous or not, and the agent can be held responsible accordingly. If these are compromised, we mitigate or deny responsibility, especially in terms of judging the character of the agent involved.

Aristotle gives an example of a ship's captain who decides to throw the ship's cargo overboard as the ship goes into a storm.

Under normal circumstances, he would not do such a thing, but he judges it necessary to save the ship given the storm. This is a case of a mixed action since the captain retains agency, but there are also limiting factors on that agency; accordingly, we would mitigate responsibility in this case. If the action is mixed or involuntary, these judgments and responsibility are compromised and mitigated. If a person is to be held responsible for his actions, they need to be ones over which the person has significant agency; the decision and actions involved need to be a product of the individual's own deliberation and judgment and not due to outside forces.

To ground this account of judgment and discretion, we must consider the degree and type of moral agency (and the accompanying right and ability to effectively exercise judgment and discretion) one surrenders when taking the oath and entering the military community of practice or when agreeing to obey and render loyalty as a citizen in a political community. It cannot be the case that military members and citizens are surrendering all aspects of their moral agency and judgment/discretion as individuals, since disobedience is allowed and viewed as permissible and expected in certain narrow cases; therefore, they must retain some individual moral agency and perhaps even collective moral agency. The question becomes how we decide the circumstances and limits we will put on this agency. The answer to this question matters, because it will also impact the type and extent of responsibility and accountability they retain and the actions others will be held responsible for within these communities of practice. In this chapter, we will consider the differences between looking at agency in collective and individual ways and lay out a more detailed account of what judgment and discretion look like—its sources, components, how it is developed, judged, and policed within a community of practice—to set the groundwork for our case study of critical obedience as negotiation in the exercise of judgment and discretion.

COLLECTIVES AND INDIVIDUALS

How do we decide whether and when to exercise moral agency—either collective or individual? We have already discussed how just war thinking gives us a framework to think about collective agency and when individuals ought to exercise it in the name of the state or others in need. The kinds of agency we value for individuals to retain are integral to their basic humanity and human rights and as important checks on collective power—especially of the state, which, when unchecked, can cause significant harm to its own citizens, as well as other political and military communities of practice.

In many ways, this discussion comes down to a larger debate about individualism and collectivism, notably in terms of moral agency and rights. As an individual, I might want to say that I have a right to make moral decisions about a range of things in my life, but I also bear moral responsibility and should be held accountable by others for those decisions. I have the right to buy a gas-guzzling truck, but I should also take responsibility for the various costs associated with that choice and not try and pass those off to others. However, these individual rights and responsibilities are bounded and limited by the rights and concerns of others, as instantiated in law, morality, and other social norms. When I act not as an individual only in my own name and out of my own interest but as a member of and on behalf of a larger social group or community, then things change—in terms of both the rights I may exercise and my responsibilities. Even if I am willing to bear the higher cost of the gas and maintenance on my truck, I am not alone in bearing the costs of increased environmental damage, more traffic congestion, and adverse impacts on the quality of life for others. As a member of a community of practice, I do have an obligation to the others in my community (as they have to me) that is about more than just my individual rights and obligations.

As a citizen, I might decide that I am not particularly interested in voting, that my one vote does not make a big difference, or that in refusing to vote, I am protesting a limited and corrupt system. Therefore, as an individual, I am exercising my right to not vote, and I do have reasons for this individual choice and exercise of agency. However, the problem is not just my vote (or lack thereof) in isolation, but the impact of my exercise of agency, taken together with that of others doing the same (even if it is not coordinated, although coordination would certainly increase the impact), on the political community. In some cases, it might be enough to change the course of elections and the policies that result from them and even to undermine the long-term viability of the values and norms of our political community of practice. A minimum threshold of voting participation seems necessary to still have a democracy, which can be compromised if enough people make the individual decision not to vote.

In the case of war, Michael Walzer argues that members of the military act as agents of the state but still preserve a measure of agency; they are morally responsible for following the requirements of jus in bello but not for jus ad bellum, which rests with the state.[5] This classical view is designed to articulate the collectivist nature of war—that is, war is an act of individuals who are acting not only in their own interests, but rather as members of and on behalf of a political community (like the state) with the intention of furthering the aims of that political community. On the other hand, it is still important to preserve some individual moral responsibility in war, so the question becomes where that individual agency and responsibility lie. Walzer's view locates them in the sphere in which the individual soldiers have power and control—their conduct and actions within the war, as opposed to the resort to war. In this sphere, they have desire, they deliberate, and they make decisions on how to act, and they exercise control over those actions in a way that is meaningful enough for moral responsibility.

On the other hand, we can recall from our earlier discussion that Jeff McMahan rejects both the agency argument and this division of moral labor, claiming the members of the military are not just responsible for the requirements of jus in bello, but also are morally culpable for acting if the cause of the war (jus ad bellum) is not just.[6] In his view, this judgment does not reside with the state alone; each individual citizen (military or civilian) must also judge and consider their actions in light of the justice of the war. McMahan does not think that collectives can have moral responsibility or act as moral agents—only individuals can do so. On this ground, he would consider selective conscientious objector Ehren Watada correct in trying to exercise this individual agency by refusing to deploy to Iraq because he viewed the war there as unjust, even though in Walzer's view, this aspect of the morality of war is not his responsibility.

One could also, as James Pattison does, take the individualistic view further and argue that one is morally responsible for (and therefore ought to be making moral judgments about) not only whether the war is just, but also about whether one's individual contribution to the war is just: "[T]he justifiability of an individual's participation depends, simply, on the merits and demerits of that contribution, rather than on the war more generally."[7] This view furthers the question of one's contribution to a just or unjust war, not simply whether the war itself is just or unjust, which Pattison argues is about the individual and judges the individual according to their membership in a group.[8] This dispute between two revisionists is important for our purposes because it underlines the difficulty in really separating individual and collective agency, particularly in political and military communities of practice. If MacIntyre and other authors we have discussed in prior chapters are right, individual and collective agencies are intertwined, although not reducible to one another.

McMahan's and other revisionists' views also seem at odds with the presumption in favor of general obedience, even at the higher levels. This argument posits that the state ought to be able to depend upon the obedience of its citizens and soldiers in order to effectively function and carry out its tasks, which include protecting the life, property, and well-being of citizens as well as the state itself. To return to John Locke, Thomas Hobbes, and social contract theory, the assumption is that when citizens enter the social contract, they agree to surrender certain (though not all) rights to the state in return for certain protections that the state will provide. This requires obedience on the part of citizens when it becomes necessary to wage war. In McMahan's view, citizens do not and cannot surrender their agency and right to moral agency to the state. This makes the obligation to obedience a much weaker condition than it does for Walzer.

McMahan's criticisms and these recent philosophical developments reinforce the idea that there is increasingly an expectation of more moral agency and responsibility by the individual citizen and military member than in the classical, limited picture put forward by Walzer. Much recent writing and discussion agree that the nature, development, and practice of professional judgment and discretion in the military (and critical judgment and discretion for citizens) are essential to the ethical exercise of military professionalism and expertise. However, not much in-depth attention has been given to exactly what this looks like and how it would work. This chapter is designed to begin to fill in some of these gaps, although it is not intended to be exhaustive.

MISSION COMMAND AND TEST CASES

Before moving to the details on the account of judgment and discretion, let's consider a few cases and concrete examples to see why the account is necessary. In the film *Kill Team,* we can see what happens to an individual's moral psyche when their agency and judgment are overpowered and restricted by the collective and meaningful moral agency is compromised. In this film, the main character attempts to alert the military to war crimes being committed by fellow members of his unit, resulting in his own isolation, threats of harm, and moral injury. A similar issue is raised in the film *Fury,* when one of the characters physically forces another character to execute a prisoner of war (by putting his hand over the hand of another character and forcing him to pull the trigger on a gun) after the character had refused to do so.[9] In both cases, war crimes resulted from an ability of individuals to exercise their moral agency in the face of pressure and coercion from members of a collective acting on behalf of the state.

The idea of mission command and the older concept of the strategic corporal are both examples within the military community of pushing back against the conventional view that obedience is the presumption and that certain kinds of moral and other judgments are outside the domain of the individual member of the military or citizen.[10] These accounts suggest that individual military members, even junior and enlisted ones, can and should act more autonomously at times and exercise their individual moral agency if that is necessary to accomplishing the mission. These ideas are vested in claiming more agency (and judgment and discretion) for the individual soldier, although remaining within the collectivist context as a way to further the mission, avoid errors, and develop cohesion and community.

The idea here is that within the commander's intent, members of the military ought to be able to use judgment and discretion in how that intent gets accomplished. This is primarily an issue about giving leeway on the how, which is different from other ideas such as command by negation, which says that I am doing a certain action unless you tell me not to. In both cases, a fair amount of individual agency is necessary, as is trust on the part of the command structure in allowing room for that agency. Command and control are necessary in the military, but both these ideas are about how much and what kinds of agency and autonomy can be trusted to subordinates. Trust is critical to both concepts, but how do you build trust without judgment and discretion and the ability to practice that and learn from experience?

In the political communities of practice, we can see the moral agency debate as coming down to which liberties we are inclined to let people have, as opposed to the decisions that we want the state to be able to give guidance on or mandate for the common good. Political communities have placed limits on how and whether parents can educate their children and make decisions about healthcare; these would be examples where we limit agency. The same is true with safety issues such as seatbelts, child restraint systems, and helmets (for bicycles and motorcycles). Generally, we want to restrict liberty and agency in cases where the exercise of individual agency can adversely impact other people beyond a threshold. On the other hand, we are inclined to allow more agency in areas that impact only a few people or are related to basic political values and liberties central to the identity and value of the community of practice: free speech, religion, voting.

In all of these cases and examples, we can see the overlap of questions about how much and what kinds of judgment and discretion (as part of the exercise of individual moral agency) collectives will permit. Trust and reliability are important issues in this discussion and will accordingly frame the account of judgment and discretion below.

PRUDENCE/PRACTICAL REASONING

For our purposes, judgment and discretion are a subset of a broader category of prudence or practical reasoning. As we have noted, Aristotle argues that the virtuous person is one who exhibits virtues of both thought and character.[11] The question then becomes the kind of thought that is necessary to have virtue of character and actions that reflect that character. For Aristotle, prudence (or practical reasoning) is the relevant virtue of thought: "[P]rudence is a state grasping the truth, involving reason, concerned with action about things that are good or bad for a human being."[12] A prudent person is able to deliberate about what sorts of means and ends promote living well; an important caveat is that these things must be achievable in action.

In addition, good deliberation and experience are important: "The reason is that prudence is concerned with particulars as well as universals, and particulars become known from experience, but a young person lacks experience, since some length of time is needed to produce it."[13] Good deliberation will be the kind that achieves its end in action, and time is not necessarily determinative: "One person may deliberate a long time before reaching the right thing to do, while another reaches it quickly. . . . [G]ood deliberation is correctness that accords with what is beneficial, about the right thing, in the right way, and at the right time."[14]

Moral agency requires this ability to apply practical reasoning in ways that allow the person to make judgments and apply their discretion about what to do in a particular context (based upon experience and an understanding of the norms and values of the community of practice in question) and then decide which action can be taken. Prudence is prescriptive in that it is orienting us toward what we ought to do, not just making a judgment. This last point is very important, since for Aristotle, if one is vicious or lacking virtue, this will show in their prudence; in order to correctly see the good, one must also be good: "Full virtue cannot be acquired without prudence."[15] All of the virtues of character require deliberation about means to an end, the end itself, and both universals and particulars, but especially the particulars that will lead to good, achievable actions. He gives the example of someone knowing that light meats are digestible and therefore healthy but not knowing which meats count as light meats and will also produce health, since not all light meats are healthy. Prudence requires the deeper, second kind of nuanced and applied knowledge to make the best decision to achieve the end of health.

How does prudence work? It allows an agent to deliberate about what is excess and deficient in a particular case, to isolate the mean, and then to decide upon that mean in virtuous action. Prudence also allows us to discern which habits we should take up relative to virtue for the good life and which exemplars to follow and be mentored by. All of these kinds of deliberations and judgments require experience to inform prudence and the assessment of the universals, the particulars, and the specific context. While we normally think of reasoning and deliberation as linear and clarifying, I would stress that prudence involves necessary messiness and nuance before it gets to clarity. We must think about the link between healthy digestion and lighter food (universals), and once we decide (via experience, following the advice of exemplars, or community) that light meats are healthier, we then need to assess which light meats are most digestible and also have other traits that lead them to be healthy. Once we decide that, we will make the judgment that because of these factors we ought to eat light meats x, y, and z, but not a and b. This judgment will be relative to other judgments about what is healthy and the role that health plays in the good life.

Stanislas Petrov noted four points that went into his decision to wait on alerting his superiors about a potential enemy missile launch: the launch detection system was new; in his view, the system was not yet trustworthy; the message passed through thirty layers of verification too quickly; and even minutes later, there was no corroboration from the ground radar.[16] These were the particulars related to his training and experience that led him to think that there was something wrong with the message and indication of an incoming attack, combined with more universals or assumptions and understandings about U.S. nuclear strategy and how an attack was likely to occur. He also had to assess what the likely impact would be (probably the launching of counterstrikes) if he reported what the system was telling him, which clearly weighed significantly in his hesitation.

In the case of the political community, we might take the example of reciting the Pledge of Allegiance in schools and whether students should be allowed to opt out or take a knee as a form of protest. What are the factors that prudence would need to consider? Part of the education system is the process of educating future citizens, which ought to include values of patriotism and respect for the rituals of the community of practice. We also ought to consider whether students know enough about civics and political debates to make informed choices as future citizens. We might also consider whether students have the right to practice their citizenship, and with protest being an important form of this, such protests allow students to participate in and practice their citizenship.

These cases show how prudence must consider the elements of both universals and particulars, as well as the issue of experience (or lack of it) in deliberating which course of action to take and its consequences and implications. Consideration of long- and short-term consequences of the actions and the relation of the action to the good life, especially in terms of the community of practice and its norms and values, are also important.

ELEMENTS AND NATURE OF JUDGMENT AND DISCRETION

Taking Aristotle's conception of prudence/practical reasoning as our basis, we are now in a position to consider in finer detail what judgment and discretion (as a form of prudence) look like in communities of practice. For the military and political communities of practice, what are the nature and important components of judgment and discretion?

First, we ought to consider what we mean by judgment and discretion, how they are developed, judged, and policed. In the case of the military, such judgment and discretion will be informed and bounded by military professionalism and the moral norms of the community of practice. The standard understanding of professionalism I use here is in terms of unique activities, requiring expertise and training undertaken for the public and engaged in by professionals chosen and regulated according to internal community standards.[17]

What are judgment and discretion? Aristotle argued that prudence (practical reasoning) was the kind of virtue of thought that was necessary for virtue of character; therefore, it is both a precondition and virtue itself since Aristotle argues that the virtues go together. Virtue of character requires the ability to deliberate about means and ends relative to action and to weigh various courses of action, and experience was critical to this.[18] Judgment and discretion are one part of prudence and practical reasoning related to actions where we may need to depart from the accepted norms (following orders) or values (protest on a particular issue) of the community of practice. Judgment and discretion are required in these gray zones, which represent a kind of decision in action relative to virtue that for various reasons falls outside the norm of more straightforward moral decisionmaking, as we have seen in many of the cases we have discussed thus far.

Next, let us consider the relevant components of prudence. At a minimum, it requires defining the end (including deliberating or judging that it *is* a desirable end) and thinking about various means to that end. Considering means to the end requires being able to think through and assess the viability, desirability, and consequences/outcomes of the various means relative to the end in terms of actual action. This usually involves gathering information, reflecting upon experience relative to each means, and drawing on prior knowledge and experience as well as communal knowledge. The military has a body of professional knowledge, expertise, and tradition that would presumably be a part of this deliberation process and would frame what might count as good ends and reasonable means to pursue them. (Military professionalism and ethics would also restrict and exclude certain ends, such as a war of civilian extermination or an unjustified war.) Data, reflection, and critical thinking/questioning could all play a part in the process in relation to a specific action that will need to be put into effect in ways that support virtue.

It is important to note that different skills or strategies may be appropriate depending on the nature of the issue at stake. This is not a formula or a checklist, but rather a menu of options from which one selects. This also means that part of judgment and discretion will mean (with experience) knowing which of the skills and strategies ought to be applied in thinking through a particular situation or case. Therefore, judgment and discretion can happen on multiple levels, one of which will include meta-thinking about which skills or strategies are best suited in a given case, as well as concrete reflection on the particular elements in the situation, which directly connects with Aristotle's idea that prudence is concerned with both universals and particulars.

Past experience is critical and foundational here, since we must also be able to think about how the current context is similar to or different from the past and how that impacts our deliberation and judgment process: Is there new information, assumptions, pressures, or concerns that need to be taken into account? Let's say that I go to my physician with an ailment. In my appointment, she will ask about my symptoms, take certain vital signs and gather other empirical data, ask about health history, and consult my prior documented history. These actions are all taken according to best practices in the medical community and would be relatively the same at another health provider following professional standards. After gathering all the data and asking questions, she will render a possible diagnosis or narrow to several options, perhaps asking for tests to confirm or prescribing a course of treatment to address the issue. This will be rooted in her experience with other patients with similar symptoms and her professional knowledge and expertise on the ailment in question, possibility in consultation with other medical professionals and members of her community of practice.

Another example might be learning to parallel park my full-sized truck. Initially, I do not have much success with this; I might hit other vehicles, park crooked, or end up too far from or too near the curb. It may take numerous attempts, and I may give up and go to the parking garage or avoid situations where I know I will need to parallel park. If this is an end or goal that is important to me, I might ask others for help and feedback and reflect upon my parking from the point of view of those who are more competent at it. I might learn what mistakes I am making; perhaps I am bad at judging distance or knowing when and how to turn the steering wheel, or I am starting from a bad position. Over time, I will practice and incorporate feedback and, hopefully, with better judgment and discretion, become better at parking.

These examples all highlight a fairly complex process involved in using judgment and discretion (as a form of prudence) to deliberate and make decisions about what actions to take in the context of certain normatively prescribed activities. There is a sense in each example about what a good practice or decision looks like, and there is a community of practice (including guides and exemplars skilled at the activity in question) that one can consult in using judgment and discretion to produce good actions. There is also a relatively stable shared sense of what success (good actions) looks like for that specific context. Good parallel parking and good medicine do not necessarily share traits, but we can say what "good" in each case looks like and develop ways to achieve it.

DEVELOPING JUDGMENT AND DISCRETION

Now we can turn to the question of how we develop the capacities necessary for the good exercise of judgment and discretion—what Aristotle calls "good deliberation." One might wonder why this needs to be developed: Isn't it just natural? If it isn't natural, how do you educate and train for its development and exercise? A cursory look at human decisionmaking (much of it bad) seems to suggest it is problematic to think that people come with these capacities hardwired in some way; they must be developed and learned relative to a specific context, community of practice, and set of norms and ethical considerations. Difference in norms and results of deliberation and decisionmaking across time, culture, and context, and the diversity of these underline the intuition that this cannot be abstract but is informed by experience and environment. If this is correct, then the context—both normative and experiential—is critical to building the capacity for judgment and discretion specifically and prudence more generally.

In the case of the mission command philosophy, the judgment and discretion will be reflected in that an order contains commander's intent (something that the commander wants accomplished), and there is permission to use various means to do this, provided the intent is carried out: "Mission command is the exercise of authority and direction by the commander using mission orders to enable disciplined initiative within the commander's intent to empower agile and adaptive leaders in the conduct of unified land operations."[19] In the context of rapidly evolving and changing combat conditions, as long as the actions taken still reflect and would accomplish commander's intent, a variety of courses of action could be followed. Judgment and discretion would be required to work through which courses of action made the most sense in the specific situation while still fulfilling the normative conditions set by the commander's intent.

To take another example with some import for the military, the report *Lying to Ourselves* indicated that lying or other forms of deception and less than candor is endemic, expected, and even accepted in the military in the pursuit of various aims and missions. If we examine a particular case to see if it is truly an instance of deception or lying as opposed to someone using judgment and discretion to assess what the situation required in terms of disclosure, we need to ask some of the following questions:

- What is the intent of the lie/deception?
- What is likely to be the effect or collateral damage/ implications of the deception?
- What is the context in which it will occur, including whether one instance or multiple instances will be required to achieve the end?
- To what degree is expertise necessary/required for the deception—is the deception required to effectively carry out one's professional duties?
- To what degree is the deception or lie socially known and acknowledged, even implicitly?

In this example of questions related to judgment and discretion, there clearly will be some overlap between these kinds of considerations and those of just war thinking, which shows the intersection of the ethical and professional considerations in the exercise of judgment and discretion.[20] The answers to these questions should also involve the below components of professional judgment and discretion and draw on unique skills related to moral judgment:

- critical thinking and analysis
- situational/contextual assessment
- weighing the relative obligations, duties, rules, and principles involved
- knowledge and expertise that are brought to bear
- exercise of the public trust on behalf of another— not on one's own behalf, for one's own benefit, or for selfish ends.

For a unit saddled with unachievable training requirements, some of which are not directly related to mission accomplishment, the leader who makes decisions about which training elements to complete and which to ignore on the basis of the good of her unit and preparation for mission readiness, and the impact of such decisions on moral, professional, and institutional integrity, could be seen as exercising professional judgment and discretion. This would be different from someone who made similar decisions based upon outside pressures, laziness, or a desire to subvert or undermine leadership or institutional integrity. The above questions and criteria should make it clear that it is possible to distinguish on the basis of the deliberation what went into the judgment and discretion and resulting choices and actions.

With this example, we can see that what judgment and discretion look like for the medical professional will, at least to some degree, differ from how they look for the military professional or the civilian citizen because of differences in context and experience. For example, medicine is practiced in the context of an insurance system where approval is required for some forms of treatment. Monetary considerations will be important, along with other considerations such as side effects, quality of life, and patient autonomy. In the military, many of those considerations about cost and profit do not apply directly, but there are considerations about combat effectiveness, unit cohesion, morale, and public trust that are directly relevant to the exercise of professional judgment and discretion. Context and communal norms matter.

BEST PRACTICES

Keeping context in mind, we can look at best practices for the exercise of judgment and discretion in the military community of practice, with some modifications for a different context and obligations in the political community of practice. First, practice and more practice! The idea of rehearsal with feedback will be important: the after-action review is well suited for this, as are gaming and simulations that offer practice making decisions, in addition to having to work out the process for decisions and their implementation. We have good ideas about what judgment and discretion look like in other professions (such as law and medicine), where decisions are subject to review by ethics boards or other peer groups with similar expertise and experience. Others who have experience with driving and parking in a similar way can judge the assessments that I make in parallel parking. With feedback from others possessing the requisite experience and knowledge and with practice that incorporates their ideas, I should get better. I may consult a driving instructor as well, especially if the advice that I get is conflicting or I am having trouble practicing on my own.

Second, we should say no to decision trees and all other mechanical input/output models or flowcharts, along with check-list approaches. While these methods are popular and have the advantage of the agent not needing to bring in their own knowledge or experience, engaging in this kind of moral reasoning is more art and nuance, which will mean there is uncertainty, ambiguity, and the possibility of failure. Such mechanical approaches cannot take context into consideration or be reflective and critical in the way needed for good decision, and they do not allow for experience and expertise, which necessarily vary for each person. The point here is not only the correct action but also the development of moral habits and skills to get one to the correct action regularly and consistently.

Third, we need to approach judgment and discretion from a holistic point of view. The elements discussed above work together and inform one another in a mutual feedback loop. Skills and content are interconnected and inform one another; they cannot be worked on in isolation and can only be effectively developed together. In the case of developing judgment and discretion in the political context to decide when to protest and engage in acts of civil disobedience, we would have to use the questions related to just war thinking (or their corollary), as well as skills and capacities such as critical thinking, assessing context, and weighing expertise, knowledge, and moral norms and considerations. How important is the aim to be achieved, and how serious is the injustice involved? What will be involved in making the protest, and what is the likely collateral damage? Are there other long-term strategies that could have greater effect, even if they take longer?

Fourth, judgment and discretion in the military and political contexts being discussed should be informed by what I call the "narrative pivot"—critical reflection upon literature, art, film, blogging, history, and case studies (including personal experiences). These are required to build the empathy and moral imagination that are critical not just to strategic thinking but also to making moral decisions in communal contexts beyond individual short-term self-interest. In the earlier example of the training requirements, empathizing with the needs and sufferings of those under one's care or using moral imagination to think about other ways to achieve the ends in the commander's intent in the mission command case both hold out ways to think about the moral norms of a community of practice as something other than mere rules or principles that must be followed unquestioningly.

David Hume argues that the moral person must develop the general point of view by learning to enter into the sentiments of others (sympathy/empathy) in order to mitigate self-interest and narrowness of concern that we discussed in terms of the atrocity literature.[21] He notes that we have natural empathy or connection with those that resemble us and those in our physical proximity because of the role the senses and observation play in motivating our sentiments. Watching a speaker have a coughing fit or crying in the same room with us has a stronger impact on us than someone we are watching on a video. Hume also thinks the resemblance that makes empathy stronger can take many forms—but it could certainly explain our preference for biological children or family members (we can observe a similarity/connection) and certain kinds of racial or gender bias. In the case of sexual assault, women who have had a similar experience identify with a female victim, where men may have a harder time with empathy if they have not had that experience or do not know someone who has. Men may identify with another male accused of sexual assault, whereas women may find it harder to empathize unless they know someone who has been in a similar situation.

Engagement with art and literature (part of the narrative pivot) is one important way to develop the moral imagination that is necessary for empathy, since resemblance and physical proximity will only take us so far. Engaging with such material can expand our sphere of identification and help us develop empathy for people we would not have natural empathy for. Being exposed through theater and music to the experience of gay men in the 1980s was instrumental in shaping and eventually changing attitudes about AIDS and same-sex marriage. One of the arguments about the "tribal" partisan politics after the presidential election in 2016 is that there has been a movement away from empathizing or trying via moral imagination to understand the world of the "other"; instead, we are making political choices expressly because our choice causes irritation, pain, or suffering for the other, even when this may not be in our own interest. Our judgment and discretion in this case has explicitly been skewed, as in the case of war crimes literature, by narrow empathy and loyalty.

Another important piece of the narrative pivot is the nature of moral obligations and virtue relative to relationships. The ethics of care tradition also builds on some of these ideas to make the claim that morality is about discernment within the context of relationships; this view is quite amenable to both the military and political contexts under discussion here.[22] Ethics of care is not just about natural caring as an emotion, but about ethical care based upon a recognition of some kind of relationship or web of relationships in which a person is embedded. I may not, on a given morning, feel motivated to take my dog for his walk, but I might engage in an act of ethical caring because I have obligations to him in virtue of our relationship. We can see the same kind of ethical obligation functioning within both the military and political communities of practice. Members of a unit have specific responsibilities to one another based upon their relationship, just as citizens of a community have specific duties based upon their membership.

The narrative pivot is important because it helps us develop empathy and moral imagination, which can help us think about and broaden our conceptions of our relational obligations that we see as operant in critical obedience and loyalty. In fact, it will be difficult to have any kind of ethical or critical obedience and loyalty without some of these capacities as part of judgment and discretion. Judgment and discretion are a necessary form of prudence in precisely those situations where we are forced to confront a moral issue or decision that is outside the usual communal norm; we have to be able to think outside our usual conceptions and loyalties.

Finally, failure is a friend and is necessary to this process, especially reflection upon and deep understanding of what went wrong, why, and what assumptions were at play in leading to that failure. We need to learn to overcorrect for our tendencies, blind spots, and biases and acknowledge that individual experience can be helpful, but it is also necessarily limited, as Hume and the ethics of care both highlight. Of course, there are different kinds of failure and different levels of impact and severity. A failure in parallel parking is survivable, and I can learn from it (possibly with some expense and embarrassment), but failure in combat has much higher costs. Typically, we don't start with the actions that have a high chance of serious and fatal failure; we start with contexts in which we can make decisions that have lower stakes and increase autonomy as experience and aptitude increase. We do not give teens the keys to a car and let them drive independently without a great deal of practice and training in driving, nor do we let toddlers cross a busy street without assistance. They have to develop judgment and discretion in order to do those things well, and practice and experience guided by exemplars and a community of practice are necessary over time for that development.

JUDGING AND POLICING JUDGMENT AND DISCRETION

Of course, it is not as simple as people exercising their moral agency through judgment and discretion in isolation; these judgments are happening in the context of a community of practice where they will be judged and policed by peers and the results of these actions. For the military as a profession, being self-regulating is essential, so we will find this judging and policing to be more explicit than we might see in the political community, where the judgment and policing are more indirect. In the military, those who fail the standards of integrity, leadership, or other norms may be expelled from the profession, whereas in the political community of practice, moral failure may result in social exclusion or loss of reputation or power, with the notable exceptions of sedition and treason.

How do we judge whether someone used their judgment and discretion correctly? On what basis are these judgments made? Typically, we will make our assessment on the basis of results (which are much easier to see from an external perspective), but we may also judge on the basis of how the person in question made the decision to the degree that we can ascertain that. The Petrov case is a good example of how, even many years after the event, we judge and police the judgment and discretion of someone relative to the norms of the community of practice. In this case, we think he made the right decision and so he is held up as an exemplar for others to follow.

Communal critique and adjustment are also important as one considers norms and communal standards. However, this raises the question of how we decide who to seek out and which critiques to follow, especially if they are conflicting. What if we get bad advice? How will we know? Over time and with practice, we do develop our own radar for who is "good" at a given thing and whether the feedback and advice they are giving are useful to improving our judgment and discretion. This assumes a certain level at which we can individually and collectively assess whether a given judgment or exercise of discretion turned out to be right in a given context. It is also important to note that we can and do revise our judgments about these things as norms change or new information comes to light. Exclusion of women from combat or the internment of Japanese Americans may have been judged to be necessary and good in the past, but many members of those communities of practice have since revised those judgments.

There will be times when standards need to change and be renegotiated within the community of practice. Changing ideas of gender standards in the military community or citizen engagement by teenagers on gun control on the grounds that adults are not getting the job done might be two examples showing the necessity of this renegotiation. It is important to stress that it is often some of the norms within the community (coming into conflict or tension with other norms or changes in circumstances) that provide the impetus for these changes over time. They are not arbitrary or quick, easy changes.

Finally, there is the issue of the policing of judgment and discretion within a particular community of practice. What happens when one is right? What happens when one is wrong? How do we make decisions about what happens? As with judgment, the policing—which usually comes in the aftermath of judgment—is going to be communally rooted, oriented, and negotiated based upon the norms, history, and priorities of the communities of practice. Those who are wrong will generally be sanctioned or punished, in ways one hopes that are consistent with the communal norms and the severity of the harm caused or trust and reliability sacrificed. Those who are right will be rewarded one hopes in similar ways, unless the community thinks that the results were anomalous, based upon luck or some other intervening condition that does not warrant increased trust or faith in the reliability of that person's judgment and discretion.

OBJECTIONS AND REPLIES

Before concluding this chapter, I want to consider a couple of objections. First, particularly in the military context, the problem of time pressure seems to preclude the kind of judgment and discretion that I have argued for in this chapter. Second, one might think that such exercise of judgment and discretion is fine under "normal" circumstances but will break down as emotion or instinct takes over in extreme situations. In short, the applicability and practicability of this account of judgment and discretion are much more limited than they look at first.

The answer to both of these objections lies in the Stoic idea of rehearsal and practice.[23] Activities such as training and wargaming and even simulations that rehearse actions as well as the decisionmaking processes involved are critical here. For a combat context, this could include scenarios with checkpoints, targeting using proportionality and discrimination problems; these scenarios need to be ones into which nuance and complexity, changing circumstances, limited information, emotional intensity, and time-constrained decisionmaking processes can be built.

In order for judgment and discretion to be developed, they must be properly habituated, which requires community critique, feedback, and exemplars to follow and avoid; at the end of the day, however, each person has to develop their own style and abilities. Within the political community, we might see participation in public discourse (either in person or on social media) as the kind of practice and development of skills that are similar to wargaming or military role-playing. There is communal feedback (sometimes strong and adversarial) and discussion of community norms, practices, and values, which other members of the community hope will regulate and shape the development and practice of judgment and discretion in the future.

In the military, this idea seems more intuitive; since we train every other aspect of the profession, it makes sense that we would also rehearse the skills involved in judgment and discretion, beginning with fairly low-stakes contexts and moving to higher stakes situations as one gains experience and proficiency as recognized by both the individual and other members of the community.

In conclusion, judgment and discretion are not mechanical and automatic things that can be applied without a great deal of reflection, experience, and other forms of data and consideration; they are more art than science. This is why we tend to reserve judgment and discretion for adults, professionals, and those with some kind of experience and expertise. There are issues of trust and reliability, which relate explicitly to the debate about loyalty and implicitly to obedience within communities of practice that are important to consider. This is why McMahan and the revisionists' arguments about the moral agency of the individual are problematic to some degree. They are correct in that we need to expect more individual agency and responsibility; one cannot cede that to the state. However, it is important to remember that such agency is still exercised within the context of a community of practice, within a collective context that is relevant and impacts how that agency is conceived and what the limits on it will be. In the next chapter, we will see the application of this tension between individual and collective agency, as well as the ideas about judgment and discretion in negotiating the boundaries and limits of obedience.

CHAPTER 8

OBEDIENCE AS NEGOTIATION

The problem was more that soldiers were beginning to view themselves as incarcerated in the trenches, potentially in perpetuity. In short, trench warfare at Les Eparges was coming to bear a conspicuous resemblance to pitched battle at Verdun.
— Leonard Smith[1]

If I had been told to do so, like [Paul] Meadlo was ordered by Lt. Calley, I would have refused because I know that it is a war crime.
— Gregory Olsen[2]

"The harsh fact of individual moral failure" was inadequate explanation for why the vast majority of Charlie Company had turned into killers.
— Michael Bilton and Kevin Sim[3]

IMAGINE YOURSELF IN THE ALLIED TRENCHES on the Western Front in 1915. A series of offensives to break through the German lines have failed, but the leadership insists that the next attempt will be successful: "The strategy is good. The men need to try harder." Each time the casualties are worse than the time before with little apparent gain or success. Quiet discussion and not-so-quiet grumbling and despair take place among the ranks about how to continue, when it will end, and whether defeat would at least be an end to the suffering. The strategy is madness. It is a machine for eating up human lives with no end or progress in sight. Defeat or endless war seem the most likely options, and the men feel trapped. Given these assessments of proportionality and reasonable chance of success—do you obey the orders to attack? How much energy are you willing to put into, or have your men put into, the attack? What do you say to your superiors?

In an article on mission command, a commander practicing radio silence notes the changes in his leadership style and the behavior of those he leads as a result of having less direction: "Here I discovered that radios had made me lazy in my briefing because I knew I could control it well during the action." On the other hand, he notices that his people are making and carrying out good decisions without intervention: "This time I witnessed several changes in the unit. I saw junior commanders making decisions, good decisions, without any direction from me. One of the teams missed their pick up and rather than speak on the radio trying to rearrange it they carried out their task on foot successfully. Other teams encountered difficulties during the mission, but they knew the intent and end state and were able to complete their tasks without further direction for thirty-six hours of radio silence."[4]

As a matter of leadership, the radio silence required judgment and discretion (and some innovation as circumstances on the ground changed) on the part of the teams, and it required trust on the part of the commander. As those under command demonstrate competency in judgment and discretion oriented to mission completion, the commander gives more trust, which builds confidence both in those exercising the judgment and discretion and in the commander, who knows he can exercise authority and leadership in a less invasive and direct way. For proponents of mission command, this is exactly what is supposed to happen and reflects what they see as the well-demonstrated benefits of such an approach.

Having laid the foundation of the capacity for judgment and discretion in the last chapter (especially in the military context), we can now return to the question of how much and what kind of moral agency are maintained and surrendered by consenting to be part of certain communities of practice. This chapter argues that obedience is "negotiated" between authorities and members of a community being commanded (although on occasion as individuals) relative to certain normative restraints that inform and limit that process. We will need to address the nature of negotiation and discuss why it is the best way to think about obedience; in short, negotiation provides a structured way to think about how we would instantiate critical obedience, especially in the borderline cases that require exercise of judgment and discretion and may require kinds of obedience other than the conventional expectation of directly doing what one is told in the way one is instructed. To do this in more granular detail, we will look at some case studies—in particular, the case of the French 5th Infantry Division on the Western Front in World War I and various activities in response to the conditions there, which ultimately led to mutinies in 1917.

In most circumstances, this process of negotiation will appear automatic and relatively uncontroversial, because it will be clear that obedience is reasonable and there are not circumstances that require negotiation. But in other circumstances, the process of rendering (or refusing) obedience may require judgment and discretion to determine what is appropriate, and actions may be on a continuum of obedience, nonobedience, less than obedience, or even disobedience—rather than the conventional either/or in the straightforward presumptive case. We typically think of these cases as the relatively rare illegal or immoral order, but such borderline cases are much more common that we might expect and occur in both normal and extreme circumstances.

We will also have to consider whether loyalty is different in that it is not negotiated in this way. If obedience is negotiated, why is it that loyalty cannot be, since they are related concepts with some overlap? We will consider this point at the end of this chapter as well as the issue of dual roles—military member and citizen—that are occupied and must be navigated. Someone who is loyal can still be disobedient, so loyalty does not need to be negotiated in action in the same way as obedience, unless the disobedience is a reoccurring issue over a long period of time.

DEFINING NEGOTIATION

The image that the word negotiation normally invokes is of the wheeling-dealing businessperson closing a deal with another such character. The main characters in such films as *Wall Street*, *Boiler Room*, and *The Wolf of Wall Street* come to mind, although those characters are not necessarily acting in an ethical fashion. In *Boiler Room* salespeople use high-pressure tactics, deception, manipulation, and emotional appeals to convince clients to invest their money in what is effectively a pyramid scheme. In this case there is a great deal of asymmetry of knowledge on the part of the customers, and those doing the selling have most of the control in the situation, along with the immoral intention of exploiting their clients for profit with no client return on the investments.

In the ethical practice of negotiating in business, we suppose that the two parties are in roughly equal power positions and that each side is trying to gain the most advantageous terms relative to their desired outcome. We also suppose that there is no coercion and roughly symmetrical information, so that each side is making free and informed choices as they negotiate for their own advantage. In an unethical negotiation such as presented in *Boiler Room*, however, coercion, lack of information, deception, or some other unequal power relation creates suboptimal circumstances for one of the parties. In the film, the manipulation, emotion, and asymmetry of information impacted the clients' ability to effectively engage in symmetrical negotiation, and those who were selling had set the circumstances specifically for that end. At its basis, ethical negotiation involves a relationship in which each side uses its power and information to try and influence the behavior of the other side to gain advantage relative to an end. If I have apples to sell and you want to buy them, we will negotiate to settle on a fair price given the condition of the apples, their qualities for cooking, making cider, or eating, and other relevant considerations that may impact the price that we are both willing to settle on. Presumably we reach an agreement from which we both benefit in some way, or we would not choose to strike a deal.

For our purposes, negotiation is more complicated; whether we are discussing the military context or that of the citizen and the state, the relationship has a basic power inequality and a lack of symmetrical information, which impacts the question of consent and the level of free will or voluntary nature of the action. While the business model is not necessarily the picture of negotiation that we will use, the idea of negotiation is useful because each side still retains some power in the relationship and can impact the behavior of the other party; there is an interdependency that can be leveraged to mitigate the inequalities in certain cases that define the community of practice. In the case of *Boiler Room*, what is missing is this community of practice with a shared history, identity norms, and values, as well as shared intentions and aims that are rooted not in profit and exploitation but in shared lives, projects, and meanings.

We need a different model of negotiation and different standards by which to judge the process. We want something more like an ethical model of negotiation, but in the communities of practice that we are discussing, we cannot have the symmetry usually associated with that; we must acknowledge the inequities of power and knowledge without sliding into the unethical form of negotiation. As we will see in the World War I case study, a level of presumption in favor of obedience by those commanded toward those in authority based upon moral and legal authority and the threat of punishment complicated the usual picture of negotiation. However, those who are commanded do have a range of choices, agency, and powers and must consent at different points in the process for commanders to be successful in their ends.

As events on the ground and judgments about those events and actions relative to reasonable chance of success, proportionality, and just cause evolve, those commanded may conclude that obedience is not justified or that only partial or provisional obedience is justified. If this situation continues or worsens, nonobedience or disobedience may be justified relative to these three ethical principles and within the context of the norms and ideas of the community of practice and/or professionalism that defines that community. The judgment and discretion discussed in the last chapter will be critical to this process of negotiation. Judgment and discretion are necessary first to discern the particulars and then to assess them against universals such as moral norms and values of the community of practice (for example, reasonable chance of success and proportionality)—both in general terms and in specific application in a context to decide whether or to what extent obedience is appropriate.

Clearly, negotiation is more of a process than a discrete event with a beginning and end; the defined temporal structure of the deal discussed above may be a series of discrete events and decisions over time. A change in one case may require and impact further negotiations; we need to think about the cumulative effect of these actions and not just one action in isolation. In the case of the draft protests during the Vietnam War, individual decisions, like those made by Tim O'Brien, were important in themselves but took on greater importance as they came to be coordinated with the decisions of others, which would manifest in protests and more widespread draft refusals. The decisions to refuse to serve at the beginning of the war when few were doing so were different than those decisions later in the war, when the political landscape and communal sentiments about the conflict were shifting.

Negotiation is more complicated than it seems at first. What we are looking at is a complex negotiation within a hierarchical structure (less so for citizens in a political community, but hierarchy still obtains), where the parties are interdependent members of a shared community of practice with different levels and types of power and agency, as well as asymmetric information impacting the question of consent and whether one's actions are mixed or fully voluntary. In these communities of practice there are constraints—things that will be at least to some degree out of one's control, and other things that will be within one's control. A new model of negotiation is needed that includes a presumption of obedience under reasonable conditions, where mixed actions and limited responsibility are the norm, but where this presumption is viewed as provisional and subject to negotiation and critical obedience in border, questionable, or difficult cases. This is precisely why judgment and discretion are needed—we need to have negotiation to decide whether and what kinds of obedience as an expression of moral agency will be appropriate in these cases.

Negotiation as a concept best captures the communal nature of the virtue of obedience while allowing for the critical, deliberative, and active aspects that are missing from the blind and passive obedience that can be so problematic. The blind and passive obedience models are oriented around individuals and their decisions, while this model of obedience takes into account that decisions about obedience are individual and collective decisions made within a community of practice. Negotiation asks those making decisions to refer to communal values and to consider not just the impact of my negotiation and individual choice about obedience, but also the communal context. This is what I see as missing in blind and passive obedience as well as the individualistically oriented revisionist accounts we have discussed. While we are not removing the presumption of obedience, we are allowing and expecting more questioning of it. This acknowledges more agency and deliberation on the part of individuals, which the presumption argument assumes is counterproductive or not realistic. It further allows us to acknowledge the range of possible actions and responses that are involved in the kind of obedience that we want to argue is a moral virtue.

WHO IS NEGOTIATING?

In this understanding of negotiation, the parties to the negotiation matter as well and differ from the conventional business model discussed above. Typically, a negotiation has two (and only two) parties, even if these parties are negotiating on behalf of, or as agents for, another party. For example, my son might represent me when I go to buy a new truck (if I am terrible at negotiations, and he is very skilled, or if I have no interest in haggling since I think car salespeople are likely to be corrupt), to make a deal on my behalf. He negotiates with the salesman with the understanding that he speaks with my authority and I will be bound by the results of the negotiations. There are two clear parties negotiating over a specific and limited end.

In the case of the military, multiple parties are the subject of commands, and both the commanded and commanding are doing so not on their own behalf but on behalf of the citizens and the state, and they are responsible to the state as well as to the other members of the community of practice bounded by norms and military professionalism. Here the negotiation relative to obedience is not the simple two-directional, two-party model and involves persons acting as representatives of the state (political community of practice) and of a profession (military community of practice) simultaneously.

The case of the citizen is more straightforward (there is a community of practice, but not a professional one), but some of the same complexities remain. This negotiation is still two-way, without the explicit agent or representational relationship as the military, but it is still representational in a different way with more individual moral agency. However, actions still happen in a communal context because of membership in a community of practice, and citizens are in relationship to one another as well as to the authority of the state. The difference is the authority is more diffuse in terms of most day-to-day actions that citizens undertake; as a citizen, I have more moral agency that I can exercise within the limits set by the state.

While individuals might be involved in this process, the contexts that we are considering do not usually have individuals acting solely in their own interests and on their behalf with no regard for others. Rather, individuals are participating in these negotiations as members of a community of practice (military, citizens, members of a political community) where they are acting in concert on behalf of others to affect some end that they may or may not personally agree with or endorse. It is not just that the individual is acting, but rather that the individual acting with other individuals in a certain way constitutes waging war. Here I agree with Walzer (against McMahan and the revisionists) that war is somehow different in terms of how we think of moral concerns. Given its permission for violence and the odd limitations on responsibility, war is a collective activity that does not bear much resemblance to other kinds of collective activities we participate in. Individuals participate in war not on their own behalf (unless they are mercenaries) or in their own direct interest, but rather on that of the state.

There is responsibility for actions in conflict but not for the cause itself and for other decisions that are rightly the realm of the state. However, I think we need to carve out alternate ground between Walzer and McMahan by returning to John Locke and his right to rebellion argument, which applies clearly to citizens but also to military members (where rebellion is clear disobedience to orders originating from the state) in the conduct of war. According to Locke, if there is a clear, egregious pattern of failing to deliver on the protection of basic rights, then the citizens may rebel and change the social contract to institute new power to rule. In the case of war, clear disobedience and actions short of that could be justified on a collective (not just individual) basis as a court of last resort to avoid harm and injustice. These are the questionable and border cases requiring judgment and discretion to determine harm and injustice (just cause and proportionality being two concerns here), as well as reasonable chance of success and last resort.

In general, citizens will assume reasonably that the causes the state asks it to fight for are just. This presumption will exist on both sides and is strongest at the beginning of the conflict.[5] McMahan even admits that the asymmetry of knowledge here is a difficulty for the level of agency he wants to advocate, even as he insists on individual moral agency both for jus in bello and jus ad bellum. I argue there is a sliding scale of agency depending upon the level of responsibility, agency, and input into the decisionmaking process. James Dubik argues for middle ground between ad bellum and in bello, reflecting the complications with Walzer's and other standard accounts but avoiding some of the problems with McMahan.[6] Dubik is especially concerned about senior military leadership, but his arguments highlight an increased connection to and responsibility for jus ad bellum as one goes up the chains of command. Senior enlisted and officers have more responsibility and agency than the average junior enlisted person on the ground because they have more knowledge, expertise, and authority to impact the outcome of events.

Dubik argues that we need to think about the justice of war waging (as an additional category within jus in bello), which includes five principles: continuous dialogue, final decision authority, managerial competence, legitimacy, and resignation. Senior officers have to give advice and carry out the orders of the civilian leaders as a basic obligation of the profession, but they can exercise some judgment and discretion by resigning if they think the civilian leaders are taking a course of action that violates norms and values of the community of practice. We can see Dubik's argument as a negotiation around obedience in terms of the civilian/military relationship and the role that senior military play in that relationship by advising senior civilian leaders but not having the final power to make the decisions. In discussing the options and obligations involved in war waging, Dubik is mirroring the negotiation processes that we will see later in this chapter, only at higher levels of responsibility.

This ground between Walzer and McMahan gives us a way to think about agency with some individual power and responsibility (especially in extremis, like the Thompson case at My Lai), where we want people to act as individuals when the other representatives of the state cannot and will not and where there is good reason to do so. There are questionable and border cases where negotiation is required to enact or work through whether to obey and what kind of obedience to render in a given situation in ways that allow for individual agency but still within the context of a community of practice and its norms, values, and history.

At the same time, we do not want to let the political community off the hook by delegating all the responsibility to the individual as an individual. If war is a collective activity, it is necessary to preserve at least some sense of collective responsibility, especially as a guard or mitigation against moral injury.[7] Too much individual agency can lead to abuses and atrocities, but it can also lead to individuals making decisions and taking on levels of moral responsibility that are inappropriate for an individual. No individual should bear the burden of the entire community when it comes to war; war is an act, and the responsibility, of the political community.

How does this work for citizens within a political community? Citizens act to some degree on their own behalf (more so than members of the military, who are agents and representatives of the state), but they are always members of a community, so their connection to the state remains, as do their communal responsibility and identity with shared values and history of a community of practice. Since they are not all members of the same profession, there are fewer permissions, less focus on the common good, and an absence of the expertise that would give greater latitude and permission in actions; citizens have more responsibility for their individual actions within the sphere granted by the state, as well as more agency in influencing how the bounds on their liberty are set by the state. As with war, the community of practice has collective responsibilities that are not reducible to those of the individual.

In the case of the Enron financial scandal, which involved various accounting violations to manipulate company value and stock prices, individuals within the company made decisions to do certain things, but there was also a collective corporate culture that facilitated, supported, and covered up such actions. Collectives can do as much or more damage and harm in ways that can have an impact disproportional to the individuals acting together or to the aggregate of the individual impact. Acting together in the name of a collective adds something to the equation that isolating responsibility only to individuals fails to capture. Institutional history, cachet, and power are distinct from and more than the individuals that make up the institution. In Enron's case, certain individuals were held liable and responsible, but that did not and could not account for the harm caused by the actions of the company. This is why we have seen increased calls after scandals such as Enron for increased corporate social responsibility that goes beyond the chief executive officers or other individuals such as stockholders.

NEGOTIATING—IN THEORY AND PRACTICE

Now we are ready to directly consider the following: To what degree is the idea of obedience a "negotiation" between the commander and the commanded based upon trust in the commander, an understanding of the mission or aim, and professional or moral and political judgments of things such as proportionality and reasonable chance of success? If this view of obedience is correct, it will help us answer the questions about the levels of moral agency and judgment and discretion that individuals retain as their own within both the military and political communities of practice. We can also then clarify how conditional the obligation to obey is and the ways the obligation is grounded in mission or end and the norms and values (such as military professionalism) of the community of practice, which puts limits on obedience that derive from the norms, values, and identity of that community.

With a more complex view of negotiation that takes into account the power and hierarchical elements of these communities, we can look at how this negotiation would look in specific practice. To do this, we turn to one case study in depth and to two more familiar ones for further exploration and discussion. This will allow us to see how decisions about obedience were made in questionable and borderline cases and also how judgment and discretion were exercised as a part of that process. An in-depth case also allows us to see how conditions evolved and changed over time such that initial actions of obedience and less than obedience eventually evolved into nonobedience and outright disobedience (mutiny and civil disobedience) in ways that crossed both the military and political roles and communities of practice.

The first case study is from World War I of the French regular army infantry division (5th Infantry Division) between 1914 and 1918 on the Western Front.[8] In his book on this case, historian Leonard Smith takes issue with the influence of the authority-generated model of obedience attributed in part to Carl von Clausewitz, who viewed disobedience of soldiers as part of the friction of war: "[C]ommand authority as explored here reflected a negotiated balance-of-power equation linking the protagonists. This settlement then set the parameters of command authority."[9] In Smith's view, these assessments were based upon the idea of proportionality, with the soldiers asking whether the means they were asked to use would achieve the ends that the commanders had in mind. Smith considers how command authority changed as these calculations of proportionality by soldiers changed and impacted their actions. These questions are also related to the issue of trust: Did the nature of command authority actually change, or was the change a matter of the perception of its binding nature and whether obedience was morally obligatory?

First, we can look at instances of breaking off attacks and resisting further calls for aggressive action within the context of pitched battle and eventually in the trenches themselves. According to Smith, the fall of 1915 was a turning point for the French forces on the Western Front, where soldiers broke off attacks when they determined they would not have the desired effect, unlike General Charles Mangin, who was determined to continue and thought things were proceeding well.[10] In September 1915 Mangin was informed that further offensive action ought not be expected from the soldiers. These actions (or resistance to action) were viewed in terms of judgments of proportionality and reasonable chance of success that soldiers had made by looking at the facts on the ground and their experiences in their theater of local combat.[11]

How do we know that soldiers were making these judgments, and what were they based upon? One of the most clear indication of these judgments was the often referenced difference between the "official" and the "hidden" transcripts of the war—the difference between what was reported officially up the chain of command and the actual lived experiences and suffering of the troops as communicated between themselves and sometimes to friends and family back home.[12] The differences in these two versions of war, as in many other wars before and since, were quite stark; the official transcript of war was optimistic and filled with data, while the hidden transcript was full of personal detail, blood, death, and existential suffering with a side of mud and chaos. The soldiers made their decisions and assessments not in individual isolation but in community, sharing their suffering and talking about it in the larger strategic context of winning the war, an aim they were committed to even as the later mutinies took place.

As French citizens and members of the military, they wanted to win the war and did not want to give up on that aim even as they wondered at various points if victory was realistic or possible.

These judgments about the breakdowns in proportionality were seen in the pitched battle at Verdun and in trench warfare at Les Eparges in 1916–17. It was not simply a matter of the numbers of casualties, but how these numbers were perceived in terms of proportionality issues and in relation to reasonable chance of success for both a particular mission and eventually the overall war effort.[13] The misery on the front and especially in the trenches came from a sense that there were two options, entrapment and defeat, and the despair that came from the situation. They did not see military utility or progress in the suffering they were experiencing, and there was a helplessness in the face of death.[14] After Verdun and Les Eparges, there was a sentiment that it would get worse before it would get better, with a hope that the 1917 offensive might bring movement and progress.[15] Even during this dire time, courts martial for desertion were fairly rare, a demonstration that negotiations around how much aggressive action they would engage in were necessary and largely successful in avoiding all-out revolt.[16]

Second, these breakdowns and refusals to fight eventually manifested themselves in a more radical form of disobedience in the mutinies of 1917; these forms of less than obedience, selective obedience, and occasional disobedience or resistance moved into full-blown disobedience. Smith argues that "the mutinies are best understood as political renegotiation around the parameters of command authority."[17] The acts of "collective indiscipline" generally included in the mutinies reflected a range of activities, including order refusal and resistance to certain demands by superiors. In these ways, soldiers expressed their power and agency as citizens, not just as soldiers that were merely agents of the state. This expression of agency was reflected by both individuals and in some collective and concerted fashion that more resembled the kinds of civil disobedience and general strikes one might see in the political community. Protests about the conduct of the war and about the conditions within the military (leave, food, etc.) were analogous to workers' protests about labor conditions during the same time period.

The critical takeaway here, as with John Locke's political theory and later in Vietnam, is that command authority derives its legitimacy from the citizens, including the soldiers themselves (both as members of the military and as citizens).[18] This reflected the dual role of the citizen and soldier, where they saw their mutiny (normally a military matter) as an act of civil disobedience or revolt as well; this points to the ways in which this negotiation was engaged in from both the military and the civilian perspective. We will discuss this issue of dual roles in more detail in the next chapter, but it is important to note here that it was part of the negotiations and informed the judgment and discretion the soldiers used in the process. This is also reflective of the Lockean social contract theory ideas as applied specifically to the military context. The state, on whose behalf they were fighting and the preservation of which made the war necessary, had failed in their view to protect their basic rights as citizens and as military members; the state had failed in its basic social contract responsibilities, and therefore obedience was not presumptive, much less obligatory.

Third, the more severe end of the negotiation (disobedience) highlighted the role of trust, based upon officers sharing the soldiers' privations and perils. Where there was trust, these issues and incidents could be resolved without more severe forms of disobedience and sanctions. Where this trust did not exist, disobedience was seen as the only reasonable option for protest and remedy. Even General Philippe Petain noted this connection: "But for the most part, soldiers became 'politicized' only when they felt let down by their leaders."[19] In addition, officers played an important role in mediating the actions of "collective indiscipline" by asking for a restrained approach in dealing with the mutineers to avoid the threat of broader political protests. They were able to do this because, as one investigator noted, "[T]here was unanimity on the part of the men in affirming their respect and their affection for their officers and NCOs. . . . [T]he only objective of their demands was to attract the attention of the government."[20] Without this affection and respect, the indiscipline certainly would have been much worse than it was, since the officers were also largely sympathetic to the mutineers and their demands.

These negotiations of obedience in different contexts demonstrated an important point for citizens and soldiers alike: that command authority does not only operate in one direction, as soldiers had the power to stop doomed offensives before they began.[21] What happened as a result of these negotiations around obedience was that the nature and grounds of obedience were changed, including new military regulations: "The commander who knows his job . . . will only ask useful efforts from his troops."[22] Communication was expected to happen in both directions; the commander had to explain reasons and context for orders, but officers were also expected to understand the emotions and experiences of their men and care for their needs. Negotiation had altered the actual ability and narrative of command control, not just the perceptions, in terms of when and under what conditions soldiers were willing to give obedience based upon judgment and discretion as a community relative to community standards (French civic identity, reasonable chance of success, and proportionality). This in turn altered what commanders could reasonably expect from their men, especially under difficult conditions where progress toward the desired and justified end was not clear. The balance of power had in some way shifted.

Two other examples, the *Lying to Ourselves* report and the case of My Lai, demonstrate a similar kind of obedience as negotiation in process, albeit in different ways and in different contexts. In the first case, the Strategic Studies Institute report on lying in the Army found extensive cases and a culture of dishonesty. The authors documented "pencil whipping" reports (especially on training), not being forthright on evaluations, and lying as a form of social lubrication to grease wheels with commanders or avoid upsetting a leader or the bureaucracy. As one person interviewed in the study noted, "The façade goes all the way up."[23] The authors attribute the divide between values and practice to two areas: ethical fading and rationalization. There is ethical fading, in their view, because many ethical decisions are "simply no longer viewed as ethical choices" because of circumstances or context.[24]

Alternatively, given the arguments we discussed with reference to the World War I example, we might think individuals recognize these as moral choices but then rationalize their decision—for example, sending a report that is less than completely candid because of other overriding concerns, such as the welfare of their soldiers, the impossibility of completing the many tasks to standard or at all, the overall mission success, or perhaps the greater good. While some of these are cases of lying and dishonesty, some could be viewed as negotiation based upon judgment and discretion rooted in considerations of military professionalism such as mission, reasonable chance of success, and proportionality relative to a specific mission. In short, some of these are instances of soldiers using professional judgment and discretion to navigate negotiations with respect to obedience. If this line of argument is correct, what we find is analogous to the official and hidden transcripts from World War I: one version of events and reality is officially reported, and another is the lived reality and experience within the military communities in question.

At My Lai in Vietnam, Hugh Thompson and others refused orders explicitly, implicitly, or in other ways, such as by walking away or failing to engage. Thompson landed his helicopter between Lieutenant Calley's troops and the targeted noncombatants and told his crew, "I'm going to go over and get them out of the bunker myself. If the squad opens up on them, shoot 'em," which facilitated the evacuation of some of the noncombatants.[25] Whether Thompson's actions are viewed as outright disobedience to Calley (who was in command) or something less than obedience/selective obedience, he clearly used judgment and discretion to fairly radically negotiate the bounds of obedience and loyalty in the situation, as did some of Calley's men.

Some of Calley's men refused orders, while others merely turned their backs on what was happening and refused to participate but did not impede the participation of others. This was a matter not simply of individual actions and their moral implications but rather a collective and communal issue, as seen in the subsequent attempts by Charlie Company and the military hierarchy to minimize and cover up the actions at My Lai, difficulties in the investigation process, and the controversy surrounding the ensuing trials. Harry Stanley, who refused Calley's orders, noted, "Even though I didn't participate I was there, and I feel like I'm just as guilty as anybody that was there. Because there was nothing I could do about the things that they did."[26] Negotiation, including judgment and discretion, is both individual and collective at the same time, as is the moral responsibility that ensues.

If these examples are suggestive of the kinds of questionable and borderline cases faced in communities of practice, then obedience is much more complicated. It may include a range of behaviors and must also include agency, judgment, and discretion on the part of those obeying, but also having impacts and implications for the community of practice. These illustrative examples of questionable and borderline cases show how border cases require judgment and discretion and were not presumptive cases of obedience. Therefore, they required negotiation to determine whether and what kinds of obedience should be rendered, based upon the context and the values and norms of the community of practice as seen through the specific (and changing) context at the time, both in the individual and collective judgment of the members.

OBJECTIONS AND REPLIES

I recognize that this line of argument is a direct challenge to and complication of the usual view of obedience that seems foundational to military training, especially in the enlisted ranks. It also presents problems to traditional arguments about the obligation of citizens to obedience within a political community. We might concede that some officers or well-educated, responsible citizens might be able to handle such obedience, but there are serious problems and objections that need to be considered and answered if we are going to make the broader argument for this view.

First, there is a concern that obedience as negotiation, supported by the exercise of judgment and discretion, will cause chaos, undermine a predictable command climate, and impede unit cohesion and therefore combat effectiveness in the military. In the political community, it could have similar impacts on the order and control that are necessary to civil society. This concern could be heightened by social media and other modes of communication that appeal to emotion, bias, and fear rather than judgment and discretion rooted in prudence. In both communities, strong and unscrupulous leaders could manipulate the situation to create chaos and undermine the ends of the community of practice for their own purposes.

Second, some object that soldiers, especially at lower and enlisted ranks, are not equipped to make these kinds of judgments. The opinion is that they do not have the expertise and may lack the intellectual capacities, experience, and big picture/contextual knowledge that would be necessary for good deliberations and decisions. Similarly, in the political community, one might object that there are serious differentials in levels of education and interest in making these judgments, especially with the advent of mass media and social media that can manipulate disengaged or less informed citizens. This account may be all well and good for a specific segment of the community of practice, but it becomes problematic when it is more broadly applied.

Third, combat offers no time to deliberate deeply or to gather the information needed to make these kinds of judgments accurately. This is less of an issue in the political community where fewer situations of this kind occur, but when events are moving quickly or there is a crisis, the same concern applies. The pressure to make a decision and to "do something" undermines the ability to perform effective deliberation.

Finally, this approach undermines a core communal understanding of the military acting as a unit, not as individuals making moral judgments on their own, which will impact command and control, esprit de corps, unit cohesion, and combat effectiveness. In the political community, there are also potential dangers to highly individualized moral agency because it erodes the idea of collective responsibility and accountability for actions that were undertaken by collective decision—voting, war, public policy. In politics, we hear the refrain, "He is not my president," or "Don't blame me, I voted for the other person," as if one is responsible in the political community for only those policies that one explicitly voted for.

In response to these overlapping objections, I would emphasize several points. First, my explanation of negotiation accounts for the difference between obedience in combat and garrison contexts. The attention in the garrison context is designed to train and set the habits, so we might tolerate a lesser degree of agency and negotiation in order to set these habits. In combat, both the commanded and commander are presumed to have had this training and proved their bona fides and ought to be trusted to exercise a greater degree of judgment and discretion and moral agency relative to proportionality and reasonable chance of success.

However, people need the opportunity to develop and practice their judgment and discretion, which suggests allowing a higher level of agency and negotiation than is currently the case. This will require lower-stakes situations where this can happen with the support of the community through feedback, correction, and learning from success and failure. These skills and the process of obedience as negotiation must be developed and practiced before they are actually needed. Doing so addresses the time pressure issue, since if these skills and capacities are already developed or developing, less time is required for deliberation in the same way that muscle memory allows physical skills to appear to be nearly automatic and instant.

Second, this account better comports with the trend toward mission command, innovation, and disciplined disobedience where justified by events to achieve the mission or other ends but still provides a more rigorous sense of what the limitations and parameters might be that constrain these judgments as departures. Obedience is important, but it is much more complicated and nuanced than we might think at first and is not an intrinsic or individual virtue. This is especially acute now with an all-volunteer force, in the context of the democratic republic and the dual role of military and citizens. The World War I example in particular reflected how the question of obedience is an issue not just for members of the military but also for citizens (regardless of whether they are also members of the military).

Shifting how we think about and discuss obedience along these lines preserves a provisionally presumptive idea of obedience in "normal" cases, which would largely preserve obedience in garrison contexts where it seems critical in the training process. However, it also acknowledges that in both garrison and combat contexts, there are questionable and border cases; it shows the necessity for judgment and discretion grounding negotiation in those contexts. Without judgment and discretion and the development of those capacities for moral agency, obedience as negotiation would be highly problematic and based merely on personal values or conscience. If this were the case, the concerns in the objections above would be very difficult to answer and surmount. However, this account is grounded in a concept of negotiation that takes seriously the communal context and collective responsibility as well as individual moral agency and responsibility.

The same is true for the application of this account to the political community. While our understanding and discussions of

obedience and civil disobedience are largely conceived of as matters of individual conscience, this account allows for a broader,
more collectively oriented view. This is important because in the
political community of practice, civil disobedience is not merely
about the exercise and expression of individual rights (although
that is part of it) but is also an attempt to persuade other members of the political community to change a policy or law. As in
the military, negotiation about the range and appropriateness of
obedience happens in a collective context.

We should return to the question of loyalty. While consistent
and regular disobedience can undermine loyalty, which is built
and sustained over time, it is less subject to the kind of negotiation oriented around professional judgement and discretion. That
said, in the case of longer term nonobedience and disobedience
based on these kinds of moral considerations, it is possible that
loyalty can be undermined. In the Vietnam and Nixon eras,
some American citizens concluded that they could not trust and
therefore continue to be loyal to the state, whereas others felt they
could continue to do so. Choices about acts and practices of civil
disobedience, nonobedience, and less than obedience (in relation
to the draft, for example) played a role in these kinds of decisions
about loyalty.

To conclude, let us consider the discussion by Ulrich Zwygart
of how obedient officers need to be.[27] He argues for what he calls
"critical obedience" based upon two considerations in any given
situation: ethics and military knowledge or expertise.[28] He posits
that for both military persons and citizens, there is an obligation
to engage critically before obeying, and in some cases critical obedience will involve not obeying. The presumption to obey is not
automatic but is predicated on certain conditions, just as Locke's
argument for the obedience of citizens and surrendering of certain
rights is conditional on obligations being met by the state. Part
of obedience must be an assessment of whether these conditions
obtain and to what degree, so it must always be critical. This view

captures in a different way the line of argument of this and the prior chapters, while setting the foundation to consider the dual role of citizen and military member and move us toward thinking about how obedience as negotiation will work in practice.

CHAPTER 9

THE MILITARY-CITIZEN DUALITY

I see an ethos that is different. . . . They talk about themselves as "we" separate from society. They see themselves as different, morally and culturally.
—Richard Kohn[1]

In many cases, this code of honor seems to hold the warrior to a higher ethical standard than that required for an ordinary citizen.
—Shannon E. French[2]

THE SATIRICAL PREMISE of the Twitter account @IamWarax is that the account owner speaks for all veterans; he takes a jab at the frequent trope of the veteran who claims authority on all veteran issues, reflecting the perspective of the military member as warrior, a separate and superior class that serves the nation and exemplifies the virtues of the country. Then–defense secretary James Mattis gave a nonsatirical expression of the same view in 2017: "Keep on fighting. . . . You are buying time. You are a great example for our country. . . . It's got some problems . . . problems we don't have in the military. . . . Hold the line until our country gets back to understanding and respecting and showing it . . . being friendly to one another."[3] This reflects the debate between the ideas of the warrior (modeled on Sparta and pop culture images of the warrior ethos) and citizen soldier. This is the tension between Achilles and Hector—between the servant of the society and a member of it, one who is the leader and set apart from that society, looking down upon fellow citizens and expecting gratitude and glory for the warrior prowess that defines one's identity.

The problem that these examples underline is that unlike in warrior societies, in which the guardian or warrior class is a distinct class or group apart, servicemembers in the United States (and arguably other societies such as Canada, Australia, and the United Kingdom) are citizens first, who will revert to civilian citizenship once they leave the military, and members of the military as a profession second. While in the military, they do not cede their citizenship; they still may vote and exercise other basic political rights with certain restrictions related to their role and rooted in the understanding of the military profession as nonpartisan. Members of the military are "political actors" of a very particular sort in their professional role; this chapter is focused on exploring that dual role as military member and citizen. This is important to consider from the standpoint of its message about obedience within both the military and political communities of practice as well as what happens when membership and obligations in these communities overlap. Does this overlap change the conception of citizenship that military members occupy in ways that are different from their civilian compatriots? If so, how would this impact the account of obedience as negotiation?

The classical view of military professionalism is that of the military as apolitical agents of the state who defer to the principle of civilian control of the military—a bedrock constitutional principle and professional obligation.[4] Anthony Hartle notes the classic view of Morris Janowitz: "The professional soldier is 'above politics' in domestic affairs."[5] He also notes the importance of the integrity of military advice (which cannot be compromised by bias and partisanship): "The advice of the military professional to military or civilian superiors must accurately reflect current situations, otherwise the consequences can be severe."[6] James Dubik builds upon this assumption in trying to carve out ethics of warmaking for senior military leaders and what their moral obligations are in giving advice, especially if they believe the civilian leaders are wrong. Given this view, there is a limited and professionally circumscribed way in which military professionals are political actors, simply as agents of the state carrying out policy.

If this view of the way in which members of the military are to be political actors is accurate, it runs afoul of certain trends and practices we see in contemporary political discourse. Retired generals and flag officers (and other prominent veterans) have endorsed political candidates, especially in the presidential cycles. In social media, we see both veterans and active duty military critiquing the commander in chief and various government policies, including those they may have to carry out, and increased partisanship and identification of the military with one political party or partisan group. One might wonder why this is viewed as problematic. After all, these current and former members of the military are also citizens and part of a political community of practice.

At this point, it is helpful to make a distinction between being a political actor, particularly in one's professional role, and being personally partisan as a citizen. Any citizen who participates in the state is a political actor. When I exercise my right to free speech or to vote, I am a political actor. When I participate in political debates, I am a political actor. Since the military is an agent of the state, those who serve on its behalf are necessarily political actors; war is, as Carl von Clausewitz reminds us, politics by other means.[7] Members of the military are engaged in a collective political activity on behalf of a political community, in which they also have membership as individual, private citizens; they are political actors twice over.

The concern about the military being apolitical is really a concern about partisanship, especially on the part of individual military members on issues that may relate to their professional roles. Why is partisanship problematic for the military—both as a collective and as individual members of that community? The most pressing concern historically is the danger of coups or other military takeovers that would compromise democratic principles and the civilian control of the military. There is a further concern about adverse influence of policy by members of the military, in their individual private roles and especially in their professional roles. Our society holds the military in high esteem, and members of the public might be willing to defer their own judgment as citizens to the military or members of the military if they were to advocate in a partisan way—thus undermining rule by the citizenry as a whole and replacing it with rule by a specific segment of citizens as professionals. We will take up this concern in this chapter. I argue that personal partisanship is to be avoided, and is avoidable while still being a political actor within the context and bounds of a profession that does not reflect one's political interests.

In the last chapter, we saw how judgment and discretion (especially relative to military professionalism and a community of moral practice) were used to inform an account of obedience as negotiation between members of a community that were commanded by representatives of a larger community of practice. Now we will look at how the dual roles of citizen and military member intersect and inform how this negotiation might need to happen. I will also address the implications for the broader military/civilian relationship and life of the political community where most members of the community do not inhabit these dual identities. The central question is whether military members occupy a special kind of citizenship when they hold these dual roles and what the ramifications are for the critical obedience and loyalty that we have been discussing. In addition, we need to think about how this question impacts those members of the political community who do not occupy the dual role.

THE EVOLUTION OF DUAL ROLES

While the idea of dual roles has been with us since the beginning of the republic, the participation of formerly enslaved African Americans in the Civil War brought to the fore the relationship between military service and the training and discipline that were also necessary in citizens. Many feared that allowing African Americans (or other marginalized and disenfranchised groups) to serve would bolster their argument for increased political rights, since there was a notion of equality in fighting and dying alongside other citizens in defense of the nation. The Founding Fathers made an intentional choice to have a citizen soldier army. The experiences of the English Civil War and the Thirty Years' War, in which the standing professional armies of the European powers had acted in ways that had domestic political ramifications, were part of their collective history and made them skeptical and fearful of such armies.

The question of white male citizenship was also an issue at this point in history, but many of the same conversations would happen in the twentieth century with the integration of women and sexual minorities into the military. The underlying issue is the relationship between the roles of the military member and the citizen in terms of thinking about obedience, loyalty, and moral obligation. In her book *Willing Obedience*, Elizabeth Samet traces this evolution and discourse throughout the history and literature of the nineteenth century, and this narrative and literary account help us to think about the philosophical underpinnings and justification for the problem of the dual roles. Her work has six major themes that are important to inform my discussion of the dual role, especially the discipline necessary for citizenship and the role of justice.

First, Samet raises the question of the kind of obedience that is appropriate for the citizen soldier as opposed to the conscript without citizenship. She notes that what emerges is another kind of obedience, "one that did not preclude personal responsibility, surrender principles to persons, or sacrifice essential truths to local expedients."[8] This reflects Edmund Burke's idea of liberal obedience, rooted in patriotic love and not Hobbesian fear. It also came out of General Ulysses S. Grant's idea of the army as a thinking machine, which is in tension with the traditional ideas of unthinking obedience being required for militaries with largely uneducated conscripts.

Second, she notes that author Henry David Thoreau sees expressions of loyalty, not obedience (especially in terms of paying taxes), as the primary commitment in the transaction between the citizen and the state. This relates to the earlier discussion about obedience being focused on discrete actions in the moment, while loyalty is more concerned with actions and attitudes demonstrated over time (such as the idea of paying taxes). For Thoreau, obedience manifested in that there were two kinds of citizens—those who served the state's "head" (intellect, including politicians, lawyers, ministers), and those who served the state's "body" (with physical service).[9] He viewed soldiering as virtual enslavement of the second at the mercy of the first.[10] The soldier is surrendering his liberty and moral agency to the state and sinning on its behalf. For Thoreau, this obedience is a betrayal of man's own pacific nature as it requires "slavish compliance," but the disobedient soldier is no better since he abets the hypocrisy of the general population—he rebels so that they do not have to and serves as a salve to civilian consciences.[11]

At this point, it is interesting to note the tension between Thoreau's ideas and the account of individual agency and responsibility favored by revisionists such as Jeff McMahan.[12] He seems to argue for exactly the kind of disobedience that Thoreau finds so problematic. In effect, McMahan is asking the soldier to disobey on our behalf, when we would not be willing to do so ourselves, to make us feel better morally. This is a major problem with McMahan minimizing collective responsibility, as it ignores or rejects the way in which soldiers are agents and political actors of a particular kind. It also collectively shifts responsibility for war to the individual and away from the state, even though the war is for the state and not for the individuals directly. For Thoreau, this is moral enslavement.

Third, Samet considers the role prudence plays in obedience. In discussing *Moby Dick*, she notes that some will not disobey, even if there are good moral reasons to do so; moral reasons are not enough to counteract the habit of submission to authority, a habit that weakens autonomy and democracy.[13] Even when the characters in the book think there are good reasons to disobey, having moral or other qualms about what is going on, the collective context carries a heavy pressure toward obedience and submission. The famous Milgram and Stanford prison experiments provide qualified support for this dynamic; disobedience requires moral courage and standing up to peer pressure and conventions of uncritical obedience, which is very difficult for communally oriented human beings who care about and are dependent upon what others in the community think of them.

Fourth is the question of how much obedience is necessary for a democracy to function. Is blind or passive obedience to the rule of law necessary as a sign of enlightened citizens? Early in the Civil War, General Sherman held that such obedience was necessary for both the military and the citizenry, with the military providing a practice ground for the development of civic virtue and discipline.[14] Soldiers had to obey authority and work together in the interest of a common end as opposed to their own desires, even to the point of sacrificing their lives. This same set of practices was necessary for the citizen as well. We can see why this view would be powerful if we think about it in terms of the relation to government authority, especially in the context of the Southern rebellion. However, by 1864 Sherman's view shifted to reflect that the independence of the troops, based upon experience and being proven in battle, is viewed not as a lack of discipline, but as the virtues of innovation and initiative.[15] Sherman came to trust in the expertise and experience of his troops in ways that could be seen as reflecting ideas such as mission command. This shift would also then have implications for the necessity of a certain kind of (unquestioning) obedience as necessary for civic virtue.

Fifth, Samet highlights the idea that "military service makes men equal" because it removes the relation of arbitrary, private subjugation (slavery), which is important in the context of the Civil War.[16] We could also see this idea as related to levée en masse in the European wars of the early to mid-nineteenth century, where the idea was that the whole populace was rising up and fighting in defense of the nation as equal citizens. This is opposed to the older idea that the ruler and their aristocracy or professional army class are fighting on behalf of the state (or even of their own interests, which the state is used to execute). We find the link legitimating service as bestowing "true" citizenship in the idea of equal citizens fighting for and defending the state. Both require collective obedience to the state as a political authority, having the same shared values and participation in a moral community. The discipline of the military service is the discipline of obedient citizenship.

Finally, the observation has been made that the navy (or any military branch) exists to preserve democracy, not to practice it, as a way to justify systems of training, discipline, and punishment that are ostensibly necessary for good order and combat effectiveness.[17] However, this is in tension with philosopher David Hume's claim about the link between obedience and justice: "In a word, OBEDIENCE is a new duty which must be invented to support that of JUSTICE; the types of equity must be corroborated by those of allegiance."[18] Just cause is necessary, not just obedience alone as a virtue; this requires the rejection of the blind or passive obedience supported by an extensive system of corporal or other strict punishments designed to keep unwilling and largely uneducated people in line. Sherman's recognition of the role of the experience that is acquired in war is an important critique of the idea that the military cannot practice the democracy it defends, but it does not go as far as Hume does in centering justice relative to obedience. This is a theme that is central to developing critical obedience and loyalty.

In these six themes, we see a tension between the effects on command and submission on the psyche and moral character of the individual, which seem to be part of the discipline of the military but which may undermine the very values necessary for the functioning of the political community—values that the military is designed to protect and foster in its citizens. On the other hand, obedience is often seen for both the military and citizen as a way to demonstrate loyalty, especially to the political community. The military does provide structure, discipline, practice at obedience, and opportunities for disobedience (or a more critical obedience with experience and changes in the social context). The questions are: How important is this discipline for good citizenship, and are there other ways that these traits can be developed? This tension at its best can be creative and provide for innovation; at its worst, it can devolve into the drawing of political battle lines, as we will see with the issue of military and veteran exceptionalism.

THE OBLIGATIONS OF CITIZENS

At this point, we want to consider the moral obligations of citizens who are not members of the military, which returns us to our earlier discussion of the interaction between obedience and loyalty in the political community. With the points that Samet outlined in mind, we can ask: Why and how are obedience and loyalty owed by citizens to the state? What is the conception of these ideas that we are working with for the community of practice and for the individual citizen?

In terms of loyalty, we usually take citizens as owing loyalty to one state or political community at a time, and the state can expect citizens to be more partial and endorsing of their projects over those of other states and political communities. There are limits on both the loyalty and obedience that the state can ask, but obedience is more oriented toward action, and loyalty toward belief and attitude, while refraining from certain (disloyal) actions. Loyalty involves more sustained attitudes and preferential treatment over time; it is less about actions and more about commitments and attitudes toward shared projects and values.

On the other hand, obedience in the political context is an obligation to a community, not to a specific individual or institution, since it is a social rather than an individual virtue. A failure of obedience can endanger or impair the community in part because of the way in which obedience is based upon oaths, promises, and other agreements between members of the community (as a community) and the state and builds reliability and ultimately trust between those members. Obedience is oriented around actions directed toward a specific end or purpose in the interest of the common good of that political community and its members.

Traditionally, military virtue sees obedience as presumptive except in certain circumstances, and the judgments about that must be informed by norms in the community of practice and military professionalism. There is significant resistance to allowing individual discretion and responsibility here—thus, the problems with McMahan's account, selective conscientious objection, and other concerns such as exercises of individual religious liberty, which might be viewed as selfishness and lack of concern for the community even at the expense of self. In theory, civilian virtue has operated or is supposed to operate in roughly the same way, although with more tolerance for individual judgment and discretion, moral agency, and liberty on political and moral matters within certain bounds and limits. Journalist Sebastian Junger points out that with increased individualism, atomization, and consumerism, those limits are fraying and worse; many are effectively opting out of the social contract or selectively participating in parts of it as it suits their individual tastes and preferences.[19] There is no longer a shared common life or sense of values that citizens are willing to act upon, even if they verbally express loyalty to certain ideas or values.

Accordingly, we find a weakening of the idea of obligations of the citizen; even historically basic duties such as defense of the nation and voting are increasingly viewed as rights but not obligations. It seems that paying taxes and obeying the law remain as shared obligations for citizens, along with the occasional patriotic displays. Paying taxes is still the major contribution that citizens make toward the state, but this is automatic for most citizens and requires no expenditure of effort or thought. On the other hand, voting and patriotic displays or participation in national rituals as a sign of loyalty are much more fleeting and transient; some participate intensely and others not at all, with a full range between those extremes. In the last presidential election cycle, at least 40 percent of eligible citizens did not vote in the general election, which is similar to past presidential year elections and a lower percentage than primary and off-year/midterm elections. This shows that a central right of citizenship is not taken as an obligation by a significant portion of the political community.

The weakening of communal identity and obligations is important for our discussion since it is an analogous gap to the one McMahan and the revisionists are trying to fill in terms of shifting the moral responsibility for war away from the state and political community as a whole toward the individual. These gaps provide the opening for military and veteran exceptionalism and at least a partial surrendering of the civic virtues of loyalty and obedience to the military community of practice, with the civil versions being appreciably weaker and even optional, no longer defining what citizenship in the political community means.

SOCIAL CONTRACT AND UNLIMITED LIABILITY CONTRACT

Understanding the civilian side of citizenship relative to obedience and loyalty, we can now ask what the intersection between these two roles looks like for members of the military who are also citizens. In particular, we need to consider what the intersections and tensions are between the social contract that the individual citizen is party to and the oath and legal contract (the unlimited liability contract) that functions as an entrance into a new moral community of professional practice for the military, with unlimited liability to the state.[20] For members of the military, this also means that some of their political rights (speech, assembly, movement) are more restricted and circumscribed, even as they still are members of the political community of practice (but in a new and different way). While their citizenship has not been revoked, it is tempting to think they have become a different kind of citizen.

One is (usually) born into the role of citizen, where consent is seen as implicit rather than explicit. The military, on the other hand, requires explicit adult consent, a legal obligation, and an oath to enter into a new legal contract of unlimited liability relative to the state; one agrees to give one's life, if necessary, and face danger while being subjected to new restrictions, as well as entering into a new moral community of practical and professionalism. Do the two obligations taken together create a new third category of obligation and kind of citizenship? Or is it simply a matter that sometimes they intersect, but they are really just two different roles one may inhabit at the same time? There will be other times when one is only a citizen (since the military role is temporary), but during the military time one is still a citizen and arguably not a different kind of citizen than other civilian citizens, even if one has a different professional role.

The military role does involve an exchange of consideration and benefits in the same way as the citizen, so that cannot be what makes the argument for a different third role or obligation. Is it the unlimited liability that produces the problem and makes it different? If the unlimited liability is the issue that produces a new kind of citizenship, we should find the same issue with other social roles of unlimited liability, such as police and firefighters who are citizens asked to make sacrifices (especially of life) for the state. We might think that these roles or professions are qualitatively different from other professions (law, medicine, clergy) in their intersections with citizenship and the political realm. As we will see, I think that argument is problematic, especially for civil-military relations, given civil control over the military.

Another consideration is that one occupies two public roles—military member and citizen. While others also occupy two public roles (most professionals and public servants), maybe it is the kind of public roles that one occupies that creates the issue. In his discussion of whether and to what extent we owe gratitude to veterans, Stephen Kershnar considers the "super citizen" status of the veteran (and military member).[21] He takes issue with the traditional argument that veterans and the military occupy a different moral space and are to be accorded more gratitude because of the sacrifices that they are asked to make (unlimited liability contract). Accordingly, he rejects this special status and gratitude as being different or more laudatory than gratitude that we ought to have for other public servants such as garbage collectors, school teachers, civil servants, or law enforcement personnel. Clearly, for Kershnar, neither occupying two public roles nor the nature of the public roles would explain this unique status of super citizen.

I think it is the combination of the unlimited liability issue (we do give law enforcement and rescue professionals who may die in the line of duty similar preferential treatment and deference of judgment as we do the military) and the nature of the profession that gives permission for killing and destruction in ways that no other profession is given. Defense of the nation and the political community is the core task of both of these professions, and as such, they and their members do seem to occupy a unique moral space that is not granted to other public roles or servants who also make sacrifices, sometimes even dying in the line of work (teachers killed in school shootings, for example). The nature of the military and law enforcement has both lethal force and unlimited liability contract built into the identity of the profession, and it is understood when one enters that profession; death may come in other professions, but it is not expected as a part of fulfilling that role.

THE PROBLEM OF MILITARY AND VETERAN EXCEPTIONALISM

Since members of the military occupy this unique space in two roles, we should consider the phenomenon of military and veteran exceptionalism, which seems to suggest that a new metaphysical creation—the super citizen—is created. Military and veteran exceptionalism (MVE) is the view that those who serve sacrifice for the country and have been through experiences that other citizens have not, imbuing them with certain knowledge and moral virtues that make them better. Bruce Willis' role as the general in the film *The Siege* and Jack Nicholson's iconic character in *A Few Good Men* are examples of this, but social media is filled with discussion groups, profiles, and memes that reflect this view. These are particularly noticeable around Veterans Day and Memorial Day and whenever any controversial issue related to the military comes up—possible wars or integration of marginalized groups (especially women and transgendered persons) into the military, for example. We have already noted the warrior debate and the veneration of historic warrior cultures such as the Spartans, Vikings, and Samurai as icons, especially of masculinity, in popular culture discussions of the military and reflecting MVE.

The common valorization of the military and veterans in popular culture, including the notion that "all who serve are heroes," reflects this kind of thinking. In social media, we see the phenomenon of "vetsplaining" (veterans explaining military matters, especially to civilians) and certain kinds of judgments about the authority, morality, and citizen commitment of those who have not served, even to the point of claiming that nonveterans cannot or ought not criticize the military, foreign policy, or military culture issues (such as sexual harassment and assault or the integration of various marginalized groups). The gun control debate has increasingly seen arguments on both sides made in terms of MVE, but Veterans Day and Memorial Day often rouse the veneration of those who have served and inspire arguments about whether those who have not served in combat "count" or are of lesser status and are deserving of less respect than those who experienced combat.

The jokes on social media about "Tyfys" (Thank you for your service) and entitlement to discounts reflect a real and deep sense of a stratification between those who have served and those who have not, who are viewed as lesser citizens. In the words of Henry V in his St. Crispin's Day speech, "And gentlemen in England now abed / Shall think themselves accursed they were not here, And hold their manhoods cheap whiles any speaks / That fought with us upon Saint Crispin's day."[22] Jack Nicholson's character in *A Few Good Men* reflects a sense of moral superiority as one who has worked, endured, inflicted discipline, sacrificed, and suffered so that others can enjoy liberty and a good life.

In politics, a common judgment is that veterans who are politicians or are running for office have more expertise than civilian candidates, especially in certain areas such as foreign policy. We regularly see examples of veterans' campaign commercials that focus on military service as preparation or proxy for moral and civil virtues and bestowing increased knowledge and expertise in governing and foreign policy. Veterans on both sides of the gun control debate will often preface their policy statements by noting their service, rank, and experience as establishing their bona fides. A regular insult on social media, especially on issues of war or foreign policy, is to point out that one's adversary did not serve, with the implication that they were cowardly or inferior in some way and that they lack standing to make their claims. The regular attention in U.S. presidential elections to the question of the military service (or lack thereof) of the candidates often becomes a proxy discussion of expertise and moral character. George W. Bush, Bill Clinton, Hillary Rodham Clinton, and Donald Trump all faced questions about their military service or lack thereof and how that impacted their fitness to serve as president and commander in chief. Endorsement by veterans and veterans' organizations is seen as giving more weight to a politician's run for office, and we have already noted the role of retired and general officers and their endorsements or protests in the political process.

This exceptionalism is problematic because of its appeal to a hierarchical nature of the political community, implying that there are really two kinds of citizens and that one is better and holds (or ought to hold) more authority (especially moral and political) than the other, effectively making those who have not served second-class citizens. The argument or at least the strong implication is that the citizens who have chosen not to serve in the military are lacking the courage, discipline, and expertise that military service provides. We can see how this issue in our contemporary politics connects to Samet's discussion of the same themes in the nineteenth century. In our own time, this contributes to the civil-military culture gap and reinforces a certain view of citizenship as requiring a willingness to go to war and kill as its basis, in effect placing the military as the top priority and value of the state in terms of service. There is also an important aspect of masculinity and masculine virtues associated with this; women who are in the military participate in it (and must conform to it) rather than refuting or expanding notions of service and citizenship. Stephen Kershnar aptly points out that there are many ways to serve the political community and problematizes our privileging of this form of service above all others.[23]

In contrast to this, I would argue that one is a citizen first and military member second, since the latter role is always a temporary one and does not completely abrogate the first role. We are all citizens who participate in and benefit from the social contract, but some (voluntarily) elect to take on additional responsibilities that they consent to in the absence of the draft that would require this of all. There is, of course, a recurring debate about whether a draft and/or public service requirement should be required for all as a way to improve the civil-military culture gap; this debate can also be seen as evidence of the way in which this idea of military service is highly privileged and frames our understanding of the relationship between service and citizenship. The consent and contract for the military based upon an oath and outward signs publicly representing that oath can and likely will change a participant's own views, habits, and moral commitments in the same way that marriage does.

However, it produces (or may produce) this change only for those that take the oath and enter the community of practice. It does not lessen or change the status of the citizens who choose not to. The citizen that does not volunteer to serve in the military still has the same relationship to the state; the oath of their fellow citizen does not change or lessen the state's obligation to them or theirs to the state. In the same way, taking marriage vows does not impose burdens on those who do not take that oath, nor does it make them lesser members of the social community than those who have chosen to marry, despite the community and social goods that we might associate with and prioritize as a part of the value of marriage in society.

With an all-volunteer force, the obligation to military service is supererogatory, but that does not denote moral or political superiority any more than one's choice to eat meat or not have children denotes superiority; these are all voluntary choices entered into for a variety of reasons, not all of which have moral importance or weight. I might really like the thrill of jumping out of planes, enjoy the comradery of military life, or want the education and benefits that come with membership. The sacrifices that are made by those joining the military are consented to willingly as a part of entering into military professionalism and participating in a particular community of practice, just as with other professions, such as law enforcement, medicine, law, and clergy; presumably those who consent think the possible sacrifices worthwhile. Those other professions do not seem to come with a sense of moral or political superiority. We generally do not think of doctors, lawyers, and members of the clergy as better, as super citizens, since they also belong to a profession, even though by definition, that means they also serve the public and common good and are given special permissions by society.

At this point, we might note that law enforcement and firefighters seem to be the exception to my argument; we tend to view them in a similar way to the military. We often do think of them as super citizens and as morally and politically superior, although this is eroding to some degree with increasing attention to and protesting of racial profiling and unjust policing practices. (Firefighters have not been subject to these kinds of issues and so have preserved their higher status along with military members.) Given this fact about law enforcement and firefighters, the issue is not with membership in a profession but with the nature of the commitment and sacrifices expected from these individuals (including an unlimited liability contract that is similar to that in the military). In addition, these are professions that protect the integrity and survival of the political community and wield the lethal power of life and death over others. In short, they have a kind of power that other professions and other citizens simply do not have, which also seems to give them a kind of moral status denied to the other professions.

IMPLICATIONS FOR CIVIL-MILITARY CULTURE GAP

The dual role of military member and citizen has important implications for the civil-military culture gap.[24] Generally, the term refers to the difference in values and culture between the military and the broader civilian society, particularly in the United States after the Vietnam era. It reflects the idea that civilian society prizes and prioritizes individualism, innovation consumerism, indulgence/pleasure, free expression and thought, dissent, and even disobedience in the service of following one's own pursuit of happiness. On the other hand, military culture tends to be more conservative and bound by tradition, rules, and honor, requiring a level of mental and physical conformity and uniformity that requires discipline and values obedience and loyalty, as well as sacrifice and suffering for the community and the greater good. The concern with the gap between these cultures is that as fewer members of Congress and the civilian decisionmaking apparatus have direct experience with or knowledge of the military, it is harder for the two to work together and respect one another's perspectives and expertise. We can look at the Clinton administration's struggles with the military culture relative to the "Don't Ask, Don't Tell" policies and various military actions and interventions in which there were high tensions and, at times, open discord and distrust between the civilians making decisions and the senior military who were advising those decisions and then carrying them out.

One might wonder why and how this issue matters in a book on obedience and loyalty in both the military and political communities. Surely the topic we are addressing demonstrates some overlap and common ground between these communities of practice? While there is some overlap, we have seen how the military and political communities have differences in practices and priorities and the extent of their willingness for obedience to be negotiated using judgment and discretion. These differences can come into conflict in policymaking and can have ramifications for both communities as a result. In some ways, the World War I–era French mutinies discussed in chapter 8 speak to two different visions of negotiating obedience in these communities, with serious effects. Given this, we need to think about the ramifications of the civil-military culture gap in this particular light.

First is the civilian impulse to trust the military, producing deference and resisting the critique and oversight functions of civilian control of the military that are part of our constitutional system. The military is one of the few institutions still seen as having moral integrity and not being partisan; even the press and courts have seen their esteem eroding in these regards. This phenomenon has been especially pronounced in the post–Vietnam War era and may be to some degree an overcompensation for the treatment of the military during Vietnam. It may also reflect a gap in exposure and experience; the military is a remote institution that fewer Americans have direct knowledge of and experience with, which may make its valorization easier. Kershnar also notes that this is a highly problematic tendency—both because of the consequences of a respect verging on uncritical deference and because it is not warranted or justified in the way we think it is.[25] Due to these tendencies, the public is increasingly deferring to and being less critical of the military, even when it is warranted. Comments made online of *Time* magazine's coverage of the war crimes committed at Haditha, Iraq, in 2005 tended toward the idea that civilians ought not and cannot judge these actions in war, even though they are done in our collective name.[26] This also fits with McMahan and the revisionists' interest in shifting responsibility from the civilians to individual members of the military in terms of their participation in and/or contribution to an unjust war.

Second, the public discourse around war and foreign policy issues requires more civilian engagement and education, which then requires military willingness to engage and share responsibility not from the MVE position but as equal citizens and members of the political community. While civilians may not have the military experience and expertise that members of the profession have, civilians have perspectives, experiences, and insights that the military members do not have or cannot think about because of the normative constraints of their training and the profession. To assume that only military professionals can have an opinion or expertise on foreign policy matters, where military force is one option among many, is highly problematic and limiting. Diversity of thought, commitment, and experience matters because we want the widest possible discussion and consideration of all options for a particular policy and/or strategy to avoid the unquestioned assumptions, biases, blind spots, and habits that the exercise of judgment and discretion require we guard against and reflect upon in the deliberation process. This also requires a level of trust between the two parties, which the civil-military gap can and has made difficult at times.

Third, the issues of post-traumatic stress and, more critically, moral injury, taken with the revisionists' desire for more individual moral responsibility—as collective moral responsibility seems to be waning—highlight the concern about the gap in dramatic ways. Through the writing, testimony, and artwork of veterans wrestling with these issues, we are seeing in graphic relief the stakes involved in the overburdening of the individual and their immediate intimate circles, while the rest of us are relatively untouched or voyeurs at best. Writings such as Bryan Doerries' *Theater of War* and C. J. Chivers' *The Fighters*, Nancy Sherman's works on moral injury, and the art produced by members of the veteran community reveal a world of existential suffering and pain that is invisible to many in civilian society. While these existential pains are as old as Achilles' rage in the *Iliad* and in warfare itself, these works are the only window many civilians have into that suffering, with so few having direct connections with the military or the military experience. We have discussed the images and themes of MVE in popular culture and of the military and war more generally; this is the only contact or point of experience with military culture that many civilians have.

While Sebastian Junger is looking for a greater sense of community as a solution to these problems, the development of empathy and empathetic understanding, especially on the part of civilians toward members of the military, is a necessary precondition. Authentic engagement and concern are missing; addressing those could and would, I think, provide more motivation for the moral communal and connected vision that Junger is calling us to. Such empathy requires circumventing and undermining MVE, which actually impedes mutual engagement and understanding as well as the self-understanding each side needs to engage in within their own respective communities of practice. This empathy, which we discussed as a part of the capacity for judgment and discretion, is also critical to deal with the civil-military culture gap, especially in terms of jointly formulating and supporting policy.

A clear counterargument to this line of thought is that civilians lack the discipline of the military that is necessary for engaged, critical citizenship. The gun rights adherents of the *Molon labe* school (encompassing veneration of the Spartan warrior culture more generally) and Special Forces and other elite military/veteran communities often extoll their athletic discipline and commitment, comparing themselves to the (in their view) less fit, undisciplined, lazy, and rather ungrateful civilian community.[27] "Thank you for your service" and the @IamWarax Twitter persona have emerged as a satire of these more politically and culturally conservative groups and a voice for liberal and moderate vets who reject or are critical of MVE and its implications for the civil-military relationship.

Discipline is necessary for engaged citizenship, but it is not the same kind of discipline as required in the military, since the military is tasked with a very specific purpose that does not involve civilians in the same way. While the culture gap is troubling in some respects, in other aspects it is understandable and even necessary. I would say that a greater sense of connectedness, social virtue, and empathy would drive civilians to a greater sense of the common good, and this would require Ulrich Zwygart's "critical obedience." Civilians do need to claim their oversight and engagement roles, demonstrating respect and support but without uncritical and unearned deference. According to Foucault, discipline is about control of both souls and bodies in the interest of the state. For civilians, the kinds of control (both external and self-control) that promote the common good of the political community are quite different than those of the military, which wields the power of life and death. Critical thinking, questioning, civil critique, free expression, voting, paying taxes, and empathetic engagement with the community and the political process are all important disciplines for the civilian citizen.

However, it is also important to acknowledge the dual obligations of military members, especially those in positions of senior leadership, who are for all intents and purposes very direct political actors in ways that include space for civilians to meaningfully enter and engage. Members of the military are still citizens and as such have obligations to their fellow citizens; obligations within a political community cannot just go in one direction. James Dubik's arguments move us toward the idea that jus ad bellum and jus in bello need a bridge between them; he acknowledges the critical point that there is more of a continuum than a sharp division of labor, especially for senior officers.[28] This means that both parties have work to do in bridging the gap, work that is critical in having a robust sense of citizenship regardless of whether one serves in the military. It is important to recognize the value of various kinds of service and commitment to the nation—not just the military.

With two differentiated understandings of obedience and loyalty, the discipline, judgment, and discretion that are required for each community of practice to understand and negotiate the boundaries of moral obligation, we are now in a position to apply this account in a more granular way to the concerns and issues that arise in each community. This chapter has added to the picture of obedience as negotiation (using judgment and discretion) the important roles of military and citizen and the ways in which they can overlap, especially for those in the military who occupy both roles at the same time. This piece has important implications for the civil-military relationship that is central to the military profession, as well as for the American political community, especially in terms of empathy and the dangers of MVE.

While there is an overlapping consensus between the two communities of practice and how they need to engage in obedience and loyalty within their community, there are also important differences that reflect the aims, histories, and identities of these communities. This returns us to the earlier discussion of MacIntyre, where moral virtue and obligation must be understood contextually and within the framework of the practices contained in these communities in terms of virtues and considerations of law and justice. To see how this account works in practice, we next look at the implications of this account in a series of specific scenarios and frame the ideas of critical obedience and reasonable challenge as successful examples and incarnations of this approach.

CHAPTER 10

CASES AND CONCLUSION

Mr. President, it is not only possible, it is essential. That is the whole idea of this machine, you know. Deterrence is the art of producing in the mind of the enemy . . . the FEAR to attack. And so, because of the automated and irrevocable decisionmaking process which rules out human meddling, the Doomsday machine is terrifying and simple to understand . . . and completely credible and convincing.

—Dr. Strangelove[1]

THE FOCUS OF THIS BOOK has been on clarifying and developing a deeper and more philosophically nuanced account of obedience as a social virtue and moral obligation, on considering how it is different from other virtues such as loyalty, and on understanding why and how it is situated in the military and political communities of practice. To consider both individual moral agency and the social nature of the virtue and obligation, we centered on the idea of obedience, especially critical obedience, as a kind of negotiation within the community of practice across a range of actions—not just the binary of obedience and disobedience. In addition, we have considered what impact the roles of citizen and military professional have on this account, especially in terms of the civil-military relationship and in cases when one person occupies both of those roles. In this chapter, I want to pull together the arguments and themes discussed to consider what larger conclusions we might draw about obedience in both military and civilian contexts, with particular attention to the ideas of reasonable challenge and critical obedience.

To do this in concrete and specific terms, we will consider four scenarios related to obedience and see how the arguments in this book hold up against those contextual problems. The following cases are all hypothetical and may have limited realism in the view of the reader. However, in philosophical accounts of ethics, the point of thought experiments or hypothetical cases is to help sharpen intuitions and see how moral concepts or ideas might be applied and play out, testing those intuitions against conceptual frameworks applied to concrete situations. The idea here is to find concrete testing and illustration of the account that can help us see the value, and also potential problems, in what we have argued. This will indicate where the account I have argued for is helpful and valid as well as areas that will merit further discussion and exploration.

CASE 1: NUCLEAR LAUNCH CODE

An impulsive president has spent the last few weeks in a war of words on social media with the leader of another nation and decides a nuclear strike on an intermittently hostile, but not peer, power is necessary to make a point about U.S. resolve in the region in relation to foreign policy. Presidential advisors are split about the decision, with some in favor of the action and others against it, presumably based on consultations with their own civilian and military advisors as appropriate. The first use of nuclear weapons is a legal, ethical, and strategic problem, and it is possible that such a strike could escalate into a broader conflict as other powers decide to get involved to defend the attacked power or their own interests. The president believes that other measures would not have the same strategic and deterrent impact and is sure that the other power will back down.

The president has refused to consult congressional leaders because of concerns about leaking the plan to the press but agrees to brief them after the strike is in progress. In the end, the advisors are not willing to protest, the president's view prevails, and the order is given for a strike. If you are in the chain of command responsible for carrying out the strike, do you obey the order? What do you think your options are? Do you have any options other than obedience? What knowledge and expertise do you have that bear on the situation, and what is outside of your knowledge?

CASE 2: THE TOXIC COMMANDER/LEADER

You have a toxic leader in your command/company who over a long period of time has engaged in toxic command behavior (nothing illegal or actionable in terms of the laws and policies of your organization, as your leader is clever and knows how to stay within the lines) that is proving detrimental to morale and unit/team effectiveness. The leader publicly berates and humiliates both peers and subordinates, often undermining and micromanaging their efforts and, when challenged on it, claims that he was just kidding and trying to motivate people to do better. He acknowledges that he has high standards but thinks his people are lazy and need to be motivated to do better. He also refuses to give supportive or positive feedback, claiming that people know when they have done a good job and that he is not there to soothe egos but to get the job done.

Those up the chain of command/in higher positions of authority have been informed on numerous occasions and by a variety of parties and have elected to take only minor steps, which has increased the problem for those at the lower levels, as these efforts have only angered the leader and done nothing to limit his authority or power. Others in your command/company are complaining, getting restless at the lack of action, and threatening to leave/quit or to sabotage the projects and aims of the leader in retaliation. What counts as obedience in this context? What level of disobedience is warranted, especially given the reluctance of those in positions of authority to do anything to address the issue? What is likely to happen in this case if no further action is taken and the situation worsens?

The political version of this scenario involves a toxic political administration that is engaging in unpopular and unethical policies that in the view of his opponents violate basic moral norms and political constitutional rights, while contributing to a toxic political climate. The members of the administration insist the old norms and ways of doing things are corrupt and need to be changed in order to get things done that the people who voted for them elected them to do. In the process, the concerns and rights of the minority party and others are being violated and/or seriously impaired as some groups are targeted for impeding progress on these agenda items. Are acts of civil disobedience to protest, raise consciousness, and disrupt these policies appropriate, even though there will likely be legal and political retaliation, including being branded as the "enemy of the people" or even being charged with sedition or treason? Can violence be used as a last resort when other means have failed to bring about change?

CASE 3: THE SUCCESSFUL MISSION
You are in command of a unit tasked with securing a particular objective in a regional conflict while advising and assisting allies. It is an evolving combat mission situation, where facts and events on the ground suggest that the orders you have been given will not mean being successful in the mission. The commander's intent and briefings on the mission set out a particular plan to minimize the casualties on your side, since you are in an advisory and support role; it is also made clear that there are larger political

and strategic concerns around the mission, so the situation is a very delicate one. However, once you arrive on the scene with your unit, you and others observe that the situation on the ground is not as intelligence had suggested that it would be, and it is also evolving and fluid in ways that the planning and orders did not seem to anticipate. In order to achieve the mission and support your allies, it seems that fulfilling commander's intent will require a fairly radical change to the original plan.

What do you do? Disobedience in this context could be considered an exercise of professional judgment and discretion relative to consideration of the mission (including both military expertise and ethical consideration, but more likely the first), but the judgment of this will be purely in terms of the outcome after the fact. If you are right and the mission is achieved with reasonable costs, then all will be forgiven, but if you are wrong, the move could result in unjustified casualties and have serious impacts on your career as well as adverse strategic impacts on your allies and your ability to provide the support that they need. Are there options short of clear disobedience you would consider? Why? What is likely to be effective given the rapidly evolving situation and time constraints involved?

CASE 4: TRAINING FOR VIRTUE

In garrison contexts, there are many orders and commands that seem arbitrary, pointless, or down right counterproductive. One example is unit physical training (PT) or other unit social activities as opposed to following your own individual workouts at the gym or having social activities with colleagues of your choosing within the unit. If I can work out effectively with one other unit mate in one hour a day, why should I spend two hours a day on unit PT, which doesn't necessarily further my fitness goals? Some people in the unit are in ultra-athlete shape and do marathons and other intensive physical competitions, while others will barely (or will not) pass the physical fitness tests, even with unit PT.

Clearly there are different levels and needs. One concern driving the idea of unit PT is that it is designed to further the aim of physical fitness (part of mission readiness) and community building/unit cohesion, reinforcing and continuing habits from basic training. How important is obedience (and what counts as obedience) in this context? How is this different from the last case of the combat mission? What is the effect on the community, both in morale and practical physical terms, if every member does not participate in unit PT?

The political community version of this case is the teaching of civic virtues such as loyalty and patriotism in public schools, via assemblies and the recitation of the Pledge of Allegiance and other activities as a way to develop these virtues. Surely, a public institution funded by the government with the aim to educate citizens for participation in the political community must provide education in the history, identity, norms, and values of the political community of which they are a part. Where else are children going to learn these virtues in ways that promote unity, consistency, and a sense of shared political identity? Given the multicultural context, this is a central place for instilling these virtues as a community of practice. However, some parents object on the grounds that it is their responsibility and under their authority to decide what values their children will be taught. They feel that the way some of these virtues are taught in the public schools is insensitive or hostile to their religious or other values, and some parents and communities see this as state coercion and brainwashing of their children, a violation of their liberty to follow their vision of the good life and a rejection of their own cultural and religious traditions and identities.

THEMES AND PROBLEMS

What do these cases tell us? What kinds of themes and problems do they highlight relative to our discussion and analysis of obedience? One core element that all the cases have in common is the question of whether and/or to what extent there are places for individual judgment and discretion, but in ways that still maintain reasonable discipline, unit cohesion, and communal unity and do not compromise the mission or political aims of the communities of practice involved. To open our discussion, we want to think through each of these cases in terms of the themes and ideas from the book, with the idea that we will revise this thinking in light of the ideas of reasonable challenge and critical obedience at the end of the chapter.

The first and second cases both contain elements that call for judgment and discretion in regard to not only military expertise but also ethical principles. This means that part of the process must involve deliberation about what a good end is and why it is a good end in terms of the good life and the community of practice. We can ask whether the goal of deterrence and showing resolve is a good one, as well as questioning the means of a nuclear strike. In the second case, we might wonder whether the aims and mission of the two communities can be achieved with the leader in question; it is possible that such leadership methods are necessary to achieve the kinds of things they have in mind. In addition, there are concerns about the means in each of these cases and how they match the ends in question. These are cases that have the potential to undermine discipline (either in terms of chain of command or civilian control of the military) and unit/military cohesion, which is tied to combat effectiveness in the long term. In the case of the political community, the methods and actions of the leadership are undermining political unity and identity as some groups feel threatened and marginalized. On the other hand, both cases seem to involve the potential of serious and unsustainable (physical and otherwise) harm if they are carried out.

There are further questions of loyalty and obligation to consider in both a military and a civilian context, since in both cases the dilemma is produced by someone who is arguably acting in ways that are at odds with the values and norms of the community of practice. In both of these cases, the leaders think that their methods are required to achieve the mission or political ends desired and that consideration is more important than the harms that are occurring in that process. Here we want to consider what the dangers are in the two cases, especially if disobedience is required. What are the long-term implications for the culture and norms of the community if disobedience, nonobedience, or less than obedience is the result? What kind of cultural practice and precedent does that set for the community after these leaders are gone, and to what degree will that change the identity and practices of the community?

The third case seems the clearest instance in which disobedience or a negotiated obedience that carries out the commander's intent, while not carrying out orders that are contraindicated by events on the ground and military expertise, would be indicated to achieve the mission. It approaches the Normandy and My Lai examples discussed earlier where the facts on the ground were moving beyond what the expectations were or the situation did not match the intelligence or other planning assumptions on which the plan and orders were predicated. Such an instance seems to imperil the success of the mission unless the plans can be adapted to the new information and context.

This case also appears to have the least risk of adverse consequences for discipline and unit cohesion and may actually serve to preserve and support them since military expertise and judgment are being invoked, as opposed to some kind of ethical failing or an illegal order as was the case in My Lai. Experts can disagree about their professional judgments in their area of expertise based upon different information, experiences, and positions; this is entirely reasonable and happens in all the professions without necessarily undermining the identity of the profession or the authority of those practicing it. Considering that the intention of the disobedience or other actions is in fact to achieve the mission (which one assumes is implied if not stated in commander's intent and the planning), it is not a case of disloyalty or disrespect toward those in authority.

The final case is all about discipline and unit cohesion and the unity of the community, even if the action involved seems largely unrelated to mission accomplishments or a particular political aim. This is where there may be significant differences and where we may want to argue that the negotiation process has to be different in combat versus garrison contexts; garrison contexts prize building obedience as a habit and practice regardless of the relation of the actual actions to a specific mission. If this is correct, we ought to be more willing to admit judgment and discretion in combat (where the stakes are higher and there are fewer viable options to deal with the issue due to time and other constraints of battle) where the habits and practices should already be set and can be presumed. In the garrison context, we might think the presumption of obedience is weaker and must be established, leaving less room for judgment and discretion.

A problem with this tolerance and discretionary view is the question of where judgment and discretion and the negotiation process can be practiced if not in the garrison context. You cannot wait until combat, so there must be some place within garrison context for this, but in ways that do not undermine the building of habits, community cohesion, and trust in authority which will all be important to mission accomplishment in combat. Just as one practices the other physical and mental skills that will be necessary in combat, the skills of judgment, discretion, and moral agency also need to be practiced. That said, the concern will be how to balance the obedience needed for training for unit cohesion and combat effectiveness with developing judgment, discretion, and moral agency. These impulses seem to be in opposition or at least in tension on a regular basis. It could lead to confusion, especially among junior officers and enlisted who need to be acculturated to the community and develop practices that support its values and norms.

In the political version of the case, the needs of the community and the desire for unity and conformity in the form of shared demonstrations and understanding of civic virtues are coming into conflict with individual liberty and the right of individuals to exercise their moral agency and pursue their own vision of the good life. While civic virtue is important, there are many ways to achieve that end and a range of expressions, beliefs, and practices that would be consistent with still being a patriotic and supportive member of the state. What that looks like for one citizen (especially given moral, cultural, or religious commitments) might be different from another with different commitments, but it seems that the state can be more tolerant of the range in the name of liberty.

An analogy to parenting may be helpful in both cases. As a parent, I give judgment and discretion and moral agency to my children in direct relationship to the skills and capacities (often indexed to age and/or maturity) of the child, bearing in mind the seriousness and responsibility required for the task and the consequences of failure. I may let my teenager choose his own bedtime or to not do schoolwork because he can handle those decisions, and the consequences of making the wrong choice are reversible. Handing the keys to my car to my seven-year-old would be inappropriate on several levels; he does not have the skills and capacities needed, and the cost of failure is literally death. Since we are dealing with adults in (one hopes) a supportive community of practice, the timeline would seem accelerated, as adults have a wealth of experience on which to draw and a greater capacity for developing these habits. As people develop more experience and skills, it is more reasonable to allow more leeway on judgment, discretion, and moral agency, demonstrating our trust in them as full members of the community of practice.

REASONABLE CHALLENGE

To address the problem of how to balance these considerations in both communities of practice, we can look at the reasonable challenge model used by the military in the United Kingdom. This model was developed in response to events in the Iraq War: "The Iraq Inquiry (Chilcot) tells us that it's important to avoid 'group-think' as we develop policy, and the best antidote to that is *reasonable challenge.*"[2] The model includes action steps and dispositional attitudes for both receiving and giving the challenge in a way that is respectful of discipline and military culture and designed to support rather than undermine it.[3] For example, the person receiving the challenge is encouraged to not take it personally, seek real diversity of thought, and give ample chance for different views to be aired. The person giving the challenge is asked to do so with courtesy and politeness, be prepared to fully explain their ideas, and use discretion in choosing the moment and venue to make the challenge. The idea is to give a specific and consistent structure to this challenge process, especially in relation to policy issues, to allow discussion and debate, avoid the concern about groupthink, and produce the best ideas while still maintaining reasonable command authority and respect.

We can think about how this would work in the military community of practice (preparing for a combat mission) and the political community of practice (debating how to oppose a specific policy of the government that is viewed as unjust) where civility and being able to navigate conflict and still work together are important. Reasonable challenge provides an outline or a script for a professional or formal kind of civility that can be helpful in navigating the specific contexts where obedience and obedient action are at stake, and they must be balanced with communal values and order. (This is not to say that a general account of civility would work in political discourse; it is designed for a very specific thing within certain narrow limits.)

What is the advantage of having a systemic process for what might normally be considered a form of disobedience or even disrespect? First, this seems to fit well with the idea of negotiation we discussed in chapter 8 related to questions involving reasonable chance of success and proportionality (and other ethical principles,) but it would also be useful for challenges in relation to some issues of military expertise. Reasonable challenge gives a structured space for disagreements around expertise and/or moral values to be explored in a way that does not necessarily undermine discipline, authority, or the nature of the community of practice. Without such a process, groupthink and bad decisions—and their attendant impacts on unit cohesion, morale, and community effectiveness/goal attainment—are much more likely. It also recognizes the idea that effective and ethical command and authority depend upon the participation of those being commanded and tries to include them to some degree in that process in an explicit and structured way.

Second, within a structured system and given the norms elucidated, reasonable challenge is not merely about the individual conscience or judgment being exercised but happens within recognizable norms of the military and/or political communities of practice and professionalism. This is important because it may render less than obedience, nonobedience, or disobedience much less likely if there is another way for obedience to be negotiated. In addition, one can do so while remaining a loyal member of the community in good standing, and therefore the challenge will be less threatening and can even be a valuable contribution to the community.

This model seems to be the most useful for policy and strategy formulation or planning missions when there is time and the process of vetting ideas is critical before implementation. Will this work in combat and under fire or in circumstances of political stress or crisis? Yes, although to a more limited degree, and it would have to be reserved for serious issues that could not be delayed: to avoid committing a war crime, for targeting issues, or where emotions or other concerns seem to be motivating decisions that could compromise the mission. It is going to be more useful in the political community with deliberation and debate still under way, and less useful in a severe crisis where violence or other state actions have commenced.

Clearly, a certain level of education, training, and professionalism or commitment to the community would be necessary for this to work. Those elements would include content expertise, ethics, practice at judgment and discretion, and being able to articulate reasons and discuss in a communal setting; however, it is important to note that empathy and emotional intelligence will also be required, especially on the side of those who are challenged. This model reflects a commitment to an authentic community of practice, indicating that each person in the community can and should contribute in constructive ways. It is flatter than the stereotypical military hierarchy and can be viewed as more collaborative.

This model also directly connects to core values and other ideas of military professionalism that reflect the normative structure of that community of practice. There are two kinds of aims in adopting this kind of model: mission achievement and persuasion by a larger community of practice/political community relative to an issue of import. I would argue that all of the above cases except the combat situation (case 3) fall under the second aim, which means that they have to be approached more carefully. The question of time pressure will be important as well. Cases 1 and 3 appear to have more time pressure than cases 2 and 4, where there will be more time to negotiate and deliberate, making reasonable challenge a better option.

How does this connect with the political community values that we discussed at the end of chapter 8? This approach values individual rights/participation in the social contract but gives a more specific and structured process for dissent. In the current climate, calls for civility tend to favor the status quo. We can recall John Stuart Mill's endorsement of civility as a value productive to discourse and the discovery of truth, provided that those in power do not use it (as often happens) to exclude the marginalized.[4] On the other hand, disruptive violations of civility or other norms of the community are useful for getting attention for an issue and raising consciousness. The ACT Up movement in the 1980s was instrumental in highlighting the AIDS crisis with precisely this kind of disruptive and uncivil, even shocking, behavior. That initial success and role can only go so far; such activities are not helpful and do not further the process of getting legislative or political change codified in sustainable ways through law or policy, which in turn shape and change norms and values within the community. For this second piece, something such as reasonable challenge provides a process and specific roadmap after the disruption and civil disobedience has gotten the attention of the community for the hard work of changing the status quo.

CRITICAL OBEDIENCE

Ulrich Zwygart's concept of critical obedience is helpful at this point for both the military and civilian contexts to build on the idea of obedience as negotiation in cases where reasonable challenge is not possible or desirable.[5] Critical obedience is the idea that obedience should not be necessarily presumptive and that in fact obedience has to be justified and warranted in a particular situation to avoid the problem of blind obedience. Here there is always a judgment about whether and to what extent obedience should be rendered relative to considerations of ethics and military expertise.

In terms of the military context, it is helpful because it looks at both ethical considerations and military expertise. Conflicts or disagreements about the second (as we can see also from the reasonable challenge model) seem easier to resolve in a communal way, since there is a communally shared and agreed upon body of knowledge/expertise and facts that can be used to judge who is right. Currently we tend to view conflicts about the ethical as a matter of purely individual judgment (thanks to the Reformation and Enlightenment political philosophy), but there are problems with this in both the military and civilian contexts. The first and second considerations are not and cannot be separated because of the idea of a community of practice in which norms and ethical principles (as opposed to private moral commitments) are the domain not of the individual alone but also of the community. Ethical principles inform military professionalism and the body of expert knowledge about how to wage war and military expertise, and the body of knowledge informs the values of the community such as courage, loyalty, selfless service, and trust.

In the case of the political community of practice, the norms and values may be more loosely held by individuals within the community, but there is a minimal level of shared history and identity that can be appealed to in a similar way. In the political community, the same sense of professional expertise to appeal to is absent, so constitutional principles or other shared norms and values of the community (liberty, individual rights, the common good) would have to serve the same function for critical obedience to be effective. The National Football League protests and the civil rights movement are both examples of appealing to shared principles (dignity of each citizen, liberty of conscience) that are being used to negotiate obedience to the state and persuade fellow citizens to change the status quo and attend to an injustice. In both of these cases, those protesting are still claiming their position as citizens within the political community of practice as their starting point and as the source of their protest, as opposed to personal moral or religious conscience, whim, or pure preference.

This involves a significant shift away from the Reformation and Enlightenment notions of individual conscience as definitive and even paramount in ethical judgments. McMahan and the revisionists' views seem to move us more in this individualistic direction and away from a collectivist view, but the arguments presented in this book (especially in chapter 9) have highlighted the dangers and problems of that move with respect to both military and civil obedience. This is different than loyalty, which is still the domain of individual judgment, belief, and commitment. Since obedience requires action of a particular sort that is collective, coordinated, and aimed at a particular political goal, individual acts have to be taken together and coordinated in certain prescribed ways (just as in religious or social rituals) to have the desired effect and meaning.

We have noted that there will be difficulties, in particular the danger that collective responsibility and accountability will disappear altogether with the individual becoming solely the responsible agent within the community of practice. In addition, there is the worry that individuals will simply act or not act on whim, prejudice, personal bias, or other reasons that are not connected to and rooted in the history and identity of the community; this could potentially lead to a great deal of disagreement and chaos. The current state of political debate and the fractured multiplicity of identities would seem to give some support to this danger; many authors, including Sebastian Junger, have lamented this and seek ways to build community and a shared sense of belonging and obligation.

That said, this shift is critical for a more coherent and consistent account of obedience and disobedience grounded in collective, ethical, and professional judgment. It also allows us to take into account how these questions arise in the context of communities of practice bounded by collective norms and action, while still leaving room for appropriate individual judgment and discretion relative to action as negotiation but not in isolation. This means that obedience consists of a range of activities requiring judgment and discretion to discern what the best course of action is relative to the consequences and aims under consideration. If we return to the Petrov case, we see that there is a reasonable and communally understood way for the individual to exercise critical obedience, and this case might have benefited from reasonable challenge (although the time issue would have been a factor) to avoid great harm to the community of practice. The reasons Petrov gave for his decisions can be recognized as rooted in the expertise and practices of his profession, not just his own personal moral view or other commitments; he is appealing to things that involve shared understandings.

Taking this kind of account seriously will also require a change in military training and education models, because it will be necessary to train and educate in ways that develop skills and habits in differentiating and practicing different forms of obedience, including reasonable challenge and critical obedience. Huntington's classical model of instant and relatively uncritical obedience will be very problematic, especially for officers and NCOs. Experience and education/expertise will matter here, but so will the prudence (professional judgment and discretion) developed through practice, experience, and failure. The normative structure and ethical principles such as core values and military professionalism also do heavy lifting here, so training the trainers will be critical, since they are the ones who will model and provide feedback and policing for this process. Returning to Foucault and his idea that discipline is historically about the control of bodies and minds in service of the state, we must ask what kinds and levels of control are in fact necessary and what kinds actually are counterproductive in a given community of practice. Excessive and overly harsh discipline and control can cause revolt and resistance, actually undermining the cohesion and shared values of the community.

Ideas of power, authority, and leadership will also require reexamination and some revisions, but we already have seen how the strategic corporal and mission command have begun to shift these concepts over the last several decades. That General Milley is able to talk about disciplined disobedience and be taken seriously shows the traction and power of this shift beginning, but tradition as instantiated in rank structures, history of the military, and culture are very much oriented against this kind of model (for good reasons), and change will be understandably slow. There will also be concerns within the political community centering around civility and law and order arguments when protest and disobedience are seen as a threat to the state monopoly on violence or the identity and historical understandings of that community of practice. In both cases, there are limits on dissent, disobedience, and critical obedience that can be tolerated while still maintaining the integrity and cohesion of the community in question.

At the same time, there are those who push back on ideas such as mission command, raising concerns about how it interacts with other ideas of command, whether it can be effectively implemented, and whether it requires too much individual judgment, discretion, and moral agency.[6] In particular there are concerns with the tendency to see mission command as the preeminent mode of command to the exclusion of others, especially if this sacrifices the quality of command over concerns of time pressure and the need for adaptability. Another concern is the relationship between tactical and strategic considerations, especially in the age of social media: "Strategic implications will inevitably draw higher echelons into decision making. The trick is to develop officers who understand how to engage in these discussions in a mature and productive way."[7] Clearly there are complexities and areas of resistance that pose a challenge to increased individual judgment, discretion, and moral agency in both the military and political contexts.

However, success is the best persuasion, and the educational background of both civilians and military is in a different place than when we began as a republic, where military ideas developed for largely uneducated forces relied on conscription, physical punishment, and fear even into the nineteenth and early twentieth centuries. Mission command is neither necessarily new nor a threat to good order and discipline provided that the capacities (judgment, discretion, and moral agency) are developed that make success more likely and in ways that do not violate or undermine the history, identity, norms, and values of the community of practice. It has to make sense for that community. This is not a generic formula or checklist that can be exported—it has to be adapted and tweaked for each community and its own context.

This process of adaptation may seem to be more intuitive in the political community of practice and will shift faster as more civilians experience this process and then bring that sensibility and experience into the military community. As civilians enter the military from a society that is more used to gender fluidity and varying gender roles, body art, and piercings or has had greater engagement on a daily basis with technology, they bring that sensibility with them, and that has an impact of the military community of practice. Sometimes these shifts will be resisted as inconsistent with the nature of the military and its function and identity (gender), and in other cases, the culture of the military slowly begins to adapt itself from the influence of the civilian society.

However, as Junger points out, the kind of individualism that we currently find in the political community is largely lacking in the communal identity and values that could keep things centered, so this process will need to be balanced by ideas of communal identity, history, and responsibility. This will require much more reflection, critical attention, and engagement with understandings of obedience and loyalty in both the military and political communities of practice; this means moving away from conventional ideas of blind and passive obedience and presumed loyalty. What does it mean to be a member of this community of practice, and what do I owe to this community?

Military and civilian habits of deference and presumed obedience will then need to shift toward critical obedience and a willingness to engage in processes such as the reasonable challenge. I have tried to make the point that there is a difference between trust/respect and deference, which we might associate more with celebrity, royalty and aristocracy, rank, and class as opposed to actions and earned activities. Trust and respect as earned in a community of practice (both civilian and military) are essential to the aims and proper functioning and success/endurance of these communities. In the military, respect and trust have been shown to be critical to both unit cohesion and combat effectiveness, as well as to levels of job satisfaction and persistence in and commitment to the institution. However, both respect and trust in their best forms must be completely compatible with and even need critical obedience to flourish.[8] This, therefore, is the essence of obedience as a military professional and for the engaged citizen.

CASES RECONSIDERED

Given these two ideas of reasonable challenge and critical obedience, we now return to the cases to see how they look through those lenses. The point of this discussion is not necessarily to give a definitive answer in each scenario but rather to suggest what points or considerations would be important to consider in the process of applying judgment and discretion to each.

Case 1

In this case, the advisors have already registered their concerns and objected on the record, and presumably in this process senior military advisors have done the same as a part of the process. It would seem then that there is a case for reluctant obedience, since less than obedience and nonobedience are not really possible here. On the other hand, you may have questions about whether this is a legitimate use of force and the scale of harms that you will be responsible (at least in part) for bringing about. Due to this complicity issue, it may be that a reasonable challenge or some other form of registering protest may be in order, even if you decide to carry out the order. This will depend on what you think about the likelihood that the order, by the time it gets to you, will have gone through several layers of both the civilian and military bureaucracy (although you have no way of knowing what concerns and protests have been registered and answered). If you have trust in the professionalism of those members of the community, you may decide it is worth deferring to their judgment since you only have part of the picture; on the other hand, you may decide you cannot trust your moral agency to others, as the revisionists argue.

Case 2

Here we have many of the same issues in both the military and political versions of the case. This is a good case for reasonable challenge, but it is likely in both cases that it will be unsuccessful both with the person who is the object of the challenge and/or those who are higher in the hierarchy and have to this point not been responsive to concerns. Due to the structure and civility of the reasonable challenge, however, it is still a worthwhile strategy as it may help the parties understand the severity of the issue in a way that they did not before. Disobedience or resistance may have an impact on others to raise consciousness about the abuses and power that realistically seem the only likely mode to avoid further harm. Sometimes publicity and public knowledge can create a different situation, where abuse often requires relative secrecy, silence, and acquiescence to be effective. If the resistance or disobedience is a last resort and nonviolent, it could be justified by the harms that the leaders are engaged in and the threat they pose to the community of practice.

Case 3

The case seems a classic kind of mission command situation, so the question is whether it is feasible and advisable to mount a reasonable challenge—given constraints of time and lack of physical collocation/communication. More than likely, it is not possible. In addition, we should consider whether to mount the challenge if it is likely that the answer will be negative; is it better to just act and gamble that the facts and outcome will be on your side and, if they aren't, to ask for forgiveness, as you were acting in good faith? (This might be especially prudent if one's superiors are toxic, resistant, or entrenched in certain ways that do not take changing circumstances into account or give them appropriate weight.) If a no is possible or likely, should you engage in critical obedience but negotiate that obedience along a spectrum following your own professional judgment and discretion? Is it reasonable to give more weight to your assessment of the situation on the ground than whatever considerations (strategic and operational) your superiors may have in mind? What role does time pressure play in your decision?

Case 4

In both versions of this case, we have aims that might be of questionable value to some, except in building certain kinds of habits that may or may not be achievable by individuals on their own, as opposed to individuals developing these in community. These would be very good instances for reasonable challenge to make the case for other strategies and options to achieve the same end. Failing that, critical obedience and negotiated obedience along a range of actions would also be a reasonable response (especially in the political case) to raise others' consciousness about the issue. There is a good chance to influence the community with low-stakes consequences in ways that might continue a dialogue or foster locally differentiated solutions. (This is often what happens in cases with public schools since they are largely locally funded and controlled.) These would both be cases where judgment and discretion and negotiation seem in order and can be effective without the kinds of catastrophic effects that might be present in the first and second cases. In addition, one can argue that for some members of the community, allowing individual autonomy and agency to develop these habits would demonstrate and increase trust while still achieving the desired ends. If that is not happening in these cases, it is fairly easy to shift and change strategies or processes, which is much more difficult in the other cases.

In all these cases, we can see that there are different considerations about the likely success and accuracy of greater tolerance of individual judgment, discretion, and moral agency, as well as the likely consequences of allowing such tolerance. In some cases, we may want to limit such individual agency because the stakes are so high and catastrophic or the individual may not have access to information or considerations that would be necessary to make a good judgment. This final consideration is then not purely an individual matter, but one that the members of the community of practice must make together, considering the history, identity, norms, and values of their community. For this account to be effective and sustainable, we must recognize the roles to be played by the individual as an individual, but also by the community of practice.

CONCLUDING THOUGHTS

In short, this book has attempted to engage and come to terms with the tensions and intersections between the individual and community in regard to the issue of obedience, relative to both the military and the political contexts. First, it provides us with a nuanced philosophical treatment of aspects of obedience in both the military and civilian political communities of practice as both a social virtue and a moral obligation. Second, we have considered important connections to and contrasts with the related concept of loyalty. Third, we have argued for a conception of obedience as negotiation across a range of obedient, less than obedient, nonobedient, and disobedient actions. This idea of negotiation was supported by the idea of judgment and discretion as a form of Aristotle's prudence, the kind of reasoning necessary to be a virtuous person and to live the good life. Fourth, we considered the implications and impact of the dual roles of military member and citizen on this account, especially in terms of military and veteran exceptionalism and the civil-military relationship. Finally, we used concrete ideas such as reasonable challenge and critical obedience to show how this account might work in practice with reference to specific scenarios that engage the themes of the book. The intention is to open the conversation about how it is possible to have individual moral agency (which we take as necessary for moral responsibility and accountability) within the context of a community of practice with a history, identity, norms, and values.

However, it is also very important against the revisionists to have some level of collective responsibility and accountability as a community of practice without abrogating individual responsibility. We need space for both when it comes to obedience.

In these communities with life-and-death consequences for decisions about how to negotiate obedience, including moral injury and the integrity of the identities of these communities, we need to give attention to the development of citizens, some of whom are also military professionals. In a political community with citizen soldiers and civilian control of the military, these questions of obedience and loyalty are part of the fabric of everyday life and many of the policies that are considered. Negotiating obedience in the context of the civil-military culture gap will also require seeing discipline (albeit in a different way) as a civilian virtue, not just the domain of the military. While the military focuses heavily on physical discipline and uniformity supported by mental discipline, it is possible that for civilians it may be the other way around, where mental disobedience and dissent are a necessary practice to preserve the political community in its physical form. Rather than seeing these approaches in tension, they can inform and reinforce one another through a more equal dialogue and sense of both shared and individual agency and responsibility.

Discussion Guide

This discussion guide is designed for individual or small group settings for readers to dig more deeply into the issues in each chapter. It is not necessary to focus on every question but rather to indicate some areas of possible discussion.

CHAPTER 1. INTRODUCTION

1. What comes to mind when you think of obedience? What do you associate with this word? Why?
2. Why should we consider what obedience is? Why does this matter?
3. What is an example of something you consider disobedience? Do you think it was justified? Why or why not?
4. What do you think military and political life would be like without obedience? With less obedience?

CHAPTER 2. THE NATURE OF OBEDIENCE

1. What is your take on the room-cleaning scenario? What would count as obedience? Disobedience? Why?
2. Do you think obedience necessarily involves respect? Why? Does obedience necessarily involve deference or honor? Why?
3. Is there a presumption in favor of obedience in the military? In the political community? Should there be?
4. Do you agree that there is a difference between obedience in combat and garrison contexts? Why or why not?

CHAPTER 3. OBEDIENCE AS A VIRTUE

1. Is obedience a virtue to you? Why or why not? If it is not a virtue, what is it?
2. If you think obedience is a virtue, do you think it is a social or an individual virtue? Why?
3. What do you think of the relationship between obedience and agency discussed in this chapter? Should the level of obedience expected be tied to the level of agency a person has? Why or why not?
4. Are members of the military merely agents of the state, or do they retain some moral agency? If they do retain some agency, how much and what kind?

CHAPTER 4. MORAL GROUNDING OF OBEDIENCE

1. Do you agree that obedience is necessary for the state and/or military to function?
2. Do you agree with social contract theory that you can consent to obey?
3. What do you think of the argument at the end of the chapter about the moral grounding of obedience? Do you agree? Why or why not?
4. What other interesting ideas struck you (in either a good or not so good way)?

CHAPTER 5. DISOBEDIENCE AND DISCIPLINE

1. Does disobedience undermine discipline? If so, how?
2. What do you think is the point of giving an order?
3. Is there a link between obedience and discipline? If there is, what exactly is it? If there is not, why not?
4. What other interesting ideas struck you (in either a good or not so good way)?

CHAPTER 6. ON LOYALTY AND OBEDIENCE

1. Is there a connection between loyalty and obedience? Why or why not?
2. Can you be obedient and not be loyal? Can you be loyal and not obedient?
3. What do you think of the idea of loyal disobedience? Why?
4. What other interesting ideas struck you (in either a good or not so good way)?

CHAPTER 7. THE ROLE OF JUDGMENT AND DISCRETION

1. How much judgment and discretion do you think people ought to have / do have in making decisions? Why?
2. Do you agree with the idea that people ought to have more agency, judgment, and discretion in decisionmaking, especially in the military? Why or why not?
3. What is an example of when you used your own judgment and discretion? What were the results? Why?
4. How do you educate and train for judgment and discretion?

CHAPTER 8. OBEDIENCE AS NEGOTIATION

1. Does the idea of "negotiating" obedience make sense to you? Why or why not?
2. What are the possible problems and concerns with the idea? What are the possible benefits?
3. What do you think of the World War I case study? Why?
4. What do you think of the issues raised in the "Objections and Replies" section? What are your responses to those issues?

CHAPTER 9. THE MILITARY-CITIZEN DUALITY

1. What is your view of the relationship between military service and citizenship?
2. Are members of the military "better" citizens than those who have not served?

3. How is being a citizen and a member of the military (at the same time) different than solely being a citizen, especially with regard to the idea of obedience?
4. Do you think the characterization of military/veteran exceptionalism is fair? Why or why not?
5. What do you see as some possible solutions to the civil-military culture gap?

CHAPTER 10. CASES AND CONCLUSION

1. What are your responses to each of the cases? Why?
2. What do you think of the idea of critical obedience discussed in this chapter? Why?
3. What do you think of the idea of reasonable challenge? Why?
4. Do you agree that critical obedience is the mark of a professional member of the military (and/or good citizen) rather than blind or passive obedience? Why or why not?

Notes

CHAPTER 1. INTRODUCTION

1. William Shakespeare, *Henry V*, act IV, scene 1, https://www
   .folgerdigitaltexts.org/html/H5.html.
2. Sophocles, *The Three Theban Plays: Oedipus the King, Antigone,
   Oedipus at Colonus*, trans. Robert Fagles (New York: Penguin Books,
   1982), 62.
3. Thanks to Mark Safranski for this example. For more information see
   "Kwantung Army," https://www.globalsecurity.org/military/world
   /japan/ija-kwantung.htm.
4. I use the term "communities of practice" in this book as a way to
   delineate professional and political communities with shared histories,
   moral commitments, and other norms that govern their identity,
   boundaries, and behavior. The profession of arms (military) in the
   United States, Canada, United Kingdom, and Australia are all examples
   of one kind of community of practice, but various political communities
   (including sovereign nation-states) are also communities of practice.
5. Rob Reiner, dir., *A Few Good Men* (Los Angeles: Castle Rock
   Entertainment, 1992).
6. For more on My Lai, see Michael Bilton and Kevin Sim, *Four Hours in
   My Lai* (New York: Penguin Books, 1993).
7. Shakespeare, *Henry V*, act IV, scene 1.
8. Plato, *Euthyphro*, trans. Benjamin Jowett, http://classics.mit.edu/
   Plato/euthyfro.html.
9. John Locke, *Two Treatises of Government*, ed. C. B. Macpherson
   (Indianapolis: Hackett Publishing, 1980), chaps. 18 and 19.
10. Thomas Aquinas, *On Law, Morality, and Politics*, ed. William P.
    Baumgarth and Richard J. Regan (Indianapolis: Hackett Publishing,
    2003), 233, 243.

11. For more on this topic, see Nikki Coleman, "Does the Australian Defence Force Have a Compelling Justification for the Duty to Obey Orders?" (unpublished dissertation, University of New South Wales, Canberra, November 2016), chaps. 2 and 3. Her discussion on the legal issues in the United Kingdom and Australian militaries is particularly interesting.

12. Declaration of Independence, National Archives, https://www .archives.gov/founding-docs/declaration-transcript.

13. For the genesis of this argument, see Aristotle, *Politics*, trans. Benjamin Jowett, http://classics.mit.edu/Aristotle/politics.html.

14. Locke, *Two Treatises of Government,* 37.

15. Leonard Wong and Stephen J. Garras, *Lying to Ourselves: Dishonesty in the Army Profession* (Carlisle, PA: Strategic Studies Institute, February 2015).

16. Josh Feldman, "Trump: Military Would Not Refuse My Orders Even If They Consider Them Illegal," Mediaite.com, March 3, 2016, https://www.washingtontimes.com/news/2016/mar/3/donald-trump -says-hed-force-us-military-commit-war/.

17. C. Todd Lopes, "Future Warfare Requires 'Disciplined Disobedience,' Army Chief Says," Army.mil, May 5, 2017, https://www.army.mil/ article/187293/future_warfare_requires_disciplined_disobedience _army_chief_says.

18. On mission command, see Army Doctrine Reference Publication 6-0, *Mission Command* (Washington, DC: Headquarters Department of the Army, May 2012), https://fas.org/irp/doddir/army/adrp6_0.pdf. On the strategic corporal idea, see General Charles C. Krulak, "The Strategic Corporal: Leadership in the Three-block War," *Marines Magazine* (January 1999), http://www.au.af.mil/au/awc/awcgate/usmc/ strategic_corporal.htm.

19. Samuel P. Huntington, *The Soldier and the State: The Theory and Politics of Civil-Military Relations* (Cambridge, MA: Belknap Press, 1957), 73.

20. Michael Walzer, *Just and Unjust Wars: A Moral Argument with Historical Illustrations* (New York: Basic Books, 1977), 311.

21. Telford Taylor, "Superior Orders and Reprisals," in *War, Morality, and the Military Profession,* ed. Malham M. Wakin (Boulder, CO: Westview Press, 1979), 436.

22. U.S. Army Oath of Enlistment, Army.mil, https://www.army.mil/ values/oath.html.

23. U.S. Customs and Immigration Service, Naturalization Oath of Allegiance to the United States, https://www.uscis.gov/us-citizenship/ naturalization-test/naturalization-oath-allegiance-united-states-america.

24. Richard A. Gabriel and Paul L. Savage, *Crisis in Command: Mismanagement in the Army* (New York: Macmillan, 1979).

25. Pauline Shanks Kaurin, "Questioning Military Professionalism," in *Redefining the Modern Military: The Intersection of Profession and Ethics*, ed. Nathan K. Finney and Tyrell O. Mayfield (Annapolis, MD: Naval Institute Press, 2018).

CHAPTER 2. THE NATURE OF OBEDIENCE

1. Plato, *Laches, or Courage*, trans. Benjamin Jowett, http://classics.mit .edu/Plato/laches.html.

2. Tim O'Brien, *The Things They Carried* (New York: Broadway Books, 1990), 59.

3. Aristotle, *Nicomachean Ethics*, trans. Terrence Irwin (Indianapolis: Hackett Publishing, 1983), book III.

4. Aquinas, *On Law, Morality, and Politics*, 244.

5. Aquinas, 243.

6. Niccolò Machiavelli, *The Prince,* trans. W. K. Marriott, http://www .gutenberg.org/files/1232/1232-h/1232-h.htm.

7. Tamler Sommers, *Why Honor Matters* (New York: Basic Books, 2018), 18.

8. Huntington, *The Soldier and the State*, 73.

9. Dominick Edwards, "31 Things Your Senior Rater Would Like You to Know that He Probably Won't Tell You," Fromthegreennotebook.com, April 18, 2016, https://fromthegreennotebook.com/2016/04/18/31 -things-your-senior-rater-would-like-you-to-know-that-he-probably -wont-tell-you/.

10. See Don M. Snider, "Will Army 2025 Be a Military Profession?" *Parameters* 45, no. 4 (Winter 2015).

11. See Gabriel and Savage, *Crisis in Command*.

12. ADP 6-0, *Mission Command,* https://fas.org/irp/doddir/army/ adrp6_0.pdf.

CHAPTER 3. OBEDIENCE AS A VIRTUE

1. Attributed to a major in Frederick the Great's German Army. Cited in Keith Nightingale, "Combat, Orders and Judgment," *Small Wars Journal*, May 7, 2017.

2. Sam C. Sarkesian quoted in Anthony Hartle, *Moral Issues in Military Decision Making* (Lawrence: University Press of Kansas, 1989), 47.

3. Alasdair MacIntyre, *After Virtue* (South Bend, IN: University of Notre Dame Press, 1984), 122.

4. MacIntyre, 128.

5. MacIntyre, 132.

6. Aristotle, *Nicomachean Ethics*, book II, 1103a15.

7. Aristotle, 1115b18.

8. Deontology is often associated with the work of Immanuel Kant, especially *Grounding for the Metaphysics of Morals*, while there are various versions of consequentialism, most notably utilitarianism associated with the work of Jeremy Bentham and John Stuart Mill.

9. Immanuel Kant, *Grounding for the Metaphysics of Morals*, trans. James W. Ellington (Indianapolis: Hackett Publishing, 1981), first section.

10. Kant, 421.

11. John Stuart Mill, *Utilitarianism*, ed. George Sher (Indianapolis: Hackett Publishing, 1979), chap. 4.

12. MacIntyre, *After Virtue*, 187.

13. MacIntyre, 222.

14. MacIntyre, 151–52.

15. U.S. Army Core Values, Army.mil, https://www.army.mil/values/.

16. Coleman, "Does the Australian Defence Force Have a Compelling Justification for the Duty to Obey Orders?" chaps. 2 and 3.

17. Wakin, *War, Morality, and the Military Profession*, 205, 207.

18. Wakin, 51, 134.

19. Sebastian Junger, *Tribe: On Homecoming and Belonging* (New York: Twelve, 2016).

20. Junger, 30.

21. For more information see *Serial* podcast, season 2, episode 1, "Dustwun," https://serialpodcast.org/season-two/1/dustwun.

22. See "Stop Calling Us Warriors," angrystaffofficer.com, December 14, 2016, https://angrystaffofficer.com/2016/12/14/stop-calling-us-warriors/.

23. Wakin, *War, Morality, and the Military Profession*, 41.

24. Wakin, 180–81.

25. Martin L. Cook, *The Moral Warrior: Ethics and Service in the U.S. Military* (Albany, NY: SUNY Press, 2004), 61.

26. Walzer, *Just and Unjust Wars*, 39–40.

27. Wakin, *War, Morality, and the Military Profession*, 210–11.

28. Cook, *The Moral Warrior*, 64.

29. Shakespeare, *Henry V*, act III, scene 3.

30. Jeff McMahan, *Killing in War* (Oxford: Oxford University Press, 2011).

31. Jeff McMahan, "The Morality of War and the Law of War," in *Just and Unjust Warriors: The Moral and Legal Status of Soldiers*, ed. David Rodin and Henry Shue (New York: Oxford University Press, 2008), 22.

32. Richard Dagger, *Civic Virtues: Rights, Citizenship, and Republican Liberalism* (New York: Oxford University Press, 1997), 13–14.

33. Walzer, *Just and Unjust Wars*, 137, 311.

34. Aristotle, *Nicomachean Ethics*, book III.

CHAPTER 4. MORAL GROUNDING OF OBEDIENCE

1. John Rawls, "The Justification of Civil Disobedience," in *The Philosophy of Law: Classic and Contemporary Readings with Commentary*, ed. Fredrick Schauer and Walter Sinnott-Armstrong (New York: Oxford University Press, 1996), 260–61.

2. Thomas Hobbes, *Leviathan*, in *The English Philosophers from Bacon to Mill,* ed. Edwin A. Burtt (New York: Modern Library, 1967), 177.

3. Ted Shine, *Contribution* (New York: Dramatists Play Service, 1969), 63.

4. While these two are traditional jus ad bellum criteria in just war thinking, I am expanding them to also include political ends outside of traditional war. For more see Walzer, *Just and Unjust Wars*, chaps. 2–4.

5. Kant, *Grounding for the Metaphysics of Morals*, 400–401.

6. Dagger, *Civic Virtues*, 63.

7. Dagger, 79.

8. Aquinas, *On Law, Morality, and Politics*, 253.

9. Kenneth Kipnis, *Philosophical Issues in the Law: Cases and Materials* (Englewood Cliffs, NJ: Prentice Hall, 1977), 161.

10. Kipnis, 183.

11. Kipnis, 188.

12. Social contract theory is a name for a collection of views in political philosophy that ground the authority of government in consent. This generally includes thinkers such as Thomas Hobbes, John Locke, Jean-Jacques Rousseau, and Immanuel Kant. More recent philosophers in this tradition are John Rawls and Charles Mills.

13. See Hobbes, *Leviathan.*

14. Hobbes, 177.

15. See Locke, *Two Treatises of Government.*

16. Locke, paragraph 67.

17. Locke, 111.

18. Quoted in Elizabeth Samet, *Willing Obedience: Citizens, Soldiers, and the Progress of Consent in America, 1776–1898* (Stanford, CA: Stanford University Press, 2004), 221.

19. David Hume, *A Treatise on Human Nature*, ed. P. H. Nidditch (Oxford: Clarendon Press, 1978), 553.

20. See Cook, *The Moral Warrior*, chap. 3.

21. Walzer, *Just and Unjust Wars*, 145, 305.

22. Walzer, 311.

23. John Searle, *Speech Acts: An Essay in the Philosophy of Language* (New York: Cambridge University Press, 1970).

24. Hume, *A Treatise on Human Nature*, book III, 522.

25. Hume, 523.

26. For more on selective conscientious objection, see Paul Robinson, "Integrity and Selective Conscientious Objection," http://isme.tamu .edu/ISME08/Robinson08.html.
27. Jeremy Brecher and Brendan Smith, "The Trials of Erhen Watada," *The Nation*, June 1, 2009, https://www.thenation.com/article/trials -ehren-watada/.

CHAPTER 5. DISOBEDIENCE AND DISCIPLINE

1. Jean Norton Cru, *Témoins* (1929), quoted in Leonard V. Smith, *Between Mutiny and Obedience: The Case of the French 5th Infantry Division during World War I* (Princeton, NJ: Princeton University Press, 1994).
2. Michel Foucault, *Discipline and Punish: The Birth of the Prison*, trans. Alan Sheridan (New York: Pantheon Books, 1977), 138.
3. Cited in Jeremy S. Weber, "Whatever Happened to Military Good Order and Discipline?" *Cleveland State Law Review* 123 (2017): 38.
4. Weber, "Whatever Happened to Military Good Order and Discipline?" 2, 161.
5. Foucault, *Discipline and Punish*, 48.
6. Foucault, 128.
7. Foucault, 215.
8. Foucault, 164.
9. Mark J. Osiel, *Obeying Orders: Atrocity, Military Discipline, and the Law of War* (New York: Routledge, 2017), 26.
10. Pauline Shanks Kaurin, "Professional Disobedience: Loyalty and the Military," Thestrategybridge.org, August 8, 2017, https:// thestrategybridge.org/the-bridge/2017/8/8/professional-disobedience -loyalty-and-the-military.
11. Gabriel and Savage, *Crisis in Command*.
12. Foucault, *Discipline and Punish*.
13. Bilton and Sim, *Four Hours at My Lai*.
14. Nightingale, "Combat, Orders, and Judgment."
15. Kaurin, "Professional Disobedience."
16. Term coined by Ulrich Zywert that I will discuss in detail in chapter 10.
17. Foucault, *Discipline and Punish*.
18. Nate Boyer, a former Green Beret and veteran, is credited with making the kneeling suggestion to Colin Kaepernick.

CHAPTER 6. ON LOYALTY AND OBEDIENCE

1. Alfred A. Montapert Quotes, BrainyQuote, https://www.brainyquote .com/authors/alfred_a_montapert.
2. Josiah Royce, Stanford Encyclopedia of Philosophy, https://plato .stanford.edu/entries/royce/.

3. Shakespeare, *Henry V*, act IV, scene 3.

4. Pauline M. Kaurin, *The Warrior, Military Ethics, and Contemporary Warfare: Achilles Goes Asymmetrical* (New York: Routledge, 2014), 28.

5. Stephen Nathanson, *Patriotism, Morality, and Peace* (Lanham, MD: Rowman and Littlefield, 1993), 107.

6. U.S. Army Values.

7. David Hume, quoted in Kaurin, *The Warrior, Military Ethics, and Contemporary Warfare*, 28.

8. Nathanson, *Patriotism, Morality, and Peace*, 188.

9. Nathanson, 54–55.

10. Nathanson, 55.

11. Nathanson, 58.

12. For an earlier version of this argument see Pauline Kaurin, "Identity, Loyalty, and Combat Effectiveness: A Cautionary Tale," http://isme .tamu.edu/JSCOPE06/Kaurin06.html#.

13. Kaurin.

14. Kaurin, 30.

15. Kaurin, 39.

16. Benjamin J. Armstrong, ed., *21st Century Sims: Innovation, Education, and Leadership for the Modern Era* (Annapolis, MD: Naval Institute Press, 2015).

17. Quoted in Kaurin, "Identity, Loyalty, and Combat Effectiveness," 27.

18. See Nancy Sherman, *The Untold War: Inside the Hearts, Minds, and Souls of Our Soldiers* (New York: W. W. Norton and Company, 2011); Jonathan Shay, *Achilles in Vietnam: Combat Trauma and the Undoing of Character* (New York: Scribner, 1994).

19. Jonathan Shay, "Moral Injury in War," lecture, Chautuaqua Institution, August 17, 2016, https://www.youtube.com/watch?v=fjzWzJhkOek.

20. Lolita C. Baldor, "Mattis: Jury Is Out on Women Succeeding in Combat Jobs," September 25, 2018, Associated Press, https://www .apnews.com/04473932a9d04748bbc95c57f172ab55.

21. Kaurin, "Professional Disobedience and Loyalty in the Military."

CHAPTER 7. THE ROLE OF JUDGMENT AND DISCRETION

1. Nightingale, "Combat, Orders, and Judgment."

2. Quoted in David Barno and Nora Bensahel, "Three Things the Army Chief of Staff Wants You to Know," *War on the Rocks*, May 23, 2017, https://warontherocks.com/2017/05/three-things-the-army-chief-of -staff-wants-you-to-know/.

3. See Sewell Chan, "Stanislav Petrov, Soviet Officer Who Helped Avert Nuclear War, Is Dead at 77," *New York Times*, September 18, 2017.

4. Aristotle, *Nicomachean Ethics*, book III.

5. Walzer, *Just and Unjust Wars.*
6. McMahan, *Killing in War.*
7. James Pattison, "When Is It Right to Fight: Just War Theory and the Individual-Centric Approach," *Ethical Theory and Moral Practice* 16, no. 1 (February 2013): 39.
8. Pattison, 36.
9. David Ayre, dir., *Fury* (Los Angeles: Columbia Pictures, 2014).
10. For a discussion of the idea of the strategic corporal, see Krulak, "The Strategic Corporal."
11. Aristotle, *Nicomachean Ethics*, 1139a37.
12. Aristotle, 1140b5.
13. Aristotle, 1142a15.
14. Aristotle, 1142b25–30.
15. Aristotle, 1144b15.
16. David Hoffman, "I Had a Funny Feeling in My Gut," *Washington Post*, February 10, 1999.
17. See Finney and Mayfield, *Redefining the Modern Military*, 4–5.
18. Aristotle, *Nicomachean Ethics*, book VI.
19. James D. Sharpe Jr. and Thomas E. Creviston, "Understanding Mission Command," Army.mil, July 10, 2013, https://www.army.mil/article/106872/understanding_mission_command.
20. Just war thinking often includes the following judgments being made about the resort to force (jus ad bellum): just cause, legitimate authority, proportionality of ends, public declaration, reasonable chance of success, and last resort; about just conduct (jus in bello): discrimination including moral equality of combatants and non-combatant immunity, and proportionality of means.
21. David Hume, *An Enquiry Concerning the Principles of Morals* (1751), http://www.gutenberg.org/ebooks/4320, chaps. 6–9.
22. See Nel Noddings, "Caring," in *Justice and Care: Essential Readings in Feminist Ethics*, ed. Virginia Held (Boulder, CO: Westview Press, 1995), 7–30.
23. See Nancy Sherman, *Stoic Warriors: The Ancient Philosophy Behind the Military Mind* (New York: Oxford University Press, 2010).

CHAPTER 8. OBEDIENCE AS NEGOTIATION

1. Smith, *Between Mutiny and Obedience*, 156.
2. Gregory Olsen quoted in Bilton and Sim, *Four Hours in My Lai*, 245.
3. Bilton and Sim, 374.
4. "Radio Silence: A Lesson in Mission Command," Wavellroom.com, December 14, 2017, https://wavellroom.com/2017/12/14/radio-silence-a-lesson-in-mission-command/.

5. Francisco de Vittoria makes this point in his work. See Gregory M. Reichberg, Henrik Syse, and Endre Begby, eds., *The Ethics of War: Classic and Contemporary Readings* (Malden, MA: Blackwell, 2006), 288.

6. James M. Dubik, *Just War Reconsidered: Strategy, Ethics, and Theory* (Lexington: University Press of Kentucky, 2016).

7. Shannon French has argued that military honor and the moral constraints of war provide emotional and mental protection against the harms of war. See Shannon E. French, *The Code of the Warrior: Exploring Warrior Values Past and Present* (Lanham, MD: Routledge, 2017), chap. 1.

8. Smith, *Between Mutiny and Obedience.*

9. Smith, 13, 16.

10. Smith, 118.

11. Smith, 123.

12. Smith, 134–36.

13. Smith, 156, 162.

14. Smith, 162.

15. Smith, 170.

16. Smith, 126.

17. Smith, 179.

18. Smith, 193.

19. Smith, 194.

20. Smith, 214, 216.

21. Smith, 205.

22. Smith, 218.

23. Wong and Garras, *Lying to Ourselves,* 12–13.

24. Wong and Garras, 17.

25. "Quotations: My Lai Massacre," Alphahistory.com, http://alphahistory.com/vietnamwar/quotations-my-lai-massacre/.

26. Bilton and Sim, *Four Hours in My Lai,* 373.

27. Ulrich F. Zwygart, *How Much Obedience Does an Officer Need? Beck, Tresckow, and Stauffenberg—Examples of Integrity and Moral Courage for Today's Officer* (Fort Leavenworth, KS: Combat Studies Institute, 1993), http://www.armyupress.army.mil/Portals/7/combat -studies-institute/csi-books/ObedienceOfficerNeed_Zwygart.pdf.

28. Zwygart, 24.

CHAPTER 9. THE MILITARY-CITIZEN DUALITY

1. Richard Kohn, quoted in Thomas E. Ricks, *Making the Corps* (New York: Touchstone Books, 1998), 278.

2. French, *The Code of the Warrior,* 4.

3. Pauline Shanks Kaurin, "Just Another Mattis Pep Talk? How 'Hold the Line' Speaks to Military and Civilian Audiences," justsecurity.org, August 29, 2017, https://www.justsecurity.org/44518/mattis-pep-talk -hold-line-speaks-civilian-military-audiences/.

4. Kaurin, *The Warrior, Military Ethics, and Contemporary Warfare*, 124.

5. Quoted in Hartle, *Moral Issues in Military Decision Making*, 50.

6. Hartle, 49.

7. Carl von Clausewitz, *On War*, trans. Michael Howard and Peter Paret (Princeton, NJ: Princeton University Press, 1989), chap. 1.

8. Samet, *Willing Obedience*, 6.

9. Samet, 59.

10. Samet, 58–59.

11. Samet, 61–62.

12. See McMahan, *Killing in War*.

13. Samet, *Willing Obedience*, 91.

14. Samet, 99.

15. Samet, 101.

16. Samet, 141.

17. Samet, 180.

18. Samet, 221n58.

19. Junger, *Tribe*.

20. See Coleman, "Does the Australian Defence Force Have a Compelling Justification for the Duty to Obey Orders?" chaps. 2 and 3.

21. Stephen Kershnar, *Gratitude Towards Veterans: Why Americans Should Not Be Very Grateful to Veterans* (Lanham, MD: Lexington Books, 2014), 9, 31.

22. Shakespeare, *Henry V*, act IV, scene 3.

23. Kershnar, *Gratitude Towards Veterans*, 9.

24. This is an expansion of my arguments in *The Warrior, Military Ethics, and Contemporary Warfare*, chap. 10.

25. Kershnar, *Gratitude Towards Veterans*, 31.

26. Tim McGirk, "Collateral Damage or Civilian Massacre in Haditha?" *Time*, March 19, 2006, http://content.time.com/time/world/article /0,8599,1174649,00.html.

27. See "This Is (Not) Sparta," *War College Podcast*, February 9, 2019, https://play.acast.com/s/warcollege/thisis-not-sparta-.

28. See Dubik, *Strategy, Ethics, and Theory*. I would also posit that his argument holds for senior NCOs who function as advisors for officers.

CHAPTER 10. CASES AND CONCLUSION

1. Stanley Kubrick, dir., *Dr. Strangelove, Or: How I Learned to Stop Worrying and Love the Bomb* (Los Angeles: Columbia Pictures, 1964).

2. United Kingdom Ministry of Defence, *The Good Operation: A Handbook for Those Involved in Operational Policy and Its Implementation* (London: Ministry of Defence, 2018), 62, https:// assets.publishing.service.gov.uk/government/uploads/system/uploads/ attachment_data/file/674545/TheGoodOperation_WEB.PDF.

3. *The Good Operation.*

4. John Stuart Mill, *On Liberty* (Indianapolis: Hackett Publishers, 1978), 51.

5. Zwygart, *How Much Obedience Does an Officer Need?*

6. Andrew Hill and Heath Niemi, "The Trouble with Mission Command: Flexive Command and the Future of Command and Control," *Joint Force Quarterly* 86 (3rd Quarter 2017): 94–100.

7. Hill and Niemi, 100.

8. Michael Wheeler, "Loyalty, Honor, and the Modern Military," in Wakin, *War, Morality, and the Military Profession*, 163–78.

SELECTED BIBLIOGRAPHY

Aquinas, Thomas. *On Law, Morality, and Politics*. Edited by William P. Baumgarth and Richard J. Regan. Indianapolis: Hackett Publishing, 2003.

Aristotle. *Nicomachean Ethics*. Translated by Terrence Irwin. Indianapolis: Hackett Publishing, 1983.

Bilton, Michael, and Kevin Sim. *Four Hours at My Lai*. New York: Penguin, 1993.

Coleman, Nikki. "Does the Australian Defence Force Have a Compelling Justification for the Duty to Obey Orders?" Unpublished dissertation, University of New South Wales, Canberra, November 2016.

Cook, Martin L. *The Moral Warrior: Ethics and Service in the U.S. Military*. Albany, NY: SUNY Press, 2004.

Dagger, Richard. *Civic Virtues: Rights, Citizenship, and Republican Liberalism*. New York: Oxford University Press, 1997.

Dubik, James. *Just War Reconsidered: Strategy, Ethics, and Theory*. Lexington: University of Kentucky Press, 2016.

Finney, Nathan K., and Tyrell O. Mayfield, eds. *Redefining the Modern Military: The Intersection of Profession and Ethics*. Annapolis, MD: Naval Institute Press, 2018.

Foucault, Michael. *Discipline and Punish: The Birth of the Prison*. Translated by Alan Sheridan. New York: Pantheon Books, 1977.

Gabriel, Richard A., and Paul L. Savage. *Crisis in Command: Mismanagement in the Army*. New York: Macmillan, 1979.

Hartle, Anthony. *Moral Issues in Military Decision Making*. Lawrence: University Press of Kansas, 1989.

Held, Virginia. *Justice and Care: Essential Readings in Feminist Ethics*. Boulder, CO: Westview Press, 1995.

Hobbes, Thomas. *Leviathan*. In *The English Philosophers from Bacon to Mill,* edited by Edwin A. Burtt. New York: Modern Library, 1967.

Hume, David. *A Treatise on Human Nature*. Edited by P. H. Nidditch. Oxford: Clarendon Press, 1978.

Huntington, Samuel P. *The Soldier and the State: The Theory and Politics of Civil-Military Relations*. Cambridge, MA: Belknap Press, 1957.

Junger, Sebastian. *Tribe: On Homecoming and Belonging*. New York: Twelve, 2016.

Kant, Immanuel. *Grounding for the Metaphysics of Morals*. Translated by James W. Ellington. Indianapolis: Hackett Publishing, 1981.

Kaurin, Pauline. *The Warrior, Military Ethics, and Contemporary Warfare: Achilles Goes Asymmetric*. Burlington, VT: Ashgate, 2014.

Kipnis, Kenneth. *Philosophical Issues in the Law: Cases and Materials*. Englewood Cliffs, NJ: Prentice Hall, 1977.

Locke, John. *Two Treatises of Government*. Edited by C. B. Macpherson. Indianapolis: Hackett Publishing, 1980.

Machiavelli, Niccolò. *The Prince*. Translated by W. K. Marriott. http://www.gutenberg.org/files/1232/1232-h/1232-h.htm.

MacIntyre, Alasdair. *After Virtue*. South Bend, IN: University of Notre Dame Press, 1984.

McMahan, Jeff. *Killing in War*. Oxford: Oxford University Press, 2011.

———. "The Morality of War and the Law of War." In *Just and Unjust Warriors: The Moral and Legal Status of Soldiers*. Edited by David Rodin and Henry Shue. New York: Oxford University Press, 2008.

Mill, John Stuart. *Utilitarianism*. Edited by George Sher. Indianapolis: Hackett Publishing, 1979.

Nathanson, Stephen. *Patriotism, Morality, and Peace*. Lanham, MD: Rowman and Littlefield, 1993.

Nightingale, Keith. "Combat, Orders, and Judgment." *Small Wars Journal*, May 7, 2017.

O'Brien, Tim. *The Things They Carried*. New York: Broadway Books, 1990.

Osiel, Mark J. *Obeying Orders: Atrocity, Military Discipline, and the Law of War*. New York: Routledge, 2017.

Pattison, James. "When Is It Right to Fight: Just War Theory and the Individual-Centric Approach." *Ethical Theory and Moral Practice* 16, no. 1 (February 2013).

Plato. *Euthyphro*. Translated by Benjamin Jowett. http://classics.mit.edu/Plato/euthyfro.html.

———. *Laches, or Courage.* Translated by Benjamin Jowett. http://classics.mit.edu/Plato/laches.html.

Rawls, John. "Civil Disobedience." In *The Philosophy of Law: Classic and Contemporary Readings with Commentary.* Edited by Fredrick Schauer and Walter Sinnott-Armstrong. New York: Oxford University Press, 1996.

Reichberg, Gregory M., Henrik Syse, and Endre Begby, eds. *The Ethics of War: Classic and Contemporary Readings.* Malden, MA: Blackwell, 2006.

Reiner, Rob, dir. *A Few Good Men.* Hollywood, CA: Columbia Pictures Corporation, 1992.

Samet, Elizabeth. *Willing Obedience: Citizens, Soldiers, and the Progress of Consent in America, 1776–1898.* Stanford, CA: Stanford University Press, 2004.

Searle, John. *Speech Acts: An Essay in the Philosophy of Language.* New York: Cambridge University Press, 1970.

Shakespeare, William. *Henry V.* https://www.folgerdigitaltexts.org/html/H5.html.

Shay, Jonathan. *Achilles in Vietnam: Combat Trauma and the Undoing of Character.* New York: Scribner, 1994.

Sherman, Nancy. *Stoic Warriors: The Ancient Philosophy Behind the Military Mind.* New York: Oxford University Press, 2010.

———. *The Untold War: Inside the Hearts, Minds, and Souls of Our Soldiers.* New York: W. W. Norton and Company, 2011.

Shine, Ted. *Contribution.* New York: Dramatists Play Service, 1969.

Smith, Leonard V. *Between Mutiny and Obedience: The Case of the French 5th Infantry Division during World War I.* Princeton, NJ: Princeton University Press, 1994.

Sommers, Tamler. *Why Honor Matters.* New York: Basic Books, 2018.

Sophocles. *The Three Theban Plays: Oedipus the King, Antigone, Oedipus at Colonus.* Translated by Robert Fagles. New York: Penguin Books, 1982.

Wakin, Malham, ed. *War, Morality, and the Military Profession.* Boulder, CO: Westview Press, 1979.

Walzer, Michael. *Just and Unjust Wars: A Moral Argument with Historical Illustrations.* New York: Basic Books, 1977.

Weber, Jeremy S. "Whatever Happened to Military Good Order and Discipline?" *Cleveland State Law Review* 123 (2017).

Wong, Leonard, and Stephen J. Garras. *Lying to Ourselves: Dishonesty in the Army Profession.* Carlisle, PA: Strategic Studies Institute, February 2015.

INDEX

civil-military culture gap, 13,
209–10, 211–17, 241; culture of
dishonesty, 186–87; danger of
disobedience in, 4; definition of,
247n4; democracy preservation
not practice by, 201–2; discipline
and good order as military
foundation, 4, 97–99; education
and literacy skills of all-volunteer
force, 15; equality of military
service, 201; importance
of obedience in, 15–16, 98;
judgment revisions with changing
norms, 166–67; moral status of
obedience in, 5–7, 11–13, 15–16,
19, 20, 82, 83–84; moral virtue
of disobeying orders, 6–7, 68;
oaths taken by members of, 10,
14–15, 16, 17, 19, 63, 84–89;
obeying orders in, 5–6, 10,
11–13, 14–16; objects of war,
consent to be treated as, 84–85;
orders and why give orders,
101–6; practices and traditions
of, 231–32, 233–37, 241;
presumption of obedience in, 13–
16, 37–42, 68; proportionality,
success potential, and obedience,
82–83, 91, 93, 170–71, 182–86;
prudence/practical reasoning in,
154; restrictions on legal rights
of, 19; selective disobedience
in, 11–12; social meaning
and impact of obedience and
disobedience in, 47; training,
education, and readiness for
combat, 40–42, 44
military professionalism: civilian
control of the military, 63,
83–84; concept and definition
of, 24–25; core values, 16, 25,
58–62, 123; creeds and ethos
statements, 16, 25; ethical
and professional judgment,
160–61, 179–80, 192, 231–32,
233–35; ethical obligations, 19;

intellectual independence as
hallmark of, 67; moral agency,
66–69, 70, 146; obedience as
critical to, 63–65; practices
and traditions of, 62–65, 70,
71–72, 75–76, 83–84, 91–92,
93–95, 140–42; presumption
of competence, 63–64, 65–66;
standards and norms in, 38–40
military service: historical attitudes
toward, 15; historical contexts
for presumption of obedience, 15
military-citizen duality. *See* citizen
soldiers
Mill, John Stuart, 55–56, 57, 230,
250n8
Milley, Mark A., 100, 115, 117, 234
missile attack, 143–44, 154
mission command: adaptation
to, 235–36; concerns about
implementation and effectiveness
of, 235; disciplined disobedience
and, 13–14, 100, 234; intention
of and obedience to, 47–49,
103; judgment and discretion
in, 159, 162–63; moral agency
and, 150–51; presumption of
obedience, 13–14, 68; radio
silence and leadership style,
171–72; selective obedience and
disobedience, 21–22
mission effectiveness. *See* combat
effectiveness
Molon labe school, 215
moral injury, 134–35, 180, 214, 241,
255n7
moral practice/morality: civil
community and moral equality
of others, 129–30; empathy
and, 162–64; friendship as
precondition to moral life, 59;
just war and moral equality
of combatants, 128–29;
loyalty, moral foundation of,
125–26; moral agency, 66–69,
70, 145–50; moral failure in

ABOUT THE AUTHOR

PAULINE SHANKS KAURIN holds a PhD in philosophy from Temple University, specializing in military ethics, just war theory, and applied ethics. She is a Senior Research Associate at the Inamori International Center for Ethics and Excellence at Case Western Reserve University. She served as the Stockdale Chair and Professor of Professional Military Ethics at the U.S. Naval War College in the College of Leadership and Ethics from 2018–25. She holds a BA in philosophy and international relations from Concordia College and an MA in philosophy from the University of Manitoba. Recent publications include *Achilles Goes Asymmetrical* (2014) and *On Obedience* (Naval Institute Press, 2020). She lives in southwestern Montana.

The Naval Institute Press is the book-publishing arm of the U.S. Naval Institute, a private, nonprofit, membership society for sea service professionals and others who share an interest in naval and maritime affairs. Established in 1873 at the U.S. Naval Academy in Annapolis, Maryland, where its offices remain today, the Naval Institute has members worldwide.

Members of the Naval Institute support the education programs of the society and receive the influential monthly magazine *Proceedings* or the colorful bimonthly magazine *Naval History* and discounts on fine nautical prints and on ship and aircraft photos. They also have access to the transcripts of the Institute's Oral History Program and get discounted admission to any of the Institute-sponsored seminars offered around the country.

The Naval Institute's book-publishing program, begun in 1898 with basic guides to naval practices, has broadened its scope to include books of more general interest. Now the Naval Institute Press publishes about seventy titles each year, ranging from how-to books on boating and navigation to battle histories, biographies, ship and aircraft guides, and novels. Institute members receive significant discounts on the Press' more than eight hundred books in print.

Full-time students are eligible for special half-price membership rates. Life memberships are also available.

For more information about Naval Institute Press books that are currently available, visit www.usni.org/press/books. To learn about joining the U.S. Naval Institute, please write to:

Member Services
U.S. Naval Institute
291 Wood Road
Annapolis, MD 21402-5034
Telephone: (800) 233-8764
Fax: (410) 571-1703
Web address: www.usni.org

www.ingramcontent.com/pod-product-compliance
Lightning Source LLC
Chambersburg PA
CBHW021613120626
46545CB00001B/209